SUCCEED
IN TEFL –
CONTINUING
PROFESSIONAL
DEVELOPMENT

David Riddell

Succeed in TEFL – Continuing Professional Development

David Riddell

First published in Great Britain in 2015 by John Murray Learning. An Hachette UK company.

First published in US in 2015 by Quercus.

British Library Cataloguing in Publication Data: a catalogue record for this title is available from the British Library.

Library of Congress Catalog Card Number: on file

Paperback ISBN 978 1 444 79606 3

eBook ISBN 978 1 444 79607 0

1

Cover image © Shutterstock.com

Typeset by Cenveo® Publisher Services.

Printed and bound in Great Britain by CPI Group (UK) Ltd., Croydon, CRO 4YY.

John Murray Learning policy is to use papers that are natural, renewable and recyclable products and made from wood grown in sustainable forests. The logging and manufacturing processes are expected to conform to the environmental regulations of the country of origin.

John Murray Learning
Carmelite House
50 Victoria Embankment
EC4Y 0DZ
www.hodder.co.uk

Also available in ebook

Acknowledgements

I would like to thank Eng Sing Cheng for patiently tutoring me in Mandarin, Jeff Mohamed for his valuable input, and the following for giving me their time to be interviewed: Tim Bierley, Andrea Borsato, Jacqueline Douglas, Ifthaquar Jamil, Fiona Johnston, Jan Madakbas, Maureen McGarvey, Christopher Milnes, William Morrow, Danny Norrington-Davies, Martin Oetegenn, Dave Rea, Tara Siddall, Justin Vollmer, Clare Webster.

I would also like to thank my Commissioning Editor, Robert Williams, for all his support and encouragement, and Bryan Fletcher for his help reviewing and improving the original manuscript.

Contents

Section 4: Global views and reflections

SECTION 1

A new beginning

1

Don't sit still

What does 'Succeed in TEFL' mean?

When I asked some working teachers to give me a quick answer to the question 'What does succeeding in this profession mean for you?', I received the following range of answers:

1 'Becoming the best possible teacher that I can be'
2 'Career development in the direction I want'
3 'Being a good teacher and having a row of smiling students in front of me'
4 'Carrying a suitcase, being intrepid, and arriving at a destination somewhere to teach and begin a new adventure'
5 'Doing it well'
6 'Development and growth – it's a process'

I love the wisdom of 6, I love the simplicity of 5, I love the spirit of 4 and I love the image of 3. I love the ambition of 2 and I love the goal of 1.

Bringing all these thoughts and ideas together, what are we left with when we are defining the title 'Succeed in TEFL'? Maybe it is about just 'doing a good job and getting better at it' and in so doing helping your learners to learn, develop, cope and be more confident, to enjoy learning and be comfortable doing it. And let's not forget being professional and reliable, being a good and supportive colleague, doing the day-to-day tasks that your organization requires, and seeking out opportunities to 'get better' at what you do. If you end up enjoying it, all those other points such as travelling and having some flexibility of hours would be a bonus.

So how do you do it well and get better at it? Some time ago I interviewed a school director about this and, after saying that 'teachers need to be looking to develop themselves', he remarked that 'a teacher who is sitting still is really going backwards'. That line stuck with me and became the title for this chapter because the sentiment behind it is undoubtedly true: this is a profession where – as teachers or trainers or line managers – you have to strive continuously to develop, to do a good job, to get better. Thus we have 'continuing professional development' as the second part of this book's title. This is the key to succeeding in the profession as a teacher, and maybe then taking on new or additional roles later in your career.

What is continuing professional development?

My first book (*Teach EFL*, Hodder Education, first published in 2001 and with a fourth edition in 2014) focused on *becoming* a teacher (of English as a foreign or second language). This book concentrates on *being* a teacher and a trainer and specifically *developing* professionally and thereby getting better at what you do. It suggests routes that might be taken for developing a career in TEFL, and firmly grounds career development as contingent upon continuing (or continuous) professional development, or CPD.

CPD is, I believe, the root and catalyst of positive career progression and is the key to succeeding in this profession and to being a better teacher. Without such development a teacher becomes less effective in the classroom, less valuable to their organization, and less likely to make career progress. So CPD is the heart of this book. The book discusses ways to develop and grow, it demonstrates possible challenges to embrace, and it uncovers comfort zones to emerge from.

Keith Harding, in *Modern English Teacher* (Volume 18 Number 3, July 2009) says that what characterizes continuing professional development is that it is:

- continuous – professionals should always be looking for ways to deal with new challenges and improve performance
- the responsibility of the individual teacher who identifies his or her own needs and how to meet those needs
- evaluative rather than descriptive – so that the teacher understands the impact of the activity
- an essential component of professional life, not an extra

My experience of CPD and career progression

My students constantly remind me that I am 'of a certain age'. When they have no idea who Elvis Presley is, or never knew a time without mobile phones, or have no idea what an LP is, then I know that my journey has been quite a long one. I thought it would be beneficial to me in writing this book to think back over the years to various examples of when I have done something to further my professional growth, big things and small. Most of my students these days weren't even born when I started teaching, but that in itself is another joy of the job – you may grow older, but your students seem to remain ageless.

In my first year or two of teaching, I do not recall being aware at the time of any specific experiences of development. And yet, when I reflect further, I realize that I never stopped developing during that time because I was always teaching new classes, new students, new levels, using different books, listening to more experienced colleagues, using different resources, teaching myself unfamiliar grammar before planning how I would teach my students that same grammar, getting better at planning and at timing, and gradually growing in confidence. And the important thing is to recognize all these things because there's no point in getting better at something if you don't recognize that improvement is taking place and what you can build on.

What, then, do I remember from those early years and beyond? Here are some examples in no particular order:

- Being observed by my Director of Studies was terrifying, but then I was reassured and encouraged by his feedback and suggestions. (Thanks, John!)
- Agreeing early on to be a regular teacher of the TOEFL exam class taught me so much about language use and rules, the demands of teaching an exam class and the different approach needed compared with a regular General English class.
- Being given tips and ideas for my lessons from my colleagues in the staffroom reduced my preparation time, and added to my still-bare collection of resources for future recycling. Such professional exchange among peers remains a powerful form of development.
- I learned ways of dealing with students who were bored, unmotivated or difficult for any reason – experience helped, as did the advice of more senior colleagues. As part of this, working in different schools and encountering different nationalities and cultures have always been key aspects of my development.
- Attending some of the school's teacher development sessions provided me with more ideas and techniques to use in the classroom.
- Running some teacher development sessions myself gave me added responsibility and the chance to share my ideas with colleagues.
- Doing other courses helped me be a student again and reminded me of some of the challenges faced by my own students.
- Becoming a marker of Cambridge exam papers helped me in my own experience of teaching exam classes.
- Becoming a pre-service teacher trainer on what is now called the Cambridge ESOL CELTA course, just four years into my career, was a steep and invaluable move for me; it really helped my own teaching as well as giving me other, non-teaching skills.
- Taking up my first position in management exposed me to a new set of responsibilities and skills and brought many benefits and lessons.

- Devising new materials or even new lessons to try out for the first time, and countless occasions of using a new course book, developed my ability to use, adapt and supplement material, and to select appropriate material and tasks.
- Writing my first book forced me to revisit the basics of effective teaching, and this one is focusing my mind on further ways I can continue my own development and help others improve theirs.
- Every time I have started work in a new school I have had the opportunity to work with new colleagues in a new context.
- Becoming a Cambridge assessor, and later Joint Chief Assessor, gave me the chance to visit schools across the world and, as part of my visits, to pick up on how different schools in different contexts approached the same course, and how each school organized its timetables and classes.
- Moving into online training was a significant aspect of development for me, both in terms of the type of course and course participant I was teaching, but also because it required me to become more familiar with technology, never my strongest point!
- Working as a 'standby' teacher, where I had to go in and teach someone else's class at very short notice if that teacher rang in sick, taught me how to plan quickly and adapt to different types of class over a short period of time.
- Reading articles and publications relevant to my work and professional interests has helped me keep up to date with new ideas.
- Watching a lesson of mine that had been recorded wasn't particularly comfortable, but it highlighted features that I needed to work on.

Just making this list has been valuable as a reminder of some of the things I have done, and made me think about what I can do next...

Who is this book for?

The focus in this book is on teachers of adults, but most of what follows could apply to those teaching young learners and to those working in different contexts. I have interviewed professionals who have experienced many different working environments and their contributions will make the content diverse and relevant to a wide range of teachers of language.

The book will discuss many different ways a teacher or trainer can develop, some of the ideas being familiar but others perhaps less so. The book is aimed primarily at the following groups:

- teachers who are new or fairly new to the profession who are looking for any help and ideas to improve as they start out in their first job
- teachers of longer experience who may feel 'stuck' and be looking for fresh ways to develop
- teacher trainers of any sort who themselves are looking for CPD ideas or for ideas to suggest to those who they work with
- managers, Directors of Studies and senior teachers who line-manage staff and who need CPD suggestions for their teachers when setting targets for the year ahead

If you are new or fairly new to the teaching profession, your initial thoughts will tend to be about just surviving those first lessons and getting used to a new workplace and maybe a new country and culture. Once you have successfully steered yourself through those early steps, the danger is that you won't know how to develop and improve, that you will 'sit still'. Section 2 of this book in particular will strive to give you ideas and reassurance so that you can take that next step. In Chapters 3 and 4 we will look at how different types of observation can be as much developmental as evaluative. Chapter 5 focuses on how much we can learn from our colleagues in the staffroom. Chapter 6 discusses in-service training and teacher development sessions in the workplace.

For teachers of longer experience, it is perhaps easier to get stuck at some point in their careers, not sure maybe of how to continue their development and to remain fully motivated. Section 3 especially will discuss some suggestions and starts with Chapter 7's focus on online resources. Chapter 8 looks at how teaching exam classes can widen a teacher's skills and methodology. Chapter 9 examines the value of being part of a reading group. In Chapter 10 we discuss how attending and participating in conferences can provide a wealth of developmental opportunities, both via face-to-face and online conferences. For budding writers, Chapter 11 reveals ways of getting into writing articles, blogs and even books. In Chapter 12 we see examples of action research and discover how teachers can benefit from even the simplest research. In Chapter 13 the value of a teacher becoming a student again is highlighted, with the author giving himself a challenge. For teachers wanting to become trainers, Chapter 14 will look at possibilities and benefits. The value of being part of professional groups and reading professional journals is discussed in Chapter 15. Taking a sabbatical from work may not seem an obvious form of CPD, but contributors to Chapter 16 may change your mind. Perhaps you are hoping to go into a management role one day. If so, Chapter 17 is for you. Keeping your goals specific and realistic is part of Chapter 18 - Get SMART. And Chapter 19 pulls the preceding chapters together as we aim to 'get ahead'.

Section 4 explores more global views. Chapter 20 is an interview with a senior line manager. How does she motivate teachers who have been in the profession for many years? Chapter 21 is an interview with a school Director as he ties everything we have covered to the vision and needs of the organization as a whole.

The concluding chapter underlines the importance of reflection as a tool for development, and summarizes all that has gone before.

If you are a teacher or trainer, then this book will give you ideas and practical suggestions for development. It doesn't matter how long you have been a teacher – the development should never stop. And, if you are a manager, Director of Studies (DOS) or a senior teacher who line-manages other teachers, I hope this book will help to give you ideas when discussing future targets with teachers or planning teacher development sessions. During my time as a school DOS, I had to conduct annual appraisals and professional development interviews with teachers. As part of these, I had to help teachers think of development targets for the year ahead, and there were times when a list of possibilities might have triggered ideas on both our parts. And, of course, many managers also still teach and, even if they don't, they still need to continue their professional journey, so I hope some of the ideas in this book will be of interest to them, too.

I did not want this book to be just a description of the different types of professional development opportunity available. I wanted examples of personal journeys and personal recommendations. I interviewed many teachers and managers to provide these, and I am grateful to all of them for making everything a bit more real. I want this book to give you ideas, to encourage and motivate you, to let you read about other people sharing their own experiences, and to help you continue your own professional journey. Those professionals I interviewed have worked across the world, and their expertise and sharing of experiences provides invaluable ideas and suggestions. It is concurrent with one of the core messages of the book that sharing with and learning from others is a key component of CPD. These expert language educators share their reflections on the developmental areas discussed throughout the book. This makes my task as writer somewhat easier, but it also provides a great deal of valuable perspective. Some discuss what stimulated their development; others give useful advice on things such as taking on exam classes for the first time. I found the process of interviewing so many sharing experts to be a rich and beneficial learning experience. I believe you will also greatly benefit.

How should this book be read? Obviously, it can be read from cover to cover, but for many readers it will be more valuable to select chapters that are relevant to them. An experienced teacher, for example, will not find much value in Chapter 2 but, if they are looking for something new to try and have never experienced professional reading groups, then Chapter 9 will be worth reading.

Each chapter has 'tasks', some of which are short and simple (e.g. 'Think of a time when...') and others which are actual developmental ideas for you to try out. They are referred to as 'Thinking Task' and 'CPD Task' for clarity.

THINKING TASK

If you are currently teaching, or have ever taught, think back over your teaching journey and list anything you have done which has contributed to your own continuous professional development. Examples can be big or small, but try to list at least ten. As with my examples, your list may include ideas from both your actual teaching and from your career as a whole (e.g. attending a conference). If you are relatively new to the profession, just list as many as you can!

Summary

It should be clearer now what this book is all about. It is not about how to find a (better) job or how to earn lots of money. Instead, it is about ways of moving forward, of developing, of getting better (which might indeed help you get that better job with better money). Some of these ways will be more obvious and recognizable than others, but all of them have value. We all need to stay fresh, remain motivated and explore different paths to professional progress. In some cases opportunities will present themselves, in others you will decide on your own objectives, and sometimes things 'just happen' on a day-to-day basis. We all need to move forward and develop, and we need to be aware of the directions we want to go in and aspects of our practice we wish to improve. We also need to be aware of what we have achieved and how much we have improved.

But the message is, 'Don't sit still!'

2

Starting out

I suspect most teachers remember their first day in their first job, and they may even look back and think, 'How ever did I survive it?' For someone who finishes their training course at the end of one week and begins with their own class in a school the following week, the transition can be especially overwhelming. But it is survivable. It is more than survivable: you can look back on that first job and reflect not only on how you survived but also on how much you learned and on how far you have developed since then. When I think now of how much I have learned and how much my own career has developed, I shudder at the memory of how little I knew back on that first day, and how scared I felt.

Your career is not just 'the job' of teaching your classes but everything else that goes with it outside the classroom and outside the building where you work. Everything contributes to those first steps and the beginning of a lifetime of development, although when you first start teaching it is natural to think of it more in terms of day-to-day survival than of development.

For thousands of people every year, 'starting out' begins with an initial training course and for many this will be the Cambridge CELTA course, or the Trinity TESOL course. There are also other less widely recognized courses available, although not all include a teaching component.

In North America, teaching certificates, some of which are similar to CELTA, are offered by various private organizations. Some online courses and one-week on-site courses also exist. Many different TESOL/TESL certificate courses are offered by colleges and universities in North America and are usually offered part-time, focusing on TESL to immigrants rather than TEFL.

Masters degrees are more popular in the USA than in the UK and some people take them as pre-service training. They come with many different names: MA TESOL, MS or MA in Applied Linguistics, MAT in ESL, etc. Some have little relevance to classroom teaching. Some (even online ones) include an evaluated practicum.

Once armed with a relevant certificate and valuable training, the next stage is to find a job.

CPD TASK

Part of ongoing development is reflection, something we will focus on in the final chapter. This is when you realize what you have done and how far you have come and when you remember what it was like for you when you started out. It can also involve considering what lies ahead and how you might face future challenges. With that in mind, let's extend the previous chapter's task.

Think back to your first job if you have already taught, and especially those first few days, weeks and months. Alternatively, think ahead to your first teaching position if you are yet to begin your teaching career. Make a list of what made it or would make it difficult or challenging as well as exciting. Consider the following categories and make a list in each category of those challenges and how you dealt with or think you would deal with them.

- Teaching your own classes
- Working in and for a new organization with people you didn't know
- If appropriate, working in a country other than your own, maybe with a very different culture and an unfamiliar language

Taking all of these points into consideration, what are the main factors in your development when you start out?

Coping with starting out

In this chapter I focus on the experiences of two teachers starting out. Beginners have to develop in multiple diverse ways simultaneously – some practical, some professional, some cultural. In that respect they may be dealing with the most difficult combination of problems they ever have to deal with at one time, and in one short space of time. Starting out might involve interviewing, selecting a new employer, moving country, finding accommodation, learning a new language, learning how to teach every day and for multiple hours every day... It is an incredibly intense period. Having a set of guiding principles, which I set out in the second half of the chapter, may take away some of the stress.

TEFL careers start out in many different ways and are chosen for many different reasons. For some it might be a career change; for others it might be their first job. A group of trainees on an initial training course can include a wide range of nationalities with ages from 18 to 60 or more. They will have a variety of reasons for being there and very different future plans. Some will have teaching experience and many will have none. The diversity of each group is rich and unique, as is the composition of any staffroom. Everyone has their own individual story to tell.

Below and throughout the book you will read about the experiences of teachers and trainers. What I believe you will get from reading these interviews is information, reassurance, ideas and stimulation. From reading the interviews in this chapter with Martin and Tim, you will hear two very different stories of starting out and you will realise that starting out will be very different depending on the context you are in and the timetable that you have.

My experience: Martin Oetegenn

Martin started out in Argentina, a new country with a different language and culture from the one he was used to. How did he survive those early days?

Where were you interviewed for the job?

A friend was working at the school and helped me arrange an interview.

What was the interview like? Were there any difficult or unexpected questions?

It was actually quite tricky. None of the questions was unexpected, though. She wanted to know a lot about how I would work with children, pastoral problems, etc.

How did you find somewhere to live?

I used the Craigslist website.

How far from the school was your accommodation?

Miles away. The school was in the suburbs but I wanted to live in the centre so I chose to commute. It took about an hour and a half!

What else did you have to do to make the move from the UK to Argentina?

Not much. The school arranged the visa for me.

Were you given a welcome orientation to the school and/or to Argentina?

Not to Argentina as I got the job when I was out there. I was welcomed into the school. I had a sort of mentor.

How many teachers were there, approximately? How many were British?

It was a primary and secondary school so there were about 100 teachers. Only two of us were British.

Did you teach adults or young learners (below 16), or both?

In the school, younger learners. Outside work I also did private lessons in businesses.

How many hours a week did you teach?

About 40 hours a week, Monday to Friday. I began at about 11 and usually finished at about 8 p.m.

How long were the lessons?

About four hours each, including duties like playground cover.

How many were there in a class?

Between 25 and 30.

What levels did you teach?

Sixth-grade kids. Their level was about B2.

Did you have a course book to work from?

No, I had to design all my own materials.

What other materials were available?

We had photocopiers, printers and computers, so we had access to the Internet and printing, paper and card and so on.

What were the classrooms equipped with?

Tables, chairs, blackboard and a TV if needed.

What support were you given by managers/colleagues?

Lots. They were very supportive. We did lots of teacher development sessions.

Were you observed early on? What was this like?

Yes – it was scary but really helpful and done in a positive way.

How was the transition from your initial training to your own class?

It was very different, as I was working with younger learners. However, I could apply a lot of what I learned about skills and language to the lessons.

What was the toughest part of the whole experience?

Dealing with behavioural problems.

And the best part?

All the funny, crazy things kids do!

Finally, what tips would you give a new teacher starting out in their first teaching job in a new country?

1 Start a Facebook group with your teacher training colleagues so that you can continue to support each other
2 Keep a Dropbox folder devoted to lesson/materials that work well
3 Take it seriously. Be smart, punctual, etc
4 Scan useful activities you used/found on the training course that you can use

5 Don't be afraid to ask your new colleagues things you
   don't know

My experience: Tim Bierley

Tim was a trainee of mine on an initial teacher training course in 2013 and he had quite a different experience. Straight after finishing the course, he took up a teaching position in Spain. Some of his experiences are not typical (e.g. the lack of a real interview) but, as his story is what actually happened, it is worth hearing, especially as a contrast to Martin's account.

Where were you interviewed for the job?

On Skype.

What was the interview like? Were there any difficult or unexpected questions?

I don't think there was a single difficult question. I was effectively offered the job after making my first email contact with the academy. After asking when the interview would be, I was told 'I suppose you could have one if you want'. I was a bit worried by the blasé recruitment policy, so I suppose I did want one and we spoke informally for ten minutes. The director was friendly and funny (far more important criteria than being organized and professional), so I took the job!

How did you find somewhere to live?

I used the Spanish housing site Idealista.

How far from the school was your accommodation?

Less than ten minutes' walk.

What else did you have to do to make the move from the UK to Spain?

Spanish bureaucracy is a bit awkward – there are tariffs to pay, NIE numbers to obtain and 'residencia' forms to fill out – but it's also as inefficient as it is awkward, so you're unlikely to get chased up about any missing documents!

Were you given a welcome orientation to the school and/ or to Spain?

I sat down and had a chat with the school director and she helped me plan a few lessons for my first week. That was about as far as it went, but it felt enough.

How many teachers were there, approximately? Were they all British?

I was the only full-time teacher but there were four part-time teachers, three from the UK and another from Ireland.

Did you teach adults or young learners (below 16), or both?

I mainly taught adults – I taught some pensioners, some middle-aged folk and also had a couple of classes with 9–12 year olds and 12–14 year olds.

How many hours a week did you teach?

It was 22 altogether: I worked Mondays and Wednesdays 5–9, Tuesdays and Thursdays 10–12.30 and 5 30–9.30, and Fridays 4–8.

How long were the lessons?

Some were one hour, most were an hour-and-a-half and one was two hours.

How many were there in a class?

Between three and eight (not many!).

Author note: This is especially unusual – don't be surprised to have classes of 20, 30 or 40 in some places.

What levels did you teach?

Elementary, Pre, Mid and Upper Intermediate, and Advanced.

Did you have a course book to work from?

We had *a popular course book* but were encouraged to depart from it as much as possible. Students were expected to do reading and writing at home.

What other materials were available?

There were a couple of conversation books. I can't remember their names. We had access to photocopiers, printers and computers.

What were the classrooms equipped with?

I had a whiteboard and some of the other classes had a TV.

What support were you given by managers/colleagues?

My director was slightly odd! A couple of weeks into the job, I was struggling with the workload so I approached her for advice. She told me that, when she arrived, she taught 60 hours per week and went out every night until 7 the next morning, so really I shouldn't be over-burdened. It was true that I put a bit too much time into my lesson plans, but I could have used some better advice! Outside school matters, she was as friendly and funny as she had been during the 'interview' and we got on pretty well. She took me salsa dancing, invited me to her and her boyfriend's house, and was a good city host. Perhaps she just wasn't a very good people manager.

Were you observed early on? What was this like?

Yes, a couple of weeks after starting. The lesson went fine and I wasn't too distracted by the director's presence. She did insist on correcting students' small mistakes during free speaking practice, which was a little off-putting, but there weren't any earth-swallow-me-up moments.

How was the transition from teacher training to your own class?

The school was oriented towards speaking skills above all else. Because the language of the streets is Spanish rather than English, students have limited opportunities to speak English. Because of this, we were expected to create a lot more debates and role plays, encouraging a lot more free practice. I enjoyed being able to pursue an exercise that went well. Given that there were few observations, there was room to loosen the structure of lessons and it wasn't necessary to bring an animated discussion to an end for the sake of covering some phrasal verbs (although they would have to be studied in the next class, of course).

What was the toughest part of the whole experience?

I worked a lot. During a good week, I would work around 60 hours (including preparation) but it was often more, including a couple of decent-sized planning sessions at weekends. This was hard to adapt to, partly because I'd previously been living a student life, in which the meeting of a deadline merited a spell of wild celebration, usually lasting until the next deadline approached. There were four deadlines per day in Madrid, so I had to resist the temptation to head to the bars each time I got a lesson taught (although maybe this was the reason behind my director's impressive lifestyle during her first few years in Spain). Working 65 hours a week would probably have proved quite hard, whatever my preparation, though! It took me a long time to work out just how to compile 90 minutes' worth of teaching. The school's method was a bit odd, in that we were expected to cover two double-page spreads of a popular coursebook in one lesson, while also making sure that we didn't focus on grammar much, before adding additional role plays which used the grammar and topics covered during the lesson. Bizarre. I did give up on the format eventually, but not before I'd spent a lot of time trying to fit every ingredient on the shelf into an omelette.

Time was an issue, then. While meeting people wasn't that difficult, finding time to see them again was! And in terms of teaching, I would have liked a better grasp of grammar. I suspect my second year would have proved a breeze. Preparation took me far too long. This was in part due to my chronic procrastination, but having to create lessons from scratch would have always taken me quite a while, regardless of how easily distracted I get.

And the best part?

Teaching! I loved almost all of my students. Even the grumpy, miserable ones were interesting in their own way. One of my students, a retired engineer, spent an entire one-on-one lesson just showing me his holiday snaps. I suppose you'd need to pay most people to sit through that for an hour, but it felt like easy money all the same!

Lessons were always fun, especially with the more advanced students. I taught all my students for at least three months and made some good friendships. Many of them have been in touch since I left. While preparation did take ages, I had a lot of licence to create lessons that my students (and I) would find interesting. I know they were grateful for this and we certainly had a lot of fun!

Finally, what tips would you give a new teacher starting out in their first teaching job in a new country?

Ask if you can watch a couple of lessons before you start your own.

Get a clear idea about your school's teaching methods. Ideally, get it written down so you can see whether or not it makes sense. Don't be afraid to give your own opinions.

If you have smaller classes, it's definitely worth parting with the textbook to do role plays and debates. Students tend to really enjoy them.

My director told me that a lot of students continue studying in Spain simply because they like their teacher. If you're open and friendly, they'll forgive the odd grammatical failure.

Have a back-up plan. Sometimes a lesson goes badly, or your students will be tired and in no mood for complicated grammar. You need to have extra material to save you from floundering. It's a good idea to have a folder of back-up lessons in your class.

Make use of your colleagues. If you have doubts, always ask.

Give yourself personal deadlines for lesson plans. I know my CELTA tutor mentioned that a lot of first-year teachers spend many hours in the staffroom, so the problem isn't only mine! Make other plans so that you have to stop working.

Your first teaching job

If you are looking for or about to set off to your first teaching position, perhaps in a different country or a different part of the country, what do you need to consider or be aware of? As well as the advice, information and tips given by Tim and Martin, here are some more general points to consider as you start out.

THE JOB APPLICATION AND INTERVIEW

1 Before the interview, find out more about the place you are applying to and show an interest in the organization.

2 When answering questions, demonstrate your enthusiasm for and commitment to teaching when asked why you want the job (rather than saying 'I want to work in a hot country').

3 Even if your only teaching experience is from your training course, talk positively about what you have learned, the materials you have used and the areas in your own teaching that you are working on.

4 Ask a few relevant questions to make sure you have all the information you need before agreeing to anything. If the interviewer hasn't told you something you want to know, ask. Obviously, you want to know how much you will be paid, but don't be taken in by what might seem a lot of money – what's the cost of living where you are going to be living?

5 Read any contract carefully and ask about anything you are unsure of regarding your terms and conditions.

6 Make sure you know about hours and location of work – you might be working a split shift, maybe at different locations. Don't be surprised if you are teaching 30+ hours a week.

7 If relevant, find out about getting a visa. Is your passport up to date?

8 If relevant, find out whether the school will help you find accommodation, or seek advice on the best places to look.

9 Find out what materials and resources are available.

10 Ask what age groups you will be teaching and at what levels and how long for.

Bear in mind, too, that some organizations may ask you to teach a demo lesson as part of the interview process. Generally, very few interview processes are as casual as the one Tim had!

PREPARATION AND TEACHING

1 Keep materials you have created or found and used that worked well, so that you can use them again in the future. You may need to change them a little from class to class, but building up a bank of material in this way will still save a huge amount of planning time, as Martin said.

2 If you have a course book, find out whether you are expected to work your way through it systematically or whether you can adapt and supplement it with other materials.

3 Don't be afraid to ask more experienced colleagues for help with your planning. Remember, every teacher has to start somewhere so the colleagues you work with are there to share their experience, knowledge and expertise – just choose an appropriate moment to ask them!

4 Make sure you know what is expected of you as a teacher. Do you have to use the book? Do you have to give homework? Do you have to give progress tests? If you are teaching young learners, what are you allowed and not allowed to do in terms of discipline?

5 Find out what might be expected of you in terms of teaching styles and methodology.

6 Ask whether you can observe a class before you start, to get an idea of the kinds of lessons teachers at the school deliver.

7 Never plan a lesson that relies on technology working because it may not. Always have a Plan B.

8 Always plan to keep your students busy, interested and challenged by your lessons, and make sure that each lesson – as well as each part of the lesson – has a clear aim or learning objective. Students want to see that they are making progress, so plan your lessons to ensure this.

9 Enjoy your students! Find out about them as people, respond to their needs and interests, and try to plan lessons that will

be useful, interesting and relevant to them. Of course you will be nervous when you first start, but the students you teach will usually be the best part of the job, so enjoy them and the experience. And remember, every teacher has to start somewhere and your continuous professional development starts on your first day and should never end.

WORKING IN A NEW ORGANIZATION

1 It can be scary at first but you'll get used to it in time.

2 The school will probably give you a full induction first to help you prepare, but, if it doesn't, ask to be shown around and introduced to key people.

3 Don't be afraid to ask colleagues or managers for help, clarification, advice and guidance at any time about any aspect of your job.

4 When you first arrive, find out whether there is a particular person that you can initially go to for help with anything, such as a mentor or your immediate line manager, and never hesitate to ask if you do need help.

5 Explore the building and find out quickly how to use basic resources in the school, such as the photocopier, the computers, the interactive whiteboard if there is one, and where all the materials and books are kept.

6 You will be observed teaching early on; treat observations as an opportunity for reassurance and development. Feedback on any observation should be a two-way process, so ask about anything to do with the lesson or your planning and teaching that is going to help you develop.

7 Try to get to know who people are – their names and what they do. Don't be afraid to introduce yourself and start to build relationships; you will learn as much from your colleagues on a day- to-day basis in the staffroom as anywhere else.

8 If your organization uses another site and you have to teach there, find out where it is, how to get there and whether you have to pay for the transport to get there.

9 Check what you are expected to do. For example, when do you need to be in the building? When can you leave? Are you allowed to take your class out? Are you allowed to have one-to-one lessons outside school or socialize with the students outside work? May you wear shorts to work? Most schools will have some kind of teachers' handbook or code of professional conduct, so find out about this.

10 Once you are settled and feel you 'belong', you can help other new teachers starting work there, remembering what it was like for you and how others helped you.

WORKING IN A COUNTRY WITH A DIFFERENT CULTURE AND LANGUAGE

Are you going to a country you haven't been to before and know little about? It is challenging to start teaching in an unfamiliar foreign country, but give it time and you will soon find that you settle down and start to enjoy where you are living as well as where you are working. This is a job that allows you to travel, so make the most of that opportunity.

1 Find out as much about the country as you can before you go, so that you can see whether you will be happy living there. Consider whether it is too far away for you if you think you will feel homesick. It happens.

2 Learn the basics of the local language if you don't already know it.

3 Once you've settled in, consider taking some lessons in the language to improve your use of it and thereby make your day-to-day life in the country less stressful.

4 Try to find out in advance about the culture of the country, including information about inappropriate body language and gestures.

5 As soon as you can, explore the local area and the transport system. Find out the route to work, to shops, and to places to visit during your time off.

6 Ask colleagues for any information and advice you need – they already live there, so rely on them for guidance.

7 Find out more from your students – why not do a lesson in which they have to give you advice, tips and warnings (e.g. 'Whatever you do, don't...')?

8 During your time off, explore the local area and beyond. This is a great opportunity to experience a new country and all that it offers and will help you feel much more that this is now home as well as where you work.

9 Try to make friends who are local to the area so you don't feel isolated, especially at first.

Summary

Don't walk into the first job you are offered without considering all the advice given above. When you do start, it won't be easy, and it might even be a bit overwhelming at times, but with help, support, and hard work you will get through those first few weeks and start to grow into your new role and feel more comfortable in your new workplace and, maybe, a new country. Above all, don't feel that you have to cope alone. And enjoy the thrill of having your own class for the first time. Let your new career begin...

SECTION 2

First steps

3

Being observed

'I need to come and observe you.'

Few words are more likely to create more anxiety, or even dread, than these, especially for a less experienced teacher, but they are words all teachers will hear at various times throughout their careers. We read in Chapter 2 about teachers starting out and often feeling overwhelmed by the whole experience of having their own class and working in a new environment. In this chapter we go on to examine what for most new teachers is the first true taste of CPD, being observed. Observations of your teaching will continue throughout your careers and, whether you have been teaching for one month or for thirty years when you are observed, the CPD journey continues through the feedback that you receive and the actions that you take following the observation process.

But is being observed an event to dread or an event to welcome? Is it designed only to check up on your standards or to help you develop as a teacher? In other words, to what extent is an observation evaluative, and to what extent is it developmental? When an observation is primarily evaluative, it means the lesson and the teacher are being observed to ensure that they meet the minimum standards of teaching and learning expected by the organization. When the observation is more developmental, it means that the observer wants the teacher to take from the observation feedback ways to improve and ideas to try out. Observations will often be a combination of the two, but one aspect might be focused on more than the other.

Without a doubt, the experience of being observed and the feedback received contribute enormously to a teacher's development at all stages of that teacher's career. Teaching can be a lonely experience and it is easy to fall into bad habits, or to become stale. Having someone come to observe you, to discuss your lesson with you, to tell you what you do well and what you could do better, to give you ideas to think about and try out is all a vital and invigorating contributor to a teacher's development. All teachers need reassurance and ideas and to be guided and even inspired by an observer's comments and suggestions. This peer dialogue is one of the most valuable forms of CPD that there is, so whether you are starting out and facing your first observation, or are very experienced and need to be shown how observations remain important to you, then you need to read this chapter.

First, you should read the views of the three teachers below discussing their general thoughts about observations. Are your thoughts similar? Then read about the different types of observation before going on to how to get the most from an observation. As part of this, you will read an interview with an experienced teacher discussing what she gained from a recent observation which will confirm to you the value of being observed.

I asked three teachers for their general thoughts about being observed. Their teaching experience ranged from five years to twenty years. This is what they had to say.

Teacher 1

'I think the purpose of being observed is partly to make sure that the standards of the school are being maintained, but I think it should also be developmental – you should get some kind of development as a teacher. Being in the classroom by yourself can be lonely; you've only got yourself to reflect on your development as a teacher. Observation works best when both parties know the purpose of being there and this can often be done with a little discussion about the observation, with the two sides deciding what is going to be looked at.

'Even though I've been teaching for many years, I still get nervous about being observed. It's because, when I teach, it is very much "my space" and my students' space and suddenly you've got someone else in there and it doesn't matter how many times you are told "This is not evaluative", it's hard for you not to think that it is.

'Observations have helped me develop as a teacher because they prompt me to think really carefully about what I'm doing and then get someone else to confirm that I'm doing what I think I'm doing – it's that extra pair of eyes.'

Teacher 2

'The purpose is developmental and evaluative, but probably more evaluative, to be honest: if they see something that's not good, they can give you feedback on how to improve it.

'Most of the times I've been observed I've taken away something from it – something I could have done better or just a different way of doing a particular activity. I've had some really useful feedback before. I do get nervous, but that just shows that you care about what you do, and feedback is always constructive.'

Teacher 3

'The purpose is to keep you on track. I think of teaching like driving – you are helped to pass the test and then you're on your own. It's just about making sure you remember what you've learned and learning some new things along the way. They develop you as a teacher. It's difficult to be critical about your own teaching because you're too close to yourself, but just having someone there to state the obvious, you just need someone to tell you sometimes, "You could have done it that way."

'Every time I get observed, I think "I wish I was observed more often", even though I dread it a bit beforehand. Sometimes you feel you want to show everything you can in one lesson, but that's impossible. All the observer can get is a snapshot.'

We can see from these comments that, however experienced you are, it is still normal to feel nervous so, if that is how you feel, then you are not alone! We can also see the recognition of the role of observations as being twofold: evaluative and developmental, with the degree of emphasis given to each varying according both to personal perception and reality.

Types of observation

Let's briefly consider the various types of observation and reasons for your being observed in your teaching before expanding on the developmental aspects of observations.

FORMAL EVALUATIVE OBSERVATIONS

This is the most common and familiar type of observation, and the one that all teachers will experience throughout their careers. Typically, it will occur once a year but it may be more or less often. The primary focus is to evaluate your teaching to ensure that it meets the overall standards expected by the organization. You would usually be expected to complete a full lesson plan and then be observed for around 60 minutes. Oral and written feedback follows.

You may be observed within the first month or two of starting at a school, and sometimes your continued employment will depend on satisfactory feedback. Ideally, though, the feedback received would include some developmental tips, too. These are often the most fear-inducing observations because you know that your teaching is being assessed according to minimum criteria of required standards. While the primary focus is evaluation, confirming that you are teaching to a satisfactory standard – or not (coupled with how to improve) – means that there is also an important element of development in these observations (and we can see evidence of this later in the chapter when we read Tara's experience of being observed).

POP-INS AND DROP-INS

With these observations – sometimes also called 'buzz observations' – you won't know when the observer is coming in. The observation is often much shorter (as short as ten minutes in some cases) than a formal evaluative observation, which teachers know about in advance and for which they will sometimes prepare a special lesson. With pop-ins and drop-ins, the observer will see more of a normal day-to-day part of a lesson and is unlikely to expect a full plan.

Sometimes observers in a pop-in say they are focusing on the students or just looking for a general flavour of the class (and this may be part of a series of pop-ins of many other classes in a particular period). Feedback is rare and teachers can sometimes feel unclear about the real reason for the visit. Pop-ins are often intended to benefit the organization more than the individual teacher and, as a result, their developmental aspect, if no feedback is given, is minimal at best.

However, if the observer(s) of the various classes draws up a list of common areas where teaching could be improved, and follows these with teacher development sessions (INSETT – in-service training for teachers), then the developmental aspect can be significant and for the benefit of all teachers. For example, let's say that a series of observations revealed that a number of teachers were missing opportunities for language feedback and reformulation in their lessons. A subsequent INSETT session focusing on this would benefit the teachers, their students, and the organization as a whole in the longer term.

Confirmation, too, of common strengths in lessons observed is also beneficial because teachers need reassurance sometimes that what they are doing *is* working. This is especially true if you have been working on a previously weak area of your teaching. To have an observer confirm that you have made progress in this area shows development on your part.

FILMED OBSERVATIONS

Some teachers welcome the opportunity to have their lesson filmed and others don't, although it is possible to have just a very small camera in the room that doesn't distract either the teacher or the students very much. The observation itself may be a formal one or entirely the personal choice of the teacher. Either way, there is the (sometimes painful) advantage of being able to watch your lesson back afterwards and to see for yourself the strengths and weaknesses of your teaching.

'Teaching' does not mean that the focus is always entirely on the teacher. Observations, of whatever kind, need to be focused as much, if not more, on the students – the learners – as on the teacher him- or herself. In a filmed observation you can do this very well by having the camera focused on the students during the lesson. From this you can see when viewing the recording how students respond at various stages, how well they appear to be learning, how motivated they seem to be and how well they are doing overall – in other words, to observe how effective the learning process seems to be. And in any kind of observation, a good observer will be watching the students in order to assess how their learning process is affected by the teaching. After all, observations should be about helping the teacher to help the students.

OBSERVATION IN RESPONSE TO A COMPLAINT

This can happen to anybody at some time, unpleasant though it is. Ideally, though, even if the observation confirms a problem, the observer can help you improve and develop in the future.

AN 'UNOBSERVED' OBSERVATION

An 'unobserved' observation might seem a strange concept, or maybe one just in need of an alternative name, but in basic terms it means that the 'observer' will talk to you before and after the lesson but not actually watch the lesson itself. This can be very beneficial in terms of development without the accompanying stress of someone coming to watch you teach. Instead, the 'observer' will rely on your account of what happened and together you will discuss the lesson and the class and focus on particular areas of the teaching and learning that took place.

It is best beforehand to identify an area or areas that you will be working on in the lesson (e.g. trying out a new approach, making better use of the interactive whiteboard or increasing student involvement), so that you and the 'observer' can follow up on this in the post-lesson discussion.

Unobserved observations are a very valuable addition to, but not a replacement for, formal observation, and they can certainly focus on developmental aspects without the usual anxiety that comes with someone watching you teach.

TRAINEE OBSERVATIONS

If you work at a centre that runs training courses, such as Cambridge ESOL CELTA courses (pre-service training), you will have trainees coming to watch lessons as part of their course. The trainees wouldn't be expected to give feedback beyond general praise or particular questions they might have, but their presence in the lesson can give you the opportunity to try out something different to show them and in so doing add to your own development.

EXTERNAL OBSERVATIONS

All schools will have external inspections every few years from a recognized body such as the British Council. An inspector will come into your class for 20 to 30 minutes, but usually at an unspecified time. They do not give feedback to individual teachers, but instead report back to the management on the overall standard of teaching. This gives the organization the opportunity to plan INSETT sessions based on the inspectors' feedback, especially in relation to areas identified as in need of improvement.

How to get the most out of observations

Having looked at different types of observation, we now move on to ways to benefit from being observed. You do not want the observation to end up being an event you just want to get over and done with but rather to be a constructive process from which you look forward to learning.

I have prepared a set of guidelines for various aspects of the process and rationale of observations. With these to reflect on, I hope the process will be smoother for you as well as potentially more productive.

This section concludes with another 'My experience' which will consolidate all that follows.

CLARIFYING EXPECTATIONS

Observations work best for all parties when the objectives and expectations are clear, including how the teacher will benefit from the process. This should not solely be about effective teaching but also about effective learning. You cannot separate the two – just as, in my opinion, an observation cannot easily separate the evaluative from the developmental, nor should it try to. An observer needs to know what they are looking for, and the teacher needs to know what is expected of them.

Here are one organization's published expectations of the teacher.

'The teacher should...

- plan and execute lessons which are appropriate to their learners' levels, needs and expectations
- use teaching techniques and modes of delivery appropriate to students' level, ensuring a variety of activity, timing and pace
- use learning materials which are up to date, and appropriate to the level, length and type of course being taught and

acknowledge the source of any materials photocopied or
adapted from published materials
- be familiar with language learning/teaching materials from a
wide range of sources
- encourage their students to participate actively in class and to
continue their studies outside class
- demonstrate a commitment to facilitating their students'
progress, e.g. by suggesting appropriate strategies for extending
their learning outside the classroom
- provide appropriate guidance to students on how to improve
their language level
- provide evidence that their lessons have been adequately
prepared, and that they form part of a logical scheme of work
- demonstrate an ability to apply the practical implications of the
Curriculum Document
(With thanks to International House, London, for permission to
publish this)

In other cases, there may be a more specific checklist of criteria. For
example, the observer may want to check that you provide:
- clear instructions
- a clear context for language
- an opportunity for the students to practise what they have learned
- clear feedback on tasks
- feedback on language use

Clearly, any teacher achieving all of the above is going to have
students who are themselves learning and progressing.

OVERCOMING RESISTANCE TO OBSERVATION

While it is normal to be anxious to a certain extent before any kind
of observation, some teachers can be resistant to being observed.
Reasons for such resistance might include:
- **past experience** – if you have had a bad experience of
being observed, you are going to be anxious about future
observations
- **mistrust** – some teachers think the only reason for someone
coming in is to 'check up' on them, regardless of what the
observer tells them

- **the observer** – some teachers are not keen on being observed by someone with much less teaching experience, or by someone who has not previously taught the type of class that they are being observed teaching
- **lack of information** – if teachers don't know why they are being observed, or what specifically the observer is looking for, this will add to their anxiety and, therefore, their resistance

Observers can help reassure teachers, and ensure that they get the most out of an observation, by following a clear process. This is a way to reduce resistance and to ensure that the experience is constructive for the teachers. As a teacher, you may have no control over this, but the following approach should help you when you are being observed.

Before the observation

As teachers, we always try to give our lessons and the language we are focusing on a clear context. In the same way observations also need context. As a teacher, I want my observer to know something about my class, my students and my aims before they come to observe. I also would like to suggest to my observer an aspect of my lesson that I would particularly appreciate feedback on. Ideally, the observer will want to find out all these things as well, before the observation. Not only will the observer probably expect a full lesson plan beforehand, identifying the principal objectives of the lesson and the intended stages and procedure, but he or she will also want some personal context. Having an informal conversation beforehand is therefore useful for the observer and it can also be reassuring to the teacher.

If you discover that the observation process in your organization does not include a pre-observation meeting, ask your observer for a brief chat beforehand if the observer has not already suggested one. In terms of CPD, by having your observer focus, for example, on a previously weak area or on something new you are trying out, their feedback can help you in the development process.

During the observation

Your observer is likely to sit at the back of the room but may move around the room during the lesson to see what the students are doing. They may arrive at the start of or during the lesson. Formal observations typically last for 45–60 minutes, with the observer taking notes and focusing both on you and your teaching and on the students and their learning. But what are they looking for?

In addition to any specific areas discussed beforehand with you, any part-evaluative observation will be based on criteria relating to the minimum standard of 'performance' expected. Areas that fall below standard, or which are of a satisfactory standard but with room for improvement, can form part of a subsequent plan for development. You should therefore have been told what the criteria are that you are being assessed against and what the minimum expectations are.

After the observation

After an observation, you might feel as worried as you did beforehand as you await the 'verdict'. Ideally, the oral feedback should take place within 24–48 hours of the observation if at all possible. This feedback typically includes a combination of what went well and in which areas you met or even exceeded the expected standard, and any areas where you fell below the expected standard, and why. The feedback session should also focus on those areas identified before the lesson as those you would have appreciated feedback on, and include comments on how you have improved in particular areas identified in your previous observation as points to work on. All of this can lead to your continued development, and it ensures that the observation is there to benefit you, the teacher, and not just to 'check up on you'.

Ideally, this feedback should be a two-way discussion with an opportunity for you to ask questions and contribute ideas rather than the observer simply telling you how the lesson went. This oral feedback should then be summarized in writing, agreed by both sides, and copies should be kept both for your own future reference and that of the organization (for your next observer to refer to).

A further useful aspect of this 'after' stage could be an informal meeting with your observer some time after the feedback meeting. For example, if in feedback following an observation the observer has discussed with you alternative ways of focusing on reading, you could tell the observer how well it worked once you've had a chance to try out their suggestion. If you had been having problems integrating a particular student into the lessons, you could tell the observer later whether you have made any progress. This 'keeping in touch' approach makes the process of the observation more meaningful and developmental and less the one-off 'event' that it can so often be – so less a box-ticking exercise and more a longer-term process to benefit the teacher as well as the organization.

My experience: Tara Siddall

I spoke to Tara, a colleague of mine, two days after she was formally observed and given oral and written feedback. I asked her about her feelings generally about observations, but especially about this particular observation and how she felt it had helped her own professional development.

How do you feel generally about being observed?

I quite enjoy the challenge of being observed. The general feeling of having eyes on what you're doing raises your game. It's very good to be reminded of the context in which your lesson is happening. It helps you think more carefully about what you're doing, and having the consequences of someone else's opinion allows you to step back and think about what you're doing more clearly.

Tell me about the observation you had this week.

I was observed teaching a mid-intermediate group (of adult learners). They are very strong on lexis and sophisticated ways of expressing themselves, but they have a big hole in their knowledge. I took the opportunity to try out a lesson I had been grading for different levels and on the back of a previous observation, thinking about how to deal with lexis in a reading or listening lesson. So I took this opportunity to see if it worked, because it worked in my opinion but I wanted to see whether or not the observer could give me insight, and she very much did.

So how specifically do you think this observation and feedback will help you develop your future teaching?

In feedback we discussed the ways in which I was using the text. I thought that maybe I needed slightly less text and slightly more language analysis, and she agreed that this was the case, and we discussed ways of doing that and her point to me was that I was cramming quite a lot into the lesson and there was some debate about what my focus was. Her point, which was a bit of a revelation to me, was 'Why don't you take that idea and expand it over a couple of lessons, because you've got so much? Yes, you got where you wanted to get to in your lesson, but it's a waste not to unpack all those different stages.' So, while the lesson worked, she said I could have made two or even three lessons out of the material I had.

What I will do now is create more supported staging within the lesson and see why my instincts have taken me away from using materials and developing them over a couple of days.

In general, how do observations help you develop?

Continuous professional development is the most important part of being observed for me. I think that it's an opportunity to reinforce creative ideas. The sophistication of the feedback is so high that you are given some sort of insight into further development opportunities, and it encourages teachers to take those opportunities and to know that people are mentoring you and taking an interest in what you're doing. This is vital for your teaching development and for seeing your purpose within the organization as a whole.

Tara's interview shows how feedback can offer very helpful and specific tips to enable someone to improve. This came about from discussing the lesson beforehand with the observer and telling her what she would appreciate feedback on in addition to the evaluative aspect of the feedback. Tara will now take this feedback to the next stage by trying out the suggestions with future classes. If I had been her observer, I would also make a point of catching up with Tara a few weeks later to ask her how the suggestions had worked out for her.

As a result of this process, not only has Tara had confirmation that her teaching is meeting or exceeding the required standards generally (evaluative), but she has identified a particular aspect of her teaching for future development which can be reviewed when Tara is next observed (developmental).

CPD TASK

The next time you know you are going to be observed, take the following steps:

1 Discuss your class/students and your planned lesson and aims with your observer beforehand.

2 Decide on one aspect of your planned lesson or your teaching that you would particularly like feedback on.

3 During the oral feedback, agree on at least one aspect of your teaching that, as a result of this observation, you want to work on or a new approach or idea you want to try out as part of your ongoing development.

4 A few weeks after the observation and feedback, report back to your observer on your progress and agree between you how you have shown development since the observation.

As a result of the above, be able to complete the following:

'As a result of my recent observation and feedback process, I am now able to / am better at / have improved in.................................. . This is evidenced by..................... .'

For example: 'As a result of my recent observation and feedback process, I am now better at exploiting reading texts and accompanying tasks and focusing more on some of the language in the text. This is evidenced by my spending more time in lessons using the material and associated tasks, and by my students recognizing, understanding and using useful language from the text, which they did not do in my previous reading lessons, which focused more on just answering comprehension questions.'

Summary

Teachers are observed for different reasons and these observations can take place in different ways. However, even though most observations have some focus on evaluating standards, the best observations also involve aspects of teacher development with a clear benefit to the teacher as well as to his/her students, and ultimately to the organization as a whole. Both sides need to ensure the maximum value of these observations by following a clear and transparent process that does not end once feedback is given, but which is ongoing and continuous. For this to happen, both the teacher and the observer need to embrace the process to maximize the benefits to all involved.

4

Observing others

In the previous chapter we explored the many issues relating to being observed, and how that experience, while stressful, is a key part of professional development. When teachers think of 'observations', it is the 'being observed' that they think of. However, another key aspect of CPD, and one so often overlooked, is the opportunity you have as a teacher to observe other people teach.

This chapter will focus on this 'peer observation' not just from the teachers' viewpoint (the one observing and the one being observed) but also from the manager's viewpoint, as peer observation usually requires institutional support for it to happen.

We will look at the following questions:

- What is peer observation?
- What are the benefits for the teachers involved?
- What are the benefits for the organization?
- How can it be arranged?
- What happens during a peer observation?
- How do you give feedback to the teacher?
- What are the longer-term benefits for those involved?

THINKING TASK

How would you answer the questions above? If you have done peer observations yourself, you will have a good idea; if you haven't, you can certainly consider the likely answers. Try to do this task now before moving on.

What is peer observation?

Peer observation is when one teacher observes another. There are many kinds of peer observation.

You observe a more experienced teacher.

This is possibly the most common type of peer observation. New or inexperienced teachers can feel very isolated at first and have only informal feedback from their students to guide them. The opportunity to observe other teachers has disappeared on most training courses and it is all too easy to get into a bit of a rut with your teaching and to lose confidence. By observing a more experienced teacher, you can be exposed to different approaches and different techniques, pick up ideas, be reassured and gain confidence.

You observe a teacher who is teaching a similar group to yours.

Maybe you are teaching a beginners' class and are struggling to think of ideas, or are experiencing difficulties communicating with them without using their language, or having problems knowing what and how much to cover in one lesson. By watching another teacher teaching the same level or type of group you can get lots of ideas and increase your confidence at the same time. And if you are teaching your groups simultaneously, then you can continue to liaise on a daily basis and share ideas and experiences.

You observe a teacher teaching a group you are about to teach for the first time.

Maybe the following week you are going to be teaching an IELTS or TOEFL class for the first time, for example. By going to watch an existing IELTS or TOEFL class and how the teacher teaches that class, you will gain valuable insight about how to approach such a class, which will give you more confidence when planning that first lesson.

You observe a teacher doing something of particular interest to you.

Maybe they are teaching some grammar you have never taught before, or are using a piece of technology you have never used before, or will be trying some unusual methodology that you want to find out about. Whatever it is, you will be seeing something new, which will give you the confidence to do the same at a later date. This can be particularly useful when you don't know how something can be exploited (e.g. using tablets in a lesson), how something can be taught (e.g. a lesson on cleft sentences) or how an approach can work (e.g. going into a lesson without any plan or materials).

You observe a manager.

Managers observe teachers, so why shouldn't teachers be allowed to observe their managers? This could follow a regular observation by your manager, who has identified an issue such as 'handling a big, noisy class'. Seeing the manager teach such a class (maybe the same one) can be a great way of actually seeing evidence of how a manager's suggestion might work. Such an arrangement can also build trust and respect and make observation more of an ongoing process with a clear developmental pattern, rather than just 'an observation' with no measurable benefits.

What are the benefits?

When you are the teacher observing, peer observation offers:

- a way of reducing the sense of isolation that you can feel in your classroom
- a chance to see how other teachers teach and gain new ideas and perspectives
- an opportunity to see how a different teacher teaches a type of class you teach or are about to teach
- a chance to find out how another teacher deals with something you are experiencing difficulties with in your teaching

When you are the teacher being observed, peer observation offers:

- a chance for some informal feedback on your lesson
- an opportunity to discuss ideas with the observing colleague
- a feeling that you have contributed to a colleague's development

For the organization, peer observation offers:

- short- and long-term benefits in the form of teachers learning from each other, gaining confidence, trying out new ideas and generally getting better by being part of a professional learning community
- a chance to build teacher-development workshops around issues arising from teachers' feedback
- a chance for students to see the school's teachers watching each other and learning from each other – dedicated, professional teachers

How can it be arranged?

This depends on the nature of the working context you are in. It will require either a teacher observing in their own time (and for this to work it means a school where not all teachers are teaching at the same time), or for a teacher's lesson to be covered by another teacher or manager while they do their observation. As a starting point, the teacher can ask their line manager directly whether a peer observation could be arranged, and the reason for it. If it is possible, either the teacher in question or the manager might suggest which other teacher would be a good one to be observed and for that teacher then to be asked. So it might be 'Joe, because he is also teaching IELTS', or 'Sue, because she has been teaching for 25 years', or 'Sammy, because he uses the Interactive Whiteboard (IWB) really well and confidently'.

Some schools are better than others at promoting peer observations as a form of professional development. Here is one example from a school I worked at that demonstrates how it could work. At this school the academic management team wanted to promote peer observation, but it didn't want the full responsibility of setting it up and running it. So a couple of senior teachers took on the responsibility with guidance from the managers. This responsibility was in itself a form of CPD. These teachers set up an 'open door' scheme in which, via a dedicated noticeboard in the staff area, any teacher who was willing for a colleague to come and observe their lesson, or any part of it, could write this on the board. Then another teacher could just pop in at any time when they were free by consulting the timetable of who was teaching which class and at what time. So, by 'opening your door' (i.e. putting your name down as willing to be observed), you allowed other teachers to visit at any time. The observer would usually check with the teacher in advance about the type of lesson they were teaching, and the best time to come in, etc. This often became a two-way process whereby 'A' observed 'B' one week and 'B' observed 'A' the next. The scheme was popular and had the added benefit that it was a scheme effectively run by teachers for teachers.

What happens during a peer observation?

The answer is everything and nothing. Whatever type of observation is occurring, there is sometimes a perception that the observer should be 'doing something' and that the teacher should be producing 'something special'. As we saw in the previous chapter on being observed, however, teachers should not be trying to do anything special but just delivering a 'normal lesson'. And although there is nothing wrong with the observer taking notes or completing a task, there is also nothing wrong with them simply watching and learning. By apparently doing nothing, they are learning everything just by watching and thinking.

That said, there should be some reason for the observation or else it would be hard to measure the benefits and the eventual development of that teacher. That's why it is beneficial if the teacher being observed knows why you are there. If it is to see how that teacher deals with correction, then they can ensure that you see some correction work taking place. The observing teacher will focus on why they are there (e.g. to see correction and other language feedback work) but will, of course, observe and note other areas of interest in the lesson.

> ## Tip
>
> Some observers prefer informal note taking and others prefer to use a more structured form. Either way, make sure it does not get in the way of you actually watching not only the teacher but also, of course, the students.

USING TASK SHEETS

Let's see two possible task sheets as examples of what could be used by teachers in a peer observation. The first is for an observation of language feedback (correction, reformulation of language, etc.) and the second for an observation of an IELTS class. You will notice that the second one is simpler and more open than the first, which is more structured. The key is to devise a task sheet that fits the occasion and helps you. In each example, too, there is the focus on how that observation will help the teacher develop in the future.

Observing for use of language feedback

Type of language feedback	Stage of the lesson	What was focused on and how it was dealt with	What I liked/ learned from the teacher's approach	What I will try to do when I next teach
On-the spot language feedback during whole-class work				
1–1 language feedback when monitoring				
Delayed language feedback at end of activity/lesson				

Observing an IELTS class

What I learned about teaching an IELTS class:
1
2
3
4
5
6
7
8
9
10

As a result of this observation, when I plan my first IELTS class, I will:
•
•
•
•
•

How do you give feedback to the teacher?

This is one of the trickiest aspects of peer observation. When a manager observes a teacher, there is some kind of agenda. This might be a routine check of that teacher to ensure that they are maintaining the expected standards of teaching within a school. There is also a 'hierarchy' – line manager and line managee. Feedback, therefore, has clearly defined boundaries and roles. With peer feedback, however, it is different because it involves a teacher observing a colleague. It is likely, too, that the observing teacher has no experience of observing and giving feedback, and they may well be unclear as to what feedback should be given, and how to give it.

The other factor here is the teacher being observed. For them, this is an informal observation from a colleague who is there to learn and not to assess the lesson. If the observer started giving what amounted to a critical assessment of the lesson, then their reaction would be negative and they would be unlikely ever again to agree to have a peer observe them. On the other hand, if no feedback of any kind took place, then the teacher might start to worry!

With the assumption that your colleague has agreed to you observing them, here are some guidelines:

1 Make sure the teacher knows that you are coming to watch.

2 Let them know roughly what time you will arrive and how long you would like to stay.

3 Tell them the reason for the observation.

4 Ask them where they would like you to sit.

5 If there is time, try to find out a bit about the class, what the teacher has recently done with them, and what the observed lesson or part of the lesson will be about.

6 Ask the teacher if they would like you to give feedback on any aspect of the lesson, or if they would prefer just to discuss the reason for the observation in any post-lesson chat.

7 Do not criticize or give the impression that you are criticizing any aspect of the lesson.

8 Ask questions, such as 'I was really interested in the way you adapted the book today. Why did you choose to do that?'

9 Thank the teacher afterwards and say something positive about the lesson. Ideally, show them that you have learned something and benefited from the experience. 'I loved the way you ... I really want to try that myself.'

10 Go back to the teacher at a later date and tell them how your observation of them has helped your teaching in some way. Tell your manager, too.

I described earlier the 'open door' scheme at a school I worked at. As part of that scheme, the teachers who observed went back to the dedicated peer observation noticeboard and wrote brief comments such as, 'I saw X teach and I really liked Y in the lesson / what I learned was Z.'

 Tip

Since peer observation is neither a formal observation nor a manager/managee observation, the feedback has to be simple, focused and positive. The experience needs to have a measurable result for the observer, and that result will be evidenced in improvements and development shown in your own planning and teachintg.

What are the longer-term benefits?

Since we are talking here about *continuous* professional development, the observation process must not begin and end with the observation itself, or even with the immediate feedback that follows. We have already listed the short-term benefits for all the parties involved (the observer, the observed and the school) and these benefits are also long term.

My experience: Chris Milnes

Chris is a teacher with many years' experience. This is what he said after he observed a colleague teach a Cambridge Advanced English (CAE) test preparation class:

'I've always found peer observations very useful because you get so many ideas from observing your peers. If you're apprehensive about something you haven't done before, it can boost your confidence and you think, "Maybe it won't be such a big leap for me to do this new course", for example. In our staffroom we discuss our ideas and our lessons anyway, but observing each other gives an extra dynamic.

'Last week I observed a Cambridge CAE exam class, which I have never taught before but hope to teach later this year. I've taught other exam classes, but never this one. Doing the peer observation last week has made the prospect less scary. And when I go on to do the class, I'll see it as part of my professional development. In particular, there were three things that really helped me:

- I saw the teacher use lexical notebooks in a way I hadn't thought of before and I really want to try this out. It really seemed to help the students.
- She also used mini-whiteboards to great effect, something I haven't previously done but now want to.

- I have always had a problem keeping a record of emerging language on the board, but the teacher I saw simply took a photograph of the board on the phone to refer to later. I definitely want to do this in future.
- 'For the teacher being observed it can be beneficial, too, although I wouldn't necessarily expect to get feedback afterwards. As an observer, it helps to know in advance if the teacher wants or expects some feedback, and then it helps to have an idea of what they would particularly like feedback on.
- 'It is equally valuable to watch a class without a specific purpose, especially if you don't have much experience or want to see a particular teacher maybe. What you get out of it may be something you didn't anticipate.
- 'To all teachers, I'd say, "Go for it!" It's so useful – it can revolutionize the way you teach and it can give you confidence in your own teaching. It makes observations less scary when they become part of the working culture at the school.'

Summary

Peer observations can be hard to set up, but if there is the opportunity to do it, grab that opportunity. If there isn't, watching lessons on DVD or YouTube is the next best thing. See the experience as a learning opportunity – know what you want to get out of it, and then let that observation drive you towards developing yourself as a teacher. Reflect later on the short-term benefits to your teaching, and then the long-term benefits. And when you have an appraisal or professional development interview (PDI) at work, cite this experience as part of your ongoing development. Reflect, review and evaluate.

5

Day-to-day ideas and development in the staffroom

The staffroom and your colleagues can provide one of the richest sources of development, both in terms of finding out answers to questions and the discussion of ideas and suggestions. Over the years I have worked in many staffrooms with wonderfully giving and sharing colleagues who, to this day, I learn so much from and am happy to help whenever I can. In other words, your development can be and will be furthered on an almost daily basis just through the interaction you have with your colleagues. Development is not just about improving, trying things out and learning new skills; it is also about knowledge and, particularly for a new teacher taking those first steps, building knowledge is a crucial part of development and asking colleagues questions is one way of building that knowledge.

- 'Can you tell me what a cleft sentence is?'
- 'Do you know the best book for speaking activities for low-level students?'
- 'I've got this really difficult student in my class who won't let anyone else speak – what can I do?'
- 'How can I get to teach an exam class for the first time?'
- 'Do you know any good online resources for teachers?'
- 'How can I spend less time planning?'

- 'I need to make my course book more interesting. Can you give me any tips on how best to use it?'
- 'What are the best uses of an interactive whiteboard?'
- 'I think I'm in a rut. What can I do?'
- 'Do you think role plays are useful because my students don't seem to like them?'

I have heard these ten questions in recent months in my staffroom – they are among the hundreds asked in any typical staffroom over the course of any year. These are questions asked *of* teachers *by* teachers. And then there are the ideas and suggestions made between colleagues. 'Have you thought about trying this?' 'Why don't you…?' 'The best way to become a trainer is…' 'I wouldn't do that topic if I were you, it might be culturally inappropriate.' 'Can I come and observe your class to pick up some ideas about using the interactive whiteboard?'

More specifically, and looking back on my career, I would particularly highlight the following aspects of staffroom development in order to underline just how important an aspect of every teacher's professional development staffroom interaction is. Any experienced teacher reading this will know the value of staffroom exchange, but if you actually spent a week listening and noting all the examples you hear, you might be surprised at the extent and value of these professional exchanges.

Early days

Beginning teaching, as I did, straight after finishing your training course can feel really overwhelming. What's more, if you are in a new working environment with people you don't know, you might be reluctant to ask anyone for help. It obviously showed in my case because one day in my first few weeks a colleague approached me and asked if I needed any help with my planning, as I was looking a bit lost. That was the beginning of a career's worth of staffroom support. In those early days everything was new to me – it wasn't just the obvious area of grammar (e.g. 'What on earth is a 2nd conditional sentence?') that concerned me at the time, but also issues concerning where I could find things, the correct procedures to follow and what books I was or was not able to use.

Tip

Don't wait until someone sees you looking worried and asks if you need help – just ask! This is the very beginning of your development as a teacher and your colleagues will be a huge asset at this time.

Language questions

Even beyond those first days, you will always come across new questions that you need a second opinion about – usually from looking at your course book – no matter how long you have been teaching. 'What exactly is the difference between using the present perfect simple and the present perfect continuous?' 'The book says this is the answer but I don't agree. What do you think?' 'Do you think it's OK to use "Yours truly" at the end of a formal letter?' 'Do you think there's any point teaching inversions?' 'Is it OK these days to say "less" people or does it have to be "fewer" people?'

Such questions are asked on an almost daily basis and sometimes these questions simply have 'an answer', which is itself reassuring, and sometimes they might spark a discussion (such as the one about 'less' and 'fewer'). Either way, the ensuing dialogue will help you in some way.

Sharing ideas and materials

However long you have been teaching, you need ideas. Maybe you are about to do a lesson on the active and passive voice for the 75th time and you really want a different practice activity from the one in the book but just can't think of one, or where to look for one. Or maybe you want to do a lesson on the weather with related lexis and you're not sure of the best way to go about it. Or perhaps you have spotted some lovely materials that a colleague has created and you'd like to use them yourself! Or you could be looking for the best book to look at for role-play activities.

Sharing is not one-way traffic and experienced teachers also have lots to gain from the creative ideas of newer teachers.

Advice about students

Knowing the best way to help students is another way in which staffroom colleagues' advice, opinions and experiences can be invaluable. This will often be a case of a student in your class who, for whatever reason, is proving difficult, or who has special needs. Getting general advice from a colleague or, even better, advice from a colleague who knows that student, can be a huge comfort. Just knowing you're not the only one who has students they need help with can be immensely reassuring.

More than this, though, your colleagues can also be a source of help in advising you on any matters to do with students' progress and plans. Helping students with their academic development and with their day-to-day issues is an important part of your own development, especially when you are asked a question you have never been asked before, or for information about something you don't know about or advice on a topic you are not familiar with. Learning more about your students' needs and being able to respond accordingly is a significant part of the teacher's role.

Inspiration for development

Hearing a colleague talking about their conference talk, a course they have done, an idea they have for a lesson, a book they have read about some aspect of teaching or some materials they have created can inspire you to find out more and maybe to do the same thing yourself. Just hearing about what a colleague has done and how much they have got out of it can really motivate you and give you ideas for development. Similarly, you may inspire others with your ideas or activities. Either way, share and discuss development and inspire or be inspired by the process.

Mentoring

Another important feature of staffroom development is being a 'mentor' or a 'buddy' to a fellow staff member. This usually, but not exclusively, involves a more experienced teacher mentoring a new teacher and helping that teacher during their settling-down period.

Such a person would help the new teacher with lesson preparation and the administrative requirements of the school, introduce them to other staff, show them where to find materials and how to use equipment, remind them of what they need to be doing, and just be a friendly face to call on when needed.

As well as being a great support for the new teacher, the mentor also benefits by having this important responsibility and seeing how their guidance can help and reassure a new teacher. I have been involved in such a system myself (and I wish I had had a mentor when I first started) and I find it a very rewarding responsibility, which I always enjoy. It is great to be able to help a new teacher along the way and to remind myself what it is like for that teacher starting out.

Mentoring can take other forms, too. It could involve helping a colleague who is teaching a new type of class for the first time (e.g. an exam class) that you have a lot of experience in. Or maybe you have a colleague who is struggling with a particular aspect of their teaching and could benefit from some ongoing informal guidance and support from a peer. Support of this kind might be informally arranged and agreed between colleagues or set up by the school but, however it is arranged, mentoring is a two-way development process, just as valuable to the mentor as to the mentee. So, even if your school does not operate such a system formally, the next time a new teacher joins your school, why not offer to be their buddy for a few weeks while they settle in to the new job and context? It really is a great source of staffroom development.

THINKING TASKS

Look again at the ten questions at the start of this chapter. Imagine that, over a period of time, a number of colleagues asked you these questions in the staffroom. Choose one of them. What answer would you give? If you are not sure about the answers to any of the questions yourself, see if you can find out by asking some of your colleagues.

At the same time, just make a mental note over the next few days at work of all the questions you hear or ask or get asked, or of any ideas and suggestions that are asked for or given. Alternatively, think of something you would like to find out from or discuss with a colleague. At the end of the process, what have you learned, discussed or overheard that will benefit you in some way with your work – in however small a way?

IDEAS FOR DEVELOPMENT – TEACHER EXPERIENCES

I asked a variety of teachers in one staffroom for one example of something they had done recently that furthered their development in some way and also for any other ideas for staff development that they had. These ideas are listed below in order to show how wide a range of development opportunities can be available at all times. In addition, I have included in this summary some of the suggestions made by teachers and managers in staffrooms in different countries from an online course I tutored. In some cases I have added my comments in brackets.

One idea mentioned by a few people was forming internal special interest groups (SIGs), where a few colleagues with a similar interest (e.g. pronunciation) or the desire to explore a topic in more detail get together to share ideas and thoughts, do some research and try things out (see also Chapter 9 on reading groups). This doesn't even have to be a formal group; it could just be an awareness of colleagues sharing a particular interest and talking about it from time to time. Simply talking and sharing is as valuable in a teacher's development as anything else.

'I presented at this year's IATEFL conference.' (See Chapter 10 for more about this.)

'I've done an EMod course to have another string to my bow.' (See Chapter 13 for more on the value of being a student again and doing other courses.)

'I've volunteered for an experimental project watching a video version of TP on an online CELTA course.'

'A couple of things spring to mind: I became an IELTS examiner, obviously to add another string to my bow and get some extra cash, but also to inform my teaching; and I recently did the IHYLCelta in Lisbon, which helped me manage the young learners while I was there.'

'*When I go into a class, I am always interested in reading what colleagues have left on the whiteboard and how they have laid it all out. This led to me taking pictures of my own board with my mobile phone (as well as sneaking shots of colleagues' boards). It meant I had a record of what went up in all my lessons so I could review them with students at the drop of a hat. It also helped me think about my board planning. Being on my phone, it was easier to access than the IWB so I even took pictures of that.*' (Many teachers do this and it is an excellent way not only to keep a record of work presented on the board but also to review and reflect on your board work.)

'*One of my line managees is reading regularly – he sets himself specific books/topics and a day a week to read. For me, it's writing and marking for Cambridge.*'

'*A little while ago a colleague and I conducted some informal research into the ways in which we help trainees understand complex concepts using metaphors. On another occasion I put together a lesson procedure based on dictogloss and text reconstruction and discussed the advantages and disadvantages with a colleague. I like to try out other people's material to broaden my repertoire as well!*' (Discussing lesson ideas and procedure and trying out lessons your colleagues have told you about is a great way to keep your lessons and your teaching fresh. You may feel that an idea you have tried out didn't work as well as you had hoped, or that an idea 'isn't really for you', but that in itself is part of development, and if the idea or suggestion does work well, so much the better! But just try things out.)

'*I do things that scare me and push me out of my comfort zone. It's the best way to learn for me…*' (A lot of people say this, and it is true for me to a great extent, but read the views expressed about this in Chapter 20 for a contrary view.)

'The thing that springs to mind is me updating the materials I use for CELTA and DELTA input sessions. In the case of the latter, as well as creating hopefully a more engaging and useful session for CPs, it's really about making me look more closely at the literature, especially new publications and articles. The core of the matter is I'm not really a reader, of any sorts of books, so it's a good way of forcing me to remind myself of stuff I have already looked at as well as things that may be new.' (This applies to your lessons as well as to training courses such as CELTA and DELTA. We all like to keep particular material and lessons that have worked well for us in order to use them again... and again... and again. However, you have to avoid falling into the trap of repeating it time and time again because, if you do that, there is a danger of the material, the lesson, and you becoming stale and not really focusing on the particular group of students or trainees you are working with. So adapt the material, play around with the approach, keep it (and you) fresh and know when the time has come to say 'This is out of date now, I won't use it again.' And, yes, read and look at other books and materials in order to get new material and new ideas.)

'I read Jeremy Harmer's correspondence with various commentators and learned how pundits manage their blogs and correspondence. With great courtesy is the short answer!' (There are so many blogs out there, some general and some specific to a particular topic, and it is a good way to read and contribute to an ongoing discussion about a topic or topics.)

'I found all my work as ADOS on MOOCs, iPads and digital literacies very interesting and stimulating. It was very challenging to think that I had to distil it, evaluate it and pass it on or recommend it to others, i.e. Exec teachers.'

'One thing I've done quite a lot of is reporting for a publisher. They send through the first draft of a course book and ask me to comment on it. It's not proofreading, but checking to see whether the tasks work and whether there is a good enough mix of skills, whether the material will work in class and is appropriate for the level, etc., and suggesting improvements.' (See Chapter 11 for more on this.)

'After seven years coasting comfortably at work, I confronted my technophobia and did an e-moderating course. Immediately after (and as a result of) that, I worked as tutor on the second-ever online CELTA. I then spoke about my experience at two conferences and moved into online tutoring of the Educational Management online course. One thing led to another, you could say!' (Ah, 'coasting comfortably' – we're back into that comfort zone! This could have been me as I was something of a technophobe myself but I, too, confronted this when I entered the world of online tutoring and that opened up many opportunities for me later. Confronting something may not always work out, but unless you try, you'll never know.)

'Trying things out. You're reading a book, you see an idea and you think, "So and so says that you can get students to close their eyes while you set up a task" and it says why, and you think "Oh, I'm not sure about that... no, I'll try it out." I've done that a lot recently, just giving things a go. There's nothing wrong with picking up a journal or a resource book and just flicking through it until you find something you've never done before and thinking "I'll give it a go".

'A few years ago, as part of the effort to keep teachers interested in development, we set up a number of internal special interest groups – such as Business, 1–1, Young learners, Exam classes. I was in the Pronunciation SIG

and we met every fortnight to discuss what we had been doing in class with pronunciation. We also agreed to read a methodology book and every month met to talk about what we had read. It worked out well and at the end of the period we put on what in my humble opinion was a really successful INSETT. As the CPD had a focus, and quite a narrow one, it was easy to keep track of what we were doing. I was also an area that is often neglected so it made us all examine our lessons and find ways of incorporating pronunciation into them. There was also a sense of competition that made us stay involved. I have to say that, although the Pronunciation SIG worked well, some of the others died a death. Some people felt forced into their choice of SIG so didn't feel motivated to make it work – a learning point, I'm sure.' (This is the first of a number of comments about the SIGs I referred to before.)

'I think the idea of having organizational SIGs with accompanying reading groups and INSETT sessions is a great idea. I'm sure some may not last as well as others, and it requires time and dedication on the part of participants, but even if only one or two "work" and last, then it seems to me to be a really worthwhile initiative.' (This person and the one before highlight the usefulness of one idea being part of different strands of development: SIGs, reading groups and INSETT sessions.)

'Internal SIGs are a really nice idea and might be a nice complement to what we are doing here around action research and peer observations.'

'I can see people working on similar areas setting up a group and getting together. I usually find that the chance to talk to my colleagues about teaching ideas and approaches is one of the best things to come out of INSETTs, so this is making it more focused.'

'In-house SIGs sound a good idea; we're doing something similar this week. As there are no lessons, we've divided

our teachers into four SIGs relating to young learners, adults, IT and the Resource Centre and asked them to investigate what projects they could usefully develop this week. The latter two have gone really well because the teachers themselves chose to be in those groups, and both were led by "experts". The former two are dying a death because there is no clear leader and the teachers fell into the groups by not electing to take part in any specific SIG. So I agree that SIGs must be led and motivated by "experts", and that they will only work well if the teachers themselves choose areas they're interested in.' (I'm not sure that the groups need to be led by an 'expert', but I do agree that participants need to be interested in and motivated by the topic area.)

'The Barcelona Young Learner centre where I used to work had a similar system, with each "learning group" focusing on a different teaching skill. I co-facilitated the group on learning technologies and enjoyed watching other groups' INSETTs and presentations on our in-house days. The groups lasted quite a long time – and no one had to join. I think teachers were paid admin rate for attending.'

'Piloting a new course book is an excellent way to get involved, and also it is motivating for more experienced teachers who might be getting a bit stale. This approach will work best if a) you have regular meetings with your line manager so that you can give your feedback on how the pilot process is going, b) you feel that your opinion is valued, and c) you can give some feedback on the new course book to other teachers – perhaps through a teachers' meeting. You could also make suggestions or recommendations to colleagues if the book is adopted.'

'Shadowing a staff member (e.g. teacher shadows receptionist) is not often used as part of an INSETT programme, but it can be very helpful to make different staff groups aware of what others do. Teachers may

be much more sympathetic to administrative staff, for example, once they realize first-hand the problems that missing documentation can cause. Equally, it makes sense to ask administrative staff to at least sit in on a couple of English classes at different levels, so they are better able to inform prospective clients about what actually goes on in the classes and how your organization is different from competitors. If you offer courses for younger learners, then I think all administrative staff who might have contact with parents should sit in on a couple of those classes, so they can reassure parents who might feel that the classes are "not serious enough" in contrast with their own, perhaps more traditional, language learning experiences.' (See Chapter 21 for more on organizational INSETT and the idea of shadowing a colleague. For most teachers, this might be difficult to do, but what you can do is to ask a colleague working elsewhere in the school what their role is. And as for your teaching colleagues, why not ask to observe them or be observed by them? Refer back to Chapter 4 for more on this.)

Summary

Whether it is asking or answering questions, giving or receiving ideas and suggestions, asking for or showing support, overhearing or joining in a professional discussion, or being a mentor to a colleague, day-to-day interaction in the staffroom can be a rich source of development. It is free, it is easy, it is relaxed, and you actually learn so much about your job and all its aspects from your staffroom colleagues. So don't be afraid to ask, or to contribute.

6

Taking part in INSETT sessions

In-service training for teachers (INSETT), also sometimes known as 'TD sessions' (teacher development sessions), is one of the best and most accessible forms of CPD for teachers, given that most schools offer TD sessions on a regular basis. Although this chapter is primarily about attending such sessions, we will also consider the value of leading an INSETT meeting.

Every school I have ever worked at has held INSETT sessions for its staff, though some variations will occur in terms of:

- how often they are held
- whether they are primarily 'top-down' (mostly manager-led) or primarily led by teachers and trainers, or a balance between the two
- whether the ideas for sessions come from teachers, managers, or both
- how long the sessions last
- whether they are compulsory or voluntary to attend

Some organizations offer INSETT sessions to staff on a monthly or even weekly basis, or maybe termly, depending on the nature of the organization. To give you an idea of the range of sessions possible with in-house INSETT, listed below is a selection of ten INSETT sessions held at one particular school over a period of a few months. Most of these sessions were led by teachers with a particular interest or expertise in the subject, and two were led by managers.

- **'I want to level up'** – focusing on the issues related to students who ask to go up a level when their English isn't good enough to do so. Just how do you deal with such students?
- **'Cambridge main suite exam marking'** – a session primarily for teachers of Cambridge exam classes on marking students' exam practice in class in relation to the marking of actual exams
- **'Tips for new IELTS teachers'** – aimed at teachers new to teaching IELTS classes or who want to become involved in them
- **'Blog focus group'** – looking at doing blogs with students in class and out of class and how they can be a motivational aspect of learning and practising English
- **'Let's explore the noun phrase'** – one of a number of language-focus sessions to give teachers more awareness of and confidence in using language
- **'Top tips for new teachers'** – geared towards short-term summer teachers and especially those who are not very experienced, this session included 62 top tips
- **'Intelligibility or impressions? – requests in ELF scenarios'** – a session led by a trainer who was going to be giving this talk at the forthcoming IATEFL conference and wanted to do a 'dry run' with colleagues beforehand (more on this in Chapter 10)
- **'Looking at new course books'** – a workshop looking at possible new course books to use in class
- **'Using the phonemic chart in class'** – fun ways of exploiting the chart with students
- **'Helping students with special needs'** – for example, those with dyslexia or physical disabilities

Benefits for teachers

INSETT sessions can be a valuable confidence boost. Sharing ideas and experiences with colleagues will help you realize that others also have the same thoughts, fears, questions or ideas – you're not alone. INSETT allows you to share, to reflect and to grow.

To show how INSETT sessions can both help and motivate teachers, I have focused on two in particular, one that I attended and one that I led. The INSETT session I attended, called 'Criticalthinkingarising', was led by the very experienced teacher, teacher trainer and conference speaker Danny Norrington-Davies. (Further details of this session can be found on the IH London website: www.ihlondon.com) The one I led was called 'Pace and challenge in lessons'.

THINKING TASK 1

Think back to the last time you did a lesson with a reading focus. How did you stage the lesson, and to what extent did students 'interact' with the text? What do you understand by 'critical thinking' in relation to a reading lesson?

Now read below what Danny's session was about – is this something you usually do or would now consider doing more of? What do you see as the benefits of what Danny discusses?

'Criticalthinkingarising'

When I asked Danny what this session was going to be about, he answered as follows:

'It was about adding critical thinking to a standard lesson procedure when you've doing a reading lesson – so, a lead-in, reading tasks, analysing language from the text, controlled practice such as a gap-fill and a freer speaking. I saw a CELTA trainee do this kind of lesson and it was very good and it's excellent to see a trainee create their own materials, but what I wanted was to use the feedback I gave the trainee to share with new teachers. That is, if you add thinking skills into your standard procedure, you'll get a lot more out of the lesson so students will interact more with the text, look for flaws, make conclusions or assumptions about what they've read.

'With a gap-fill, for example, you fill in the gaps but you could then discuss the context of it. In this particular lesson the text was about what you would do if you were king or queen of your country. One example was that 'chocolate would be free' and students had to respond with 'That's a terrible idea because...' so the gap-fill then becomes much more than just a simple focus on language. And then, in the freer practice, students say what they would do if they had the power and the others would challenge their ideas with 'That's a terrible idea because...' and start a discussion. So I was looking at a one-hour lesson that was really good already that could be made into three hours maybe, with a lot more conversation and genuine interaction, and a lot more language would have then emerged. Because I had a lot of experienced teachers and trainers attending, I partly turned the session into how you might encourage CELTA trainees to do this more, and this opened up other areas for discussion.'

Session feedback

After the session I asked a number of those who attended why they came and what they got out of it – especially in terms of how they felt the session would make them better teachers when it came to doing reading in class. This is what they had to say.

What was it that made you want to attend this particular session?

- The fact that Danny was leading it and I want to be like him!
- I wanted to learn more about critical thinking
- I am always keen to learn from my peers
- Critical thinking needs to be integrated into language lessons and I wanted tips on this
- Always interested in Danny's ideas

What do you think were the most interesting or useful aspects of it, and why?

- Critical thinking
- Exploiting material more
- How to encourage teachers to get students to interact more with a text
- Including higher-order thinking skills in lessons
- Seeing how the idea can be used in the classroom
- Good practical teaching ideas
- Looking at how to expand on texts in a more meaningful way
- Using comprehension questions in a more meaningful way
- That it would be something to think about on CELTA courses

What aspects of the session might influence future reading lessons that you do and benefit both you and your learners?

- Processing texts more for meaning
- Exploring the students' reactions more
- It would contribute to a more stimulating learning environment
- Trying to get students to evaluate texts and practise activities in class more
- It will raise the level of challenge
- It will make tasks more engaging
- I used the materials and ideas yesterday and they worked a treat and the students loved the opportunity to think about the text on a different level. It was very generative and we had lots of emerging language and meaningful, genuine speaking
- Doing the language analysis after the whole thing instead of doing it straight after the text
- Looking at language later
- Giving students more space for critical thinking

Why do you find INSETT sessions useful and important to you as a teacher?

- They give us good ideas
- Makes you think differently about the way you do things
- They give you fresh ideas to use in lessons
- They give you the opportunity to discuss techniques with colleagues
- It's easy to get stuck in a rut. TD sessions make me reflect and push myself
- It's nice to see that other people are in the same boat!
- There's always more to learn
- Love listening to new or different ideas/experiences

What other INSETT sessions have you recently attended?

- A session on visualization
- A session on revisiting course book texts
- A session on text cohesion
- A session on using new course books
- A session on pronunciation, which revolutionized my pronunciation teaching!

- A session on creativity
- A session on 'Punctuation as an Endangered Species'
- A session on warmers and fillers
- A session on using mini-whiteboards
- A session on using the interactive whiteboard

The benefits of leading a session

I spoke to Danny again later about delivering this particular INSETT session and how leading such sessions as well as attending them can be an aid to development. This is his response:

'The feedback I got afterwards was very positive, in that a few teachers said it had made them think about their procedure, but I also had questions and comments about how to fit this approach into the criteria for assessing lessons on a CELTA course. That was good, because it was nice for me to have some challenging questions and feedback. For example, one trainer said this idea wouldn't work for weaker candidates on a course and another asked about criteria, so it's good to get someone reining you in because I got very enthused about it all, sort of "I'm getting rid of course books in Week 1."

'Leading sessions is good for my own professional development and I do them a lot as well as speaking at conferences. I think there are two reasons for this. One is when you do something quite practical you then get other teachers who do the same thing and then they come and talk to you about it, and you realize that you've got something to share and you then start looking more deeply into what you do. I did another session recently and the teachers told me how it had worked with their students and it's nice to see when the techniques you are suggesting work for other people and this confirms your willingness to share.

'The other reason is that I'm not very good at just reading and getting information and "putting it away". I usually have to read something or see something or hear something and then talk about it to someone and then I've got it. That's why, during the 'talk, I suddenly thought, "Oh, I think I'll get rid of course books on CELTA." It was having an idea occur to me simply as a result of my sharing thoughts on critical reading. And so I decided to do a session on the handout I had on reading skills that I could have just read and filed away, to see what other people thought about it. And I saw that I can use it now that I know it works. I remember reading a quote from someone – "You can't just read and know something as teachers – you have to do something with it." It's like language teaching. I couldn't read grammar books when I was beginning and then go into a lesson and teach the grammar. I had to teach it first and then see the book; that was the only way I could do it.

'It's also equally valuable for a teacher with, say, one or two years' experience to lead a session. New teachers need to understand that they have everything that more experienced teachers don't have. I co-led a session once with quite a new teacher on study skills and she had the most amazing ideas of how to deal with a monolingual group and she just went in, took over and ran with it. Sometimes, rather than just telling a new teacher "This is interesting", if you share it, they will realize better what they can bring to a session and how more experienced teachers can benefit from their ideas. I think it's wonderful when you go in and say, "This is what I am doing, tell me what you think" and everyone confirms that what you are doing is very good. I think that the fact that you stand up in front of other teachers and do a session can give you confidence and the feedback will be positive. So I think that all teachers should lead these sessions, not just the more experienced ones.'

'Pace and challenge in lessons'

During the course of writing this book, I led an INSETT session at a summer school for teachers relatively new to the profession, and new to the school and its environment, focusing on 'pace and challenge in lessons'. Later I will reflect on how doing this session helped me as well as asking those who attended how it helped them.

In Chapter 2, on starting out, we considered some of the challenges faced by people teaching for the first time, with so much still to learn and to experience. For a very experienced teacher it can be easy to forget just how new and difficult everything was when they started, and therefore how important it is to help new teachers with 'the basics'. Having an appropriate pace and level of challenge in lessons is very important for effective teaching and learning, but these are often areas that new teachers struggle with. That, therefore, was the background to my session.

First, though, here is a task to consider some of the aspects of pace and challenge in lessons.

THINKING TASK 2

Either think about and perhaps make notes, or discuss with a colleague or colleague(s) the following questions. Ideally, try to speak with at least one colleague with different experience from you. Whether you are very experienced or quite new to teaching, pace and challenge are areas that always remain an important part of the teacher's skill.

1 What do you understand by 'pace'?
2 What are some of the factors that can affect pace in the classroom?
3 What can you do to reduce potential pace problems in the following situations?
    1 When monitoring students during an activity
    2 When dealing with a student in your class who is at a significantly lower level than the others
    3 When assessing how much time in a lesson you spend talking and explaining
    4 When faced with a dominant student
    5 When using favourite materials of yours many times
4 What do you understand by 'challenging' your students?
5 What are some of the ways you could do this in relation to:
    1 checking understanding of meaning?
    2 dealing with pronunciation?
    3 setting up a reading or listening task?

4 using your course book?

5 when faced with a student or students who usually finish tasks sooner than the others?

Session feedback

After my session I asked a few of those who attended to give some feedback on the session and how or why they found it useful as part of their ongoing development. Some of those who came were very experienced but they still felt that pace and challenge were sometimes a problem for them.

Why did you come to this session? Are pace and challenge areas you feel you have had problems with?

'I am a newly qualified teacher (I finished my CELTA less than two weeks ago) and so I am very new to the world of teaching and any information from more experienced teachers is valuable to me.'

'Pace and challenge is something I have problems with. I worry that some students aren't challenged enough at times and I can get stuck with students asking me questions about random things not always related to the task. I look around but struggle to stop a student talking to me.'

'I believe that pace and challenge in the classroom will always be a problem area for teachers new and old. The dynamics of the classroom and the ever-changing needs of students and their expectations mean that the teacher needs to be fully armed with an array of techniques to deal with these common problems.'

'I think professional development is very important and gives teachers things to think about when planning and teaching. It stops them getting into bad habits or stuck in a rut. Generally, I think it is best practice to attend training sessions.'

'As a newly qualified teacher, any teacher development is valuable. Pace and challenge was not something I recall being dealt with explicitly on my CELTA.'

What aspects of the session did you find useful or helpful?

'Going through the factors that can affect pace and challenge in a systematic way has helped me cement them in my mind and will contribute to my awareness of pace and challenge in my lessons.'

'It's good to talk with other teachers and hear that everyone has similar issues. It's helpful to review techniques to help overcome some of these issues.'

'I found the different methods of dealing with pace in particular very useful and to see that they are problems faced by other teachers put my mind at ease. It contained a lot of useful tips.'

'Relating situations to our own experience and sharing with colleagues.'

'Surprisingly, but pleasingly, the fact that other teachers are experiencing similar issues.'

How do you think the session may help you in your teaching?

'It has given me clear points to bear in mind while in the classroom.'

'It will give me the confidence to say (politely) "I'll come back to you on that," etc., when needed.'

'It definitely highlighted some areas with my teaching and has given me confidence in how to address them.'

'I will be more conscious of this in class now and prepare better.'

'I will have a better insight into students' learning and learning experience.'

'Hopefully, I will be perceived as a better teacher.'

INSETT and CPD

You may wonder how, or even if, leading such a session can also benefit a wrinkled old-timer such as myself, or someone with much less experience than those attending. Well, it can. Danny talked about how leading his session benefited him, and how it can be good for a newer teacher to also lead such sessions, and for me, too, there were a number of benefits.

It is always good to 'go back to basics' and remind yourself of them. It is easy to slip into bad habits in your own teaching, so revisiting these so-called basics can be a timely reminder and force you to re-evaluate your own teaching.

By realizing that those attending welcome your input, and see it as something which will help their own teaching, is very rewarding in itself. I don't usually devote an explicit session to pace and challenge on a pre-service CELTA course – these factors are usually dealt with as part of teaching-practice feedback – but I think from now on I will dedicate a session to this topic.

As someone currently working in a managerial role in a large school, I can easily get sucked into the day-to-day requirements of systems and procedures and not have as much time as I would like to devote to teachers. Running such a session has redressed the balance and helped me in my managerial capacity to remember always that, in my professional opinion, my first responsibility in this role is to support and develop teachers.

Not long before this session, I did an observation of a new teacher and among all the very good aspects to the lesson and to his teaching was a clear issue with pace, in that he was rushing the students and not exploiting and developing the language focus properly, leaving some students confused. By linking observations to INSETT, you can address the issues being faced by your staff, so for me this observation informed my choice of INSETT session. Ideally, observations of teachers should do this – as an observer you should identify key areas where there may be problems, or where it is felt there could be new ideas or approaches, and plan INSETT sessions accordingly. Sessions could also be as a result of recommendations made by an inspecting body, or requests from teachers, or feedback from students.

Tip

Make INSETT relevant and useful to your context and to your teachers and students.

Summary

Attending conference talks may not be possible for many staff, but in-house INSETT sessions are there on your doorstep and a golden opportunity for development in a broad range of areas that affect your teaching and more. They need to be regular as part of ongoing development and, ideally, they should be led by a variety of staff members – teachers (both newer and more experienced), managers, and occasionally speakers from outside the organization. If you're a teacher in a school that welcomes suggestions for sessions, do just that and suggest a session on a particular topic – even volunteering to run it. Newer or less confident teachers could team up with someone else and share the preparation and delivery of a session. Leading sessions is just as useful to your development as attending a session.

There should be a good range of topics, including practical teaching ideas and ideas for discussion. Some topics should arise from:

- observations of teachers – what are the common features of these observations that could be useful for teachers to have INSETT on?
- the comments or recommendations of inspecting bodies
- a recent conference talk that someone has attended and is giving feedback on.

There needs to be follow-up:

- Reflect on what you got from attending or leading a session.
- Evaluate how the session may now inform and influence your teaching or training.
- Try out the ideas you have discussed and see whether they work for you.
- Share your findings and experiences so that the session you went to doesn't simply end that day but continues in the days, weeks and months ahead. Ideally, you want to get to the point

where you can say 'As a result of that session, my teaching / my lessons / my students / my approach, etc., has benefited from the session in the following way(s)...' Just as valuable is to try out something new and on reflection decide 'No, this doesn't work for me.'

- If you have the chance, why not make it your target for the next year to lead an INSETT session for your fellow teachers?

SECTION 3

Later steps

7

Using online resources

Finding, adapting and integrating materials from other sources is an important part of CPD. Whether these sources are from colleagues (e.g. lesson plans), other books and materials in your place of work or from online sources, the important point is that you are integrating a variety of different sets of materials into your teaching and this contributes to your own development. Being able to select, adapt and supplement your course book is an important part of the teacher's repertoire and you are effectively making these 'borrowed materials' your own.

Looking online for ideas for professional development and for ideas for the classroom can be a rather overwhelming experience, given the enormous range and number of sites available, but the very fact that there is so much online professional support out there is little short of fantastic. The problem, though, can be where to start looking.

CPD TASK 1

No doubt you already have your favourite online sites. Make a list of the sites you particularly like and find useful, either in terms of ideas for lessons or more general professional development (e.g. teacher blogs and sites containing professional articles). Then ask a few colleagues for their favourites and add them to your list. If they mention sites that you are unfamiliar with, go online and explore them and decide whether you want to add any to your own list of favourites.

Useful online resources

What follows is a selection of sites that I use and like or have just discovered and which I would recommend to others. The web addresses can be found in the 'Useful web addresses' section at the end of the book. I could list more, but this list is quite wide-ranging. Two of the sites are purely for lesson ideas and materials and the others are focused more on professional development, although some of these also have teaching materials.

You will surely be familiar with some of these sites, with others less so. Since sites change from year to year, you may find some content referred to is no longer there or has changed in some way if you are reading this several years after it was written. Despite this, your searches are bound to lead you to something, somewhere that will interest you enough for you to explore them. You will find sites where you can read something new, contribute an article, sign up for a workshop or select some new material for a lesson. And, if you didn't already realize it, you will also discover just how much is available in cyber world.

I have certainly felt overwhelmed at times looking at these sites one after another and at all that is on them. The amount of material available is huge, but it is probably best to stick to your own selected favourites once you have decided what they are. Many sites are updated with new content on a regular basis, and so it is perhaps more useful and time-efficient to know your way around relatively few than to dip into a large number without ever fully exploiting what's on them.

Tip

As part of staff development, it is good to share your favourite sites, or to direct colleagues to sites you have found that contain content that would be of particular interest or use to them. Why not compile a list of everyone's favourite sites and what you find most useful on them and display this, perhaps on a staff noticeboard? For example, you could publicize sites that are particularly rich in articles for reading and discussing.

Online resources for managers

If you are a line manager or the Director of Studies, relevant websites can give you ideas to pass on to those you manage, perhaps during annual appraisals. And, of course, one idea can lead to another. So an online article could form the basis of:

- a reading group session
- a new classroom activity
- an organizational INSETT session, based on a new approach you have learned about

You might even find a talk from a conference that you have been inspired to attend, or which you have read about, and it might encourage you to do a conference talk yourself.

SITES WITH LESSON IDEAS AND MATERIALS

Handoutsonline

This site was recommended to me and I now recommend it to others. At the time of writing, the site offers more than 400 'ready-to-go' lessons: over 95 pages' worth of handouts and notes arranged according to level, topic or type (such as 'telephone English'). You can print off worksheets with teachers' notes and answers for a lesson on the present perfect, or a reading about weather for B2 learners, or a lesson on lexis to do with travel, or just about anything else you can think of.

Although you will not be able to access the worksheets without joining, you can still have a look at the site and get a good feel for what is available on it. To use the materials, you need to pay a small annual registration fee (or your school could have institutional membership).

Link: www.handoutsonline.com

Onestopenglish

This is a similar type of site, and one very popular among many colleagues I have worked with. Here again, you need to pay a small annual registration fee to access some of the materials.

Link: www.onestopenglish.com

CPD TASK 2

1 Have a general look around the Handouts website to see what you think of it.

2 Take the 'free tour' and see a sample of the worksheets on offer.

3 If you are a member, or decide to register and become one, find a worksheet or lesson that you could use with one of the classes you are teaching and download it. Try to choose a topic or language area or activity type that you are less familiar with or confident about in order to help you become more familiar. Adapt it in whatever way you feel appropriate to your class, and then do the lesson. Afterwards, reflect on the lesson and material – do you think this site could now become a source of material you could use from time to time, maybe as a change from using a course book?

CPD TASK 3

1 Have a general look around the onestopenglish website.

2 What differences do you see between this and handoutsonline? In particular, have a look at the 'community' and 'support' links and explore some of the content.

3 Search for and find out from the site something about about 'CLIL' and 'TKT' that you don't already know, and also ideas for using mobile phones in the classroom in TKT. Maybe you could try out one of the mobile phone ideas that you haven't thought of doing before with one of your classes. (At the time of writing various lesson plans are available for mobile phone lessons.)

PROFESSIONAL DEVELOPMENT SITES

Several of the following sites also contain lesson ideas, but the focus is equally – if not more – on professional development.

ESLcafe

I have used this site throughout my career and, like many of its kind, it is very hard to just dip into because it has so much information that you inevitably find five minutes online turning into a couple of hours. At the time of writing, this site includes the following sections:

- 'Jobs'
- 'Stuff for teachers'
- 'Stuff for students'
- 'Stuff for everyone'

I decided to see whether I could expand my teaching ideas a bit by choosing 'Stuff for teachers' / 'idea cookbook' / 'for the teacher' – 'pronunciation' to look for some new activities to try out in my lessons. On opening the page I discovered about 50 different links, many with intriguing titles. I chose 'minimal pairs telephone pronunciation' as I wanted a new activity to provide students with practice of this area of pronunciation. The idea was contributed by a teacher called Nick and involved having a series of minimal pairs such as 'chip' and 'cheap' next to a number. In the activity one student would give another a 'telephone number' such as 35754 and the other student would then read out the corresponding words before alternating with one student reading out a list of words and the other student giving the corresponding 'telephone number'.

I liked the idea, tried it out, and found that it worked well, and the students enjoyed it while at the same time getting some useful pronunciation practice.

On the site are hundreds of ideas contributed by teachers, largely for young learner classes, as well as forums for teacher training and students, chatrooms and much more.

Link: eslcafe.com

Teachitworld

I discovered this site only recently and I wish I had discovered it much earlier. Finding a new site gives you an enormous new source both of lesson ideas and materials and stimulating and thought-provoking articles. I spent a whole morning exploring this site and to see what is there. There are different levels of membership but even the free membership allows access to a significant amount of material and useful articles. For me it was a great discovery as I read a number of articles for both teachers and trainers, and found some easy-to-go lessons and materials, which I am now very keen to try out.

Link: www.teachitelt.com

CPD TASK 4

I suggest that you register for free membership first before exploring Teachitworld further. Once you have done that, find between three and five ready-to-use lessons that would be appropriate to your context and learners, and give them a go. Then find an article on a subject you either would like to know more about or would like to have a different perspective on. For example, at the time of writing, articles are available on subjects as diverse as the educational possibilities of hip-hop (by Alastair Pennycook) – which I probably won't be exploiting myself! – and how 'ESOL' differs from 'EFL' (by Clare Suss). I also downloaded several lessons to use with my students in study skills classes.

Tinyteflteacher

This site attracted me by its name, to be honest, and is another site I was not previously familiar with. That in itself is always a motivation for me to look, just to see what I've previously been missing out on. It has many links to lesson ideas and materials including a wealth of pronunciation activities, many of which I look forward to trying out.

Link: www.tinyteflteacher.co.uk

An A–Z of ELT

Scott Thornbury, a teacher and teacher educator with more than 30 years' experience in English language teaching, writes a fascinating and thought-provoking blog based on his book *An A–Z of ELT* (Macmillan 2006).

I looked up the entry 'Soaps' under 'S' and was reassured that it referred not to what we use in the shower but to what some of us watch on TV. Maybe my addiction to *Dallas* from 1978 until 2014 (yes, I admit it here in print) is what drew me to this entry! I was subsequently really interested to read about studies into the benefits of using soap operas as part of the learning process and how repeated and structured exposure to them and what is perhaps dubiously perceived as exposure to 'real language' can help learners with their English. I even discovered that there are books dedicated to the subject. And I got all that just from 'S'!

Link: https://scottthornbury.wordpress.com

CPD TASK 5

Go to the Scott Thornbury blog and have a read. Perhaps set yourself the target of reading a few entries each day. Make a note of any ideas or thoughts expressed that 'got you thinking' and perhaps inspired you to read more on a particular topic, or entries that suggested something new you might try in your classroom. Or just choose a letter at random and see what comes up.

English Club

English Club contains lesson materials, ideas and plans, teacher forums, articles, jobs, teaching tips and sections relating to learning difficulties and ELT management. This was a site I was not familiar with but which now will be added to my favourites. I especially liked the inclusion of sections about management and the teacher forums allowing discussion among teachers worldwide on a variety of subjects. Sites like this are a good source of articles to discuss in reading groups (see Chapter 9). 'Using memory in class' and 'Classroom – forum or arena?' were two articles that caught my attention that could be used for group discussions. An article about helping learners with dyslexia was also an interesting read that has given me greater insight into the subject.

Link: www.englishclub.com

> ### Tip
>
> These sites can sometimes be a bit overwhelming, given the rich and mind-boggling amount of content, so it can be more realistic to set yourself the aim of 'doing' one thing a day. This might be reading an article to further your awareness of a subject, finding a new idea for the classroom, or contributing to a teachers' forum.
>
> This can be more doable if you have a particular focus in mind – for example 'I want to read something about teaching very mixed-level classes so that I can help my students more' or 'I want to go to a forum because I want to start a discussion about the use of electronic dictionaries in the classroom – do they help or hinder learning?'

ELTjam

This is another interesting site I had not previously explored. It has many articles and posts from a variety of contributors, ranging from an article about 'Learnification' by Philip Kerr to one about the use of technology as an aid to learning in classrooms in Korea by David Harbinson.

Link: www.eltjam.com

Cambridge English Teacher

This excellent site has lots of professional development links.

Link: www.cambridgeenglishteacher.org

Tip

I am now realizing to an even greater extent than before just how much ELT content is 'out there' on the net! My advice is to have your selected favourite sites that you regularly dip into for lesson ideas and avenues of professional development, and to see what additional content has been added, and then every so often to dip into an unfamiliar site to discover, as I have been doing in the process of writing this chapter, new sources of content and developmental material.

INTERNATIONAL HOUSE SITES

These sites are great for discussions, blogs and ideas.

IH Teachers

IH Teachers has a section called 'Our students & classes' in which you will find articles on juggling multi-level groups, dealing with 'problem students' and student problems, and dealing with motivational issues, all of which should give you some useful tips for the classroom.

Link: www.ihlteachers.co.uk

IH London Blogs

IH London Blogs has an article 'Teaching English for digital chat and social media' by Fiona Johnston. This article is about a conference talk Fiona gave at IATEFL in 2014. She talks about this session in Chapter 10 and the two pieces together give some great ideas and insight into using digital chat and social media in the classroom, an area in which many teachers probably feel they need guidance.

Link: www.ihlondon.com/blog/posts

TEACHER TRAINING SITES

No journey into the cyber world of ELT would be complete without a visit to the **British Council** website. This site includes sections on tools for teachers, teaching resources, articles, teacher training, specialist training, blogs, special events and teacher development. This last section includes areas such as conferences, publications, research, seminars, webinars and continuous professional development. If this book is mostly about giving ideas for CPD and hearing from experienced professionals in order to encourage, persuade or even inspire you to do something to further your development, then this British Council site is an essential next step to guide you along your professional journey in a structured and detailed way.

You should also refer to **Eaquals** whether you are a teacher, a trainer or a manager.

Line managers could use both the British Council and the Eaquals links for the staff they line-manage, and either one could form the basis of ongoing INSETT within your organization.

We will return to the importance of these sites in Chapter 19: Get ahead.

Links: www.britishcouncil.org

http://eaquals.org/

CPD TASK 6

Go to the British Council site (www.britishcouncil.org) and explore the section on CPD in detail; it includes comprehensive content on all aspects of CPD for professionals at different stages of their careers, and provides many links to help you further.

Go to the Eaquals site (http://eaquals.org/pages/7104) and do a self-assessment of your professional competencies. This will give you an indication of what competencies you need to acquire or develop in three broad development stages.

Tip

Make online resources part of your professional development and that of your colleagues. All you need is a computer and Internet access and maybe a fixed hour a week to delve into the world of online CPD. It's time to log on!

Summary

We have looked at a number of sites but there are many, many more, all of which provide teachers, and learners, with material and ideas and which provide professionals with uncountable opportunities for professional development. This might be reading a professional article, contributing to a forum or finding out about a local conference you'd like to attend, or discovering a new idea for the classroom, or discovering more about learning styles... basically anything that will help you to your job better, or differently, and which will help your learners in some way.

8

Teaching exam classes

I always tell new teachers that they won't be asked to teach exam classes until they have a good deal of experience under their belt. My story was different (and definitely not one to be recommended), in that the very first class I was given was an exam class to replace the scheduled teacher who had to take sick leave. The class was a Cambridge First Certificate in English (FCE) class and I had the group for 12 weeks alongside a General English class. It was, shall we say, 'an education' for me.

So why is teaching an exam class an important developmental experience for a teacher? For a start, you will be working with a group of students with the same goal alongside high expectations and strong motivation. Teaching a General English class, by contrast, can involve students who are studying for assorted reasons, and who may be less clear about their specific learning goals. With an exam class, then, you will need to focus more on having a clear course structure and on having clear aims for every activity in every lesson that relate to the exam. Further, you will need to develop your analytical skills and ability to think like a marker/assessor in terms of viewing learning outcomes, and to understand what is required to achieve good results in any given exam. All of these factors contribute to professional growth and make teaching an exam class an important form of CPD.

These are the principal exams that will be referred to in this chapter:

- Cambridge First Certificate of English (FCE) – now more commonly known as 'Cambridge First'
- Certificate of Advanced English (CAE)
- Certificate of Proficiency in English (CPE)
- Test of English as a Foreign Language (TOEFL)
- International English Language Testing System (IELTS)

There is more information about these at the end of the chapter.

THINKING TASK 1

How much do you know about the exams listed above (and there are many others apart from these)? If you are not familiar with any of them, find out as much as you can both about them and why students take them. Once you have done this, the rest of this chapter will make more sense.

THINKING TASK 2

Do Part A if you have experience in teaching any kind of exam class, and Part B if you haven't.

Part A

Reflect on the following:

- What would you say are the principal differences between teaching a General English class and teaching an exam class?
- What do you like best about teaching exam classes?
- What are the biggest challenges and how do you overcome them?
- Why would you recommend to a teacher who has never taught an exam class that they should do so?
- What would be your top tips for teaching an exam class?

Part B

Try to find a colleague who has taught exam classes and ask them the questions above. If you cannot do this, try to imagine what the answers might be from doing the first task above.

Once you have completed one of these tasks, you should already have either reflected on your knowledge and experience of exams and teaching exam classes or increased your knowledge and awareness. Either way, that is a degree of personal development.

My experience: Andrea Borsato

As part of this encouragement of reflection as a means of development, I spoke to Andrea Borsato, an Italian teacher with considerable experience of teaching exam classes. As you read his comments, see which of the questions in Part A of the task above he discusses. Are you surprised by any of Andrea's comments? If so, why?

1. Which exam classes have you taught?

The first classes I did were Cambridge main suite exams – FCE, CAE and CPE – and recently I have been specializing in CAE and CPE and I've also done a lot of IELTS. The first one I taught, a long time ago, was an FCE class. I had always wanted to teach exam classes because I'm Italian and I learned English as a second language and so I struggled a bit with motivation when I was teaching General English, and didn't feel challenged enough, so I always then asked for exam classes in every school I taught in.

2. Were you given any kind of training, or the chance to observe an exam class first?

No, I was thrown in at the deep end, but the experience of having been a student helped me a lot and I've got good language awareness. When it came to exam strategies and stuff like that, you can get those from the exam course books and the help of more experienced teachers. When I came to this school, it helped that the first time I did exam classes was in the evenings, so classes were only twice a week, which gave me more time for preparation and marking. After doing two or three evening courses, I started doing them in the daytime, full-time, five days a week.

3. Ideally, though, you wouldn't want to be thrown in at the deep end the way you were. What do you think would be good preparation for the first-time exam teacher?

If possible, it's better to start by teaching a part-time course to give you more time, but it's always a good idea to do some observations of an exam class taught by an experienced teacher – the exam that you are going to be teaching.

4. What are the main differences between these classes and regular General English ones?

The motivation of the students tends to be higher, which for me makes the class easier to teach because they all have the same goals and the same focus – which is passing the exam – and there's a clear format and structure to follow. I enjoy teaching IELTS as well, because even though everyone says it's very dry and can be a bit too academic, the speaking part isn't academic and I try to use authentic materials a lot. I also try to promote independent learning, which is the secret to passing the exam and to improving your English, so with all these exam classes I try to show them ways they can learn to work by themselves. Also, I'm interested in a lot of the topics covered, so I find it more intellectually rewarding myself.

5. Could any teacher go on to teach an exam class?

The things I tell students they need to pass the exam are, I think, the things a teacher needs too, so, for example, if you don't read newspapers or have never read a novel in your life, then I don't think you should be teaching CPE or IELTS. You need to enjoy them, too, even IELTS – today I was doing a lesson focusing on social media and we watched a TED talk online, and I like these kinds of things. So, yes, you need to have an interest and to enjoy it otherwise you aren't going to be very good at it. You also need to know the exam itself and what it consists of and what is required, and you need to have experience of all the strategies, although I think these are very straightforward – but very important, of course – but usually it's not so difficult to learn about strategies and to teach them. The most important thing is to have an interest in the subject, the topics, and to know a lot about them and to transmit your love of the topic to the students to make it interesting and relevant. I think I enjoy teaching exam classes even more now than when I first started.

6. How do you deal with those times when you have a student in the class who, after a while, you know deep down has no realistic chance of passing?

That's interesting because I don't think that passing is always or necessarily the ultimate end in all cases, though of course for some students it is. I always tell them, 'You don't learn IELTS, or whatever; you learn English.' I remember a Spanish student in his mid-forties, who was very weak – he shouldn't have been in the CPE class really – but during those three months he improved enormously. He didn't pass the exam, but it didn't matter to him because he had really enjoyed the course and he got close to passing, which I hadn't really expected. I don't think teaching and learning are always results based, but they can give you motivation and push you. I've had students who passed the exam but didn't really progress that much and students who didn't pass but who progressed enormously and that's why I can be proud of what I'm doing – when I can help students progress. Numbers are numbers, and you also need a bit of luck as a student with exams, by the way, but passing an exam isn't the only aspect of taking an exam class.

7. How has teaching exam classes helped your own professional development?

You can bring the focus you develop when teaching exam classes to General English classes as well. I now try to organize my courses in GE in a similar way to how I organize my exam classes – so topic-based with a lot of language, and a lot of independent learning is very important. So I give GE students more focus in what they're doing, and that's what I believe they want because sometimes they can be demotivated by an apparent lack of focus in GE classes.

Teaching CPE especially, over and over again, improved my own confidence with language – especially as English isn't my first language – and that helped my confidence as a teacher as well.

8. Finally, what advice would you give a new exam teacher?

First, get totally familiar with the exam, its format and the materials.

Look at the books that you will be teaching from and see how they are structured and what useful tips and information about the exam they give.

Do some of the exercises as if you were a student, to understand the level.

Observe some classes in that exam taught by an experienced teacher.

If possible, start with a part-time course.

Be confident.

Be honest – you won't know the answer to every question they ask but say you'll check and get back to them (and make sure you do).

Keep it fresh by looking for authentic materials to supplement the course-book materials. Read a 'serious' newspaper every day to look for articles and topics.

Do it!

Teaching exam classes and CPD

Like me, Andrea felt he was 'thrown in at the deep end', hardly the best way in to teaching exam classes. However, he also talked about how his first experiences of teaching exam classes helped his own language confidence, and that was certainly the case with me, too. In particular, I learned a huge amount from my time teaching TOEFL. The TOEFL exam has changed a lot since I taught it in the 1980s when it was a purely multiple-choice exam with no speaking or writing components and a heavy focus on grammar, including a 'find the mistake' section which included 'mistakes' that even then would have been considered acceptable in spoken or even written English. I especially remember the hanging participles (or 'dangling verbs' as they were also called). It would go something like this:

Which is the mistake, 'A', 'B', 'C' or 'D'?

While <u>walking</u> home from work one day a dog ran into my path and

     A

<u>started</u> <u>barking</u> loudly at me as I <u>tried to</u> get away.

  B   C   D

The answer would have been 'A' as it was not the dog that was walking home from work but me ('While I was walking home from work…'). You get the idea – the mistake section was full of that type of question. 'The **amount** of people' would be wrong (it should be 'The **number** of people'). 'It was **very** unique' would be wrong (it should be just 'It was unique'), and so on.

Perhaps understandably, teachers were not too keen to take on this class but I agreed to teach it, three hours a day, five days a week. I ended up teaching those TOEFL classes for two years and earned the nickname 'Dr TOEFL' for my efforts. As with Andrea, teaching this class while I was still a comparatively new teacher helped me build my confidence in grammar and language, including some of the finer points of English. Analysing language is very important for the teacher to do (in any class) in order not only to teach it effectively but also to deal confidently with questions about it, questions that exam students in particular will expect you to be able to answer. Doing this will help students to do better with the exam, and that is the main reason you are there.

Any kind of test is designed to provide a sample from which an assessor can infer a full-range of language competencies. Preparing students to take tests is proven to improve results, so the new exam teacher has to develop through understanding the underlying skills being examined and tested and the steps to teaching those skills. A teacher starting out in the profession will have developed an initial set of skills in their initial training course that they can refine and develop in General English classes, but by going on to teach an exam class they are not only developing but also expanding on this range of skills and thereby demonstrating professional growth.

To this day, I credit my years teaching that exam class with my own confidence in grammar and lexis in terms of precise meanings, differences in meaning and accuracy of language. To that end, this was a much more developmental experience than the one I had teaching FCE straight off my CELTA course. (That was pure survival and I should never have been given that class, with my zero experience.) But TOEFL was different and it gave me confidence and led me towards taking on other types of exam class, principally FCE, CAE and CPE and, some years later, IELTS.

EXAM CLASSES VS GENERAL ENGLISH

Teaching FCE for the first time, also in the 1980s, I especially remember having students in my class who needed to pass the exam in order to get promotion at work (and passing would also mean having their fees for the course paid by their employer). For those students it really was all about passing the exam, but I agree with Andrea that for others just making real and identifiable progress with their English could also be a reward – and should be.

In recent years IELTS has become the biggest exam in terms of the number of students taking it, primarily but not exclusively for entrance to English-speaking universities. This exam is not about passing or failing but achieving a minimum 'band' to enter university (or for a job, or for a visa) so here, too, students are very focused and often under a lot of pressure. 'I need a Band 7 by the end of the year to get into university' is the sort of thing that teachers will often hear.

As for my own exam class experience over the years, let me give my own answers to the questions posed in Thinking Task 2 earlier in this chapter. I will give just five points for each question. These are my views and my answers won't be exhaustive, but they should give you a further flavour of what exam class teaching is like. My views, added to those earlier from Andrea, will perhaps encourage you to teach an exam class if you have yet to do so. One thing is for sure: it is a hugely developmental experience in many ways.

What would you say are the principal differences between teaching a General English class and teaching an exam class?

- The students are more focused and have one common aim
- You will have the same group of students each time (compared with a typical General English class where students might join on a weekly basis)
- As a teacher, you know exactly what the aims of the courses are and what your students want and expect from you
- You and your students need to know and understand the structure and format of the exam, including the criteria for each section – it's not just about learning English but about the exam, too
- You need to ensure that you link everything you do explicitly to a particular part of the exam. For example, 'This will help you with Speaking Part 1.'

What do you like best about teaching these classes?

- The fact that there is a clear purpose behind it makes planning easier
- You are developing a clear structure and plan for teaching the class and preparing your students to study in and out of the class, to prepare for the exam
- Because of this, there is usually a more serious and studious atmosphere
- The satisfaction of seeing students pass the exam and achieve the grade needed is considerable
- You feel you are developing as you learn more and more about the exam and how best to prepare your students to take it

What are the biggest challenges and how do you overcome them?

- Students feeling under pressure – show them the strategies that will help them and teach them what they most need to know. Reassure and encourage them throughout the process
- Needing to become familiar with the exam itself – learn as much as you can about it so that you can prepare your students well and give them the correct advice and correct answers to their questions about the exam
- Students who are not likely to pass (see what Andrea said about this earlier)

- Students struggling with the workload and the intensity – again, you need to encourage and reassure, but also sometimes to change the energy and pace and format of the lessons
- All the extra marking you have to do – you just have to do it! If it helps, just remember that you are helping people to try to achieve their goal and, when the results come out and you see people have passed, it will all feel worthwhile

Why would you recommend to a teacher who has never taught an exam class that they should do so?

- It's something new for you – a step out of that comfort zone and a very different type of teaching experience
- You will learn a lot about an exam that you didn't know before
- You will learn a lot about the best way to teach that exam
- You will have an extended period with the same group of students – more time to get to know them as learners and as people and more time to help them
- It is an opportunity for significant professional development. Do it!

What would be your top tips for teaching an exam class?

- Know the exam thoroughly and the best way to teach it (including strategies and tips for each section)
- For any task you are setting (e.g. a reading or listening comprehension, a Use of English practice, etc.), do the task yourself so you not only have the answers and the reasons for or the location of the answers, but also an understanding of what it was like to do the task
- Find out as much as possible at the start about your students, including why they are doing the exam, their hopes, expectations and future plans, and then build on this knowledge as the course progresses. Have some one-to-one tutorials during the course, too
- Give exam practice as well as strategies and tips. You are teaching them English but you are also teaching them about the exam and how to do it
- Have a clear structure and plan for every lesson and for the course as a whole. Set learning aims and link everything you ask your students to do to the exam

The exams: an overview

Here is some basic information about the exams mentioned in this chapter. Bear in mind that revisions to exam formats do take place from time to time, so always check before teaching a new class. The information about FCE, CAE, CPE and IELTS comes from the International House London website (visit http://www.ihlondon.com/exam-centre/).

To find out more about the exam structure and content and how it is graded, just look at any relevant course book for that exam, or check online.

FIRST CERTIFICATE IN ENGLISH (FCE)

Cambridge English: First, also known as First Certificate in English (FCE), is an upper-intermediate-level qualification for those who want to use everyday written and spoken English. Studying for FCE will help learners improve their language skills and use them in a wide range of contexts.

FCE is designed for learners whose command of English is adequate for everyday purposes, including business and study. Successful candidates will have a wide grasp of vocabulary, and should be able to construct an argument and use appropriate communication styles for a variety of situations. They also need to show an awareness of register and of the conventions of politeness and degrees of formality as they are expressed through language.

The FCE is taken by more than 270,000 people each year in more than 100 countries. It is a valuable qualification for anyone who wants to work or study abroad or to develop a career that requires English language skills, including business, medicine, engineering and many other professions. It is also useful preparation for higher-level examinations, such as the Cambridge Certificate in Advanced English and the Certificate of Proficiency in English.

FCE is recognized by many universities and other educational institutions as proof of intermediate-level English skills, and these institutions accept it as meeting part of their entrance requirements. Employers throughout the world recognize FCE. It indicates sufficient proficiency in English to be of practical use in clerical, secretarial and managerial jobs in many industries, in particular tourism, where contact with English speakers is required. Successful candidates have the ability to deal with routine letters and telephone enquiries, and to cope with some non-academic training courses and simple textbooks and articles.

CERTIFICATE IN ADVANCED ENGLISH (CAE)

The demand for high-level English language skills is increasing all around the world. Passing Cambridge English: Advanced (CAE) shows achievement at a high level.

The CAE is an advanced exam that tests ability to communicate with confidence in English and deal with most aspects of everyday life. The CAE is accepted by more than 3,000 educational institutions, businesses and government departments around the world as proof of high-level achievement. The course develops the language skills needed for success at this level, and the CAE can be used for university and student visa applications in the UK and Australia.

CERTIFICATE OF PROFICIENCY IN ENGLISH (CPE)

Cambridge English: Proficiency, also known as Certificate of Proficiency in English (CPE), is the most advanced qualification Cambridge offers, and it requires a high level of English ability. Candidates passing this test demonstrate that their English is good enough for them to teach English to others and to study at any British university. Over 45,000 people in more than 80 countries take the CPE exam each year.

The Cambridge Proficiency exam is the oldest of the Cambridge EFL exams. It is designed to make sure that a student doing a university course in a British university has the language skills needed to study at this level. This course deals with more academic language than the CAE; the CAE exam is aimed more at people who need to function, for example, in an English-speaking business environment.

INTERNATIONAL ENGLISH LANGUAGE TESTING SYSTEM (IELTS)

The International English Language Testing System (IELTS) is one of the world's most popular English language proficiency tests for higher education and global migration, with more than two million tests taken in 2013. IELTS evaluates reading, writing, listening and speaking skills and is designed to reflect real-life use of English.

The IELTS test has a strong international reputation and is accepted by over 8,000 organizations worldwide, including schools, universities, employers, immigration authorities and professional bodies. IELTS is the most widely accepted English language test that uses a one-to-one, face-to-face speaking test to assess English communication skills: it involves having a real-life conversation with a real person, the most effective and natural way of testing English conversation skills.

The test is designed to assess the language ability of candidates who want to work or study in countries where English is the primary language of communication. It has two modules:

- The Academic module is normally for people who want to study an undergraduate or postgraduate degree course or who wish to register with a professional body.
- The General Training module focuses on basic survival skills in a broader social and educational setting. General Training is suitable for people joining a training programme or doing work experience in English-speaking countries. It is not designed for degree level.

IELTS has a 9-band scale and each band corresponds to a level of English competence. All parts of the test and the overall band score can be reported in whole and half bands, for example 6.5, 7.0, 7.5, 8.0.

TEST OF ENGLISH AS A FOREIGN LANGUAGE (TOEFL)

The TOEFL exam measures the ability to use and understand English at university level. It evaluates how well candidates combine listening, reading, speaking and writing skills to perform academic tasks.

More than 27 million people from all over the world have taken the TOEFL test to demonstrate their English-language proficiency. More than 9,000 colleges, agencies and other institutions in more than 130 countries accept TOEFL scores. The average English skill level ranges between Intermediate and Advanced.

The test is suitable for:
- students planning to study at a higher education institution
- students needing scholarship and professional certification
- English-language learners who want to track their progress
- students and workers applying for visas

For further details, see the ETS website at www.ets.org/toefl

Summary

Teaching an exam class is an excellent way to further your own development. It will give you the chance to do a different type of teaching with an added degree of responsibility and to teach students with a very different and more focused reason for studying than General English students. As well as the satisfaction of trying to help those students achieve their specific target, you will have the chance to add a more specialized type of teaching to your previous experience and therefore to further your own development. If you have taught one exam already, try a new one if you have the chance. And if you are about to teach a particular exam class for the second time, reflect on what went well and what could be improved from the first time you did it. Reflect, learn and develop!

Reading groups

In our classrooms we usually try to make reading tasks interactive, even saying something as simple as 'Discuss your answers in pairs'. If we read a good book, we are as likely to tell someone about it and talk about it as we are to tell them about a good movie we have seen and to discuss it together, if the other person has seen the movie or read the book as well. So why not take this one stage further in our professional development and share what we have read about in an article or a book on a professional topic? We can do this by setting up a reading group or book club for colleagues to join.

First, though, let's find out more about reading groups and how they work. A strong believer in their value is Ifthaquar Jamil and he told me about a reading group at his school.

My experience: Ifthaquar Jamil

Why did you start a reading group at your school?

We started our DELTA book club a couple of years ago, to get teachers with varying experience together. Some were CELTA trainers, some were DELTA trainers and some were new teachers, all meeting and talking about language and getting some different insights and perspectives. We had up to ten teachers in the group. Some of the group were about to do their Diploma (DELTA), so they were very enthusiastic but most of us had already completed it, so for people like me it was a chance to go over things and review them – all the theories and ideas behind teaching. When you do a course like the DELTA, you don't really have that much time to process it and so you need to revisit it, but doing that by yourself is really quite boring so it's quite nice to get different people's ideas and thinking 'I never thought of it like that before.'

Getting a group together was something I had been thinking about for a while because I quite like book clubs generally and I believe that talking and sharing about something means you learn a lot more than just reading about it yourself. A colleague of mine was soon to start her DELTA, so I thought this was a good time and opportunity to start it: we could go through books and review stuff and others could learn some new ideas and theories and discuss them. I thought it would help me consolidate my knowledge about some theories about language and language teaching.

How often and where did you meet?

We met once a week and sometimes we would prepare things beforehand, perhaps reading a chapter of a book which had been chosen around the interests of the group – we were quite democratic in the whole process of it. Sometimes it was a particular issue, such as teaching phrasal verbs if someone didn't quite 'get them' – we actually spent a whole month on phrasal verbs because it was such an interesting area and so different people went away and read about different aspects of phrasal verbs and then we came back and shared our findings.

We met in the school kitchen area, so it was very informal and relaxed. We wanted other people to join, so sometimes people might just be standing there and listening to us. If you didn't want to be part of the group and to participate, you could just be silent and sit down and listen and absorb it – you didn't have to contribute. We didn't want to put pressure on people because there was the danger of some people thinking 'Oh, so-and-so is so knowledgeable, so I don't want to say anything', but the point was that there was something for everyone and different roles for different people. Most meetings lasted an hour or so and sometimes longer, depending on how engrossed we were!

What other things did you discuss?

We didn't only focus on the DELTA; we branched out and looked at some articles and some different ideas so, although it's good to have an initial focus, that focus will evolve and you all kind of branch out naturally and organically. Sometimes we would all go away and read the same article and other times we would read different articles around the same area. We would sometimes work in pairs and then come back and each pair would do a little presentation on what they had read and someone would make notes. Based on those notes, that might give us another platform to work from and we'd think, 'Oh, OK, we can explore this now' or 'Actually, we don't really understand this point very well,' and we'd all go away and research that point and then come back together and talk about it.

A reading group does need someone to co-ordinate it but it can be just a case of getting people together and making a suggestion initially of what area to focus on or what to read and not to be over-ambitious. Start with something simple to get the ball rolling and from that the needs will emerge.

Reading groups can also tie in with SIGs and this can be very useful because teachers have definite interests and concerns. Pronunciation is a good case in point, because I'd say that phonology is the weakest part of my teaching, so being able to focus on that with others who share the same interest, and to go away and add reading to our discussions and ideas, really helps you understand it. The collaborative nature of the group is its most useful aspect and it reflects what we do as teachers – we ask and talk to other people and we refer to sources and it's through the dialogue as much as through the reading that we get the understanding.

In your opinion, what makes a successful reading group?

You have to be quite open-minded.

You need to encourage an atmosphere where people are free to air their ideas.

You need to be not over-critical.

> You need to want to explore issues and to have a dialogue.
>
> You need to let people be quiet if they want to be quiet – they'll speak when they're ready or when they feel they've got something to contribute.

 Tip

If you are unable to join a real professional reading group or book club for any reason, you can join a virtual one online. Check the ELT Reading Group website: http://eltreadinggroup.weebly.com/

Reading groups and CPD

Ifthaquar considered that the reading group helped his development in a number of ways. It taught him to:

- be less prescriptive
- take on board different perspectives and ideas
- consider all the ways that different people think and how their thinking affects their teaching
- have more respect for different ideas even if he disagreed with them (something he did not expect)
- appreciate that there's more than one answer out there, depending on how you approach it

With these points in mind, you will now have the opportunity to do the same in the following task. At the end of the task we will add to the list of how reading groups can aid professional development.

CPD TASK

This task is related to the text below on Dogme ELT. In recent years there has been much discussion about whether teachers rely too much on course books. Consider the following questions about course books:

- What do you think of them?
- Do you have a preferred series? Why do you prefer it to other series?

- If you use a course book, when and why do you use it?
- What works and what doesn't?
- What do your students think of them?
- If you don't use a course book, why is this?

Now try out the reading group experience. If you can, get together with one or, preferably, more than one colleague. Ideally, at least one person should be a keen user of course books and at least one person a more sceptical user, or even a non-user. Read the following article by someone who is a keen believer in dogme over course books and then read the response to this article that follows.

Arrange a time to meet after you have all read the article and the response and then spend an hour or so discussing it. Have your views about course books or dogme changed at all as a result of reading it; if so, why? What arguments in the article caused the biggest reaction, and why? What did you most agree or disagree with, and why? You could also talk about the questions above as part of your discussion, and any other related points.

READING GROUP STIMULUS: DOGME VS COURSE BOOKS

Below is an article, reproduced by kind permission of its author, Chia Suan Chong, a keen believer in dogme over course books. (Dogme is a communicative approach to language teaching that encourages teaching without textbooks and focuses instead on conversation among learners and teacher.) A response to this article, which first appeared as a blog post on the International House London teachers' blog in 2012, from a school Director of Studies, follows.

'Making student-centred dogme student friendly' by Chia Suan Chong

It seems that some students have been complaining about their teachers not using the assigned course book and the discussion about whether the use of the course book should be encouraged/enforced has yet again risen.

With the dogme approach to language teaching becoming more widely accepted in the TEFL world in recent years, I had assumed that the debate was more or less over – that it was clear as day that a materials-light classroom where the use of students as the main resource was almost a given. I have taken for granted the fact that everyone knew that, when done correctly, such lessons are rather taxing on the multitasking dogme practitioner, and that the benefits to their language learning process were for all to see.

Perhaps it's because I've been a dogmetician teaching without a course book for over three years. Perhaps it's because Thornbury and Meddings have given the approach an official label and wrote an award-winning book, alongside countless journal articles and blogs with solid theoretical backup of the approach. Perhaps it's because I've come to see dogme not as an approach or methodology, but simply as improvised but principled eclecticism and good teaching. But all teachers apply dogme in very different ways. After all, it is what a teacher has in their 'bag of tricks' and how principled their version of improvised eclecticism is.

I have always enjoyed analysing language, and been rather systematic in the way I clarify grammar, lexis or pronunciation, and perhaps this comes through in the way I conduct my dogme classes. I have also invariably learned my foreign languages in the same fashion. Whether it be Japanese or Italian, coming into contact with the language through authentic texts and real-life communication (whether it be Japanese pop songs or arguments in Italian with my ex) had been what motivated me to put the systems I'd learned to use. Our own learning experiences undoubtedly influence how we see the language learning process. And most of our students have been students in language classrooms prior to our encounters with them. They, therefore, have certain expectations of what their classes should entail. And one of these expectations might very well be a structured journey through a course book.

But we know language learning is by no means linear, and that learners remember and use so much more of the language when they themselves have noticed the gap in their knowledge and have seen their need for it. Students clearly prefer communicating about themselves, their classmates and their teacher to doing predictions and receptive skills tasks about the faceless Johns and Janes in a course book. When I did my action research project on dogme several years ago, the students surveyed quite unanimously claimed that the dogme lessons were much more motivating and effective. So how is it that we have students complaining about the course-book-light classrooms at school?

Could it be that they find the lack of structure daunting? Could it be that they feel they are not learning anything in class? Could it be that skills work has dominated these lessons and that students are unable to recognize this as language learning when little grammar is involved? How is it that the clients of executive business classes who have never been prescribed a course book are not voicing the same complaints?

I hope I'm not preaching to the converted but here are some things that I do to try and address the above issues:

1. Needs analysis

This is crucial in a classroom where a course book is not going to be followed. A detailed needs analysis needs to be carried out on day one, and the interests of the students, their language needs and expectations need to be identified. I make sure I ask the following questions at the beginning of every course, and allow time for students to discuss them in pairs/groups:

- How long have you been here? How long will you stay?
- Why are you learning English? Why did you decide to come to this city/school?
- Who will you be speaking English to in the future? In what kind of situations?
- Do you find it more difficult to speak or to understand?
- Do you use English outside the classroom? When and who with? How do you feel when using English in these circumstances? Do you read the news or watch English TV programmes?

- Which skills would you like to work on? Speaking? Reading? Writing? Listening?
- Which systems do you think you need to work on? Grammar? Lexis? Pronunciation? Why?
- Do you find it difficult understanding native speakers? What about non-native speakers?
- What did you like about your previous language classes and what didn't you like?
- How do you think you improve your English best? How do you try to remember and use the new lexis or grammar structures that you learn?

Because our school provides free course books for General English students, when I give out these new books on day one of a GE class, I get students to turn to the contents page and discuss the topics and language areas (grammar, functions, lexis) that they wish to cover. To add to the topics in the book, I put up several topics on the board, e.g. Travel, Food, Current Affairs, Fashion, Health, Education, Politics & History, Technology, Music, etc. The negotiation process then begins. Students confer with their partners and the class votes for the topics they would like to see in the coming weeks (each student gets five votes). This allows me to steer conversations towards the areas they are interested in, to ask more questions when these topics come up, and to be ready to use the appropriate activities/methods that I need from my teaching 'bag of tricks' to address their language needs. My end-of-day-one notes will often look like this:

Student profiles

Maria – Nurse from Spain, been here two months, staying for another three.

Needs English to keep up to date with the advances in the medical field and to communicate with people from different countries when travelling.

Loves shopping and clubbing.

Lives and hangs out with other Spanish-speakers after class. Watches many English films with English subtitles.

Finds it more difficult to understand native speakers.

An organic learner who prefers to pick chunks of lexis up through frequent contact.

Thinks she needs to work on her grammar because her last teacher told her it's important and that she's bad at it.

Hates activities that require her to stand up.

Yukiko – Flight attendant from Japan, been here one month, staying for another five.

Needs English for work and loves the sound of the language, etc., etc....

Results of needs analysis and negotiation

Systems: 1. Lexis; 2. Grammar; 3. Discourse; 4. Pronunciation

Skills: 1. Speaking; 2. Listening; 3. Writing; 4. Reading

Topics: Food (10 votes); Education (8 votes); Health (8 votes); Current Affairs (5 votes), etc.

Grammar areas in course book: Conditionals 2 & 3; Relative clauses; Passive structures; Story-telling tenses, etc.

2. Explaining why I do what I do

We do sometimes walk around with a 'teacher-knows-best' attitude, assuming that our students will trust us no matter what approach we use. Students, however, often have a set idea as to how they learn best, and sometimes gently going through the hows and whys of the approach we're employing (preferably backed up with a few sentences that start with 'Scientific research into language learning has proven that...') could not only take the mystery out of this unfamiliar way of teaching and encourage them to see the benefits of it for their English, but resolve any false assumptions about language learning. I don't just do this on day one but every time I employ an activity or method I haven't done with them before, e.g.

progressive deletion, running dictations, TBL, etc. I try to provide students with the pedagogic rationale behind it.

3. Working with emergent language and corrections

Dogme has been accused of being 'winging it elevated to an art form'. For it to rise above being merely a chat in the pub, it is crucial that the teacher is noticing opportunities to feed in new language, to board and extend the language emerging, listening for the language problems that students are having and finding the right moments to work on them to the appropriate extent.

4. Drawing attention to the language covered

In order to avoid a situation where students are unsure of what language input they have been given, I find it worth highlighting to students at the end of the class what lexical/ grammatical work they have done that day ('Look at all that grammar we've done today!'). Keeping a language column on the side of the board that is gradually filled out during the lesson does help, but I also get students to tell each other what they have learned that day à la the end of a *Sesame Street* episode ('*Sesame Street* was brought to you by the letter Z and the numbers 1 to 10'). Recalling the previous day's lesson and carrying out recycling activities at the start of the next day also helps reaffirm this (shameless plug: my last blog on recycling in a dogme classroom).

5. Taking notes

If students are not using the course book, it is all the more important to get them to keep an organized notebook. My students often have three notebooks, one for taking notes in class, a lexical notebook they keep at home where the lexis covered in class is reorganized either into alphabetical order or by topic, and a grammar notebook that they also keep at home. The transferring of information from their class notebook to the home one helps students to remember and revise what they have learned that day and allows them to have the time and space to raise questions about the use of that language. It is also important to make sure students are given time in class to write down what you have boarded and clarified.

6. Controlled-practice exercises

Course book-less classrooms don't equate to fluency-focused classrooms. There can be accuracy work done too. This could take the form of pairwork, e.g. teaching an elementary level 'there is/are...some', 'there isn't/aren't...any': 'Tell your partner about the shops near where you live'; teaching a mid-int class past modals of obligation: 'Tell your partner about the rules you had when you were at school'; teaching an upp-int relative clauses: 'Bring a photo of your friends and family tomorrow and tell your partner about the people in the photo.'

'But those are semi-controlled/freer-practice activities!', I hear you exclaim. I often find that controlled gap-fills, sentence transformations, matching and categorizing activities in course books and grammar workbooks tend to use random decontextualized sentences that have absolutely nothing to do with the topic you are discussing. Making up your own enables you to exploit the context that delivered that language and helps students to focus on not just the form but the meaning and use as well.

Having said that, I recognize that, with some grammar structures, it is quite difficult to keep all the practice within context (which is probably why the books, too, find it hard to produce contextualized controlled practice). In such cases, using the students' names and their real experiences or making a friendly joke about the students in the exercises often helps memory and retention. E.g. teaching Vanessa, who is a journalist and loves celebrity gossip, relative clauses, I wrote the following sentence transformation exercise on the board: 'Vanessa wrote that article about Angelina Jolie. Angelina Jolie punched Vanessa during an interview.' This, of course, wasn't true, but following Derren Brown's maxims on memory tricks: keep it visual and make it funny!

I remember teaching a Saudi student the structure 'so+adj + that + clause) on the day after he had been to the dentist. Among the many sentence transformations about his classmates was one that read, 'Ahmed looks so gorgeous with his new teeth that everyone standing beside him now looks ugly.' Ahmed was writing the sentences on the board down in his notebook when he noticed this one and laughed, 'I'm never going to forget this structure now!'

7. Ensuring variety

We tell trainees on the CELTA in week one about different styles, and although I'm not a big fan of the VAK paradigm, the aim of that input session is to convey the message that we need to vary the activities we use in the classroom. But so many of us get lazy and start to rely on the same tricks day after day. Teachers might find their favourite boil-in-the-bag lessons much easier to execute than using a course book. As Chaz Pugliese said in his talk at IATEFL this year, 'Teachers, have fun! Or you might bore us!'

8. Not letting gimmicks and technology dictate

On a very different note from the last point, I have often seen teachers who spend a lot of time preparing their lessons and trying to spice things up, creating the most amazing materials using the plethora of features that the Internet and IWBs offer. This is hardly materials-light to classify as a dogme approach, but I simply felt that I needed to include something about that in this post. Arguably, one can still make lessons interesting and ensure variety by focusing on the lives of the students and the stories they have to tell us.

As much as I believe teachers should harness their creativity, the focus needs to be taken off the fancy tools of teaching and placed on the very people we are teaching. Several years ago, the British Council produced some telling results of focus group research they conducted, where students claimed that they felt that the use of IWBs and technology was taking their teachers' attention away from them and on to the technology. The novelty of IWB gimmicks might impress students to start with, but when that starts to take centre stage, the development of our students inevitably suffers. We are not in competition to see who can create an all-singing, all-dancing lesson about the present perfect continuous. We are in the business of helping students understand and use the structure. And I'm all for the most efficient way to go about doing this.

9. Giving homework

Homework in my classes often entails students keeping their notebooks up to date, reading an article their classmates have brought in, doing some research on a topic online, preparing presentations or writing emails/blogposts/journals/essays. Depending on the needs analysis, of course, including writing skills work is essential in giving students a 'rounded experience' of learning English. Using the controlled-practice exercises in course books as homework can also placate students who feel like their course books are going to waste, and help them to see that the language covered in the classroom does correlate to the syllabus in the course book.

10. End-of-course retrospective round-up

Speaking of correlation, at the end of my courses, after rigorous rounds of recycling and revision activities, I get my students to turn to the contents page of the course book once again, as they did on day one. I then get them to discuss with their partners which topics and which language areas in the course book they have covered over the month. Students are often pleasantly surprised to find that not only have they covered everything in the part of the book they were meant to cover, but they have also acquired structures and language beyond that syllabus.

If students are still complaining despite all this, perhaps it's simply due to the fact that they've been given a free course book that they haven't got to use. The solution then is simply: Stop giving them free course books and save the school some money. *(Wink)*

A response from a Director of Studies, Varinder Unlu

A very interesting article on dogme and why you feel that it is a good method to employ in class. However, there are a number of points I think are a little worrying.

Whether you like them or not, course books are a useful resource and students do like having them. We cannot assume that we as teachers are the only ones who know what the best approach/method is for our learners. It's surprising how much students know about their own learning styles and what they want from a course.

I am also a little alarmed that we would tell our students that 'scientific research into language learning has proven that...' to encourage them to come round to our way of doing things. L'Oreal has been telling me for years that scientific research has proven that my hair is going to look much better if I use their products!! I don't think we should be telling our learners such things.

Secondly, picking out the right 'bits' from the course book and supplementing or complementing it with my own materials has always worked for me. This way, the students feel they are progressing as they can see what they have done – and I get to be creative. I think that most students like the structure a course book offers. Being able to use a course book in this way is not an easy thing to do and it takes real skill and thought from the teacher to achieve the right balance.

Teachers should not be made to feel ashamed or embarrassed if they are using a course book and I feel that this can happen sometimes. There are a lot of approaches that work in language teaching and I would certainly not favour one particular approach more over another because, for me, variety and balance are important.

There is one point I agree with and that is the over-reliance on IWBs and technology in class. I think there is a tendency to plan lessons around the IWB and, if one is not available, it's a disaster. Technology is an important part of everyday life but it should not come in the way of what is really important: the learner.

It always comes back to one thing: the learner and their needs.

THINKING TASK

Now that you have discussed the article and response for the CPD Task , reflect on what the reading group experience was like for you. Maybe you'd like to repeat it (there is another reading task in Chapter 19) on a regular basis?

Having read the article, and hopefully been able to discuss it, what would a senior teacher or manager hope and maybe even expect you to get from the reading and sharing experience? Here are a few suggestions to reinforce or add to those made earlier by Ifthaquar:

- increased knowledge or awareness of a particular topic that relates to the profession and which might influence your teaching or thoughts in some way and add to your range of skills and approaches in the classroom
- different perspectives and ideas from discussing and debating a topic and related topics with colleagues in a more formalized fashion
- the desire to read more on that topic or others in order to keep up to date with ideas, trends, issues and methodology
- the experience of a different kind of CPD that perhaps you hadn't tried before, which in itself can be refreshing and motivating

Summary

Reading groups are an undervalued and underused source of development. Reading by yourself is great, but reading and sharing is even better because of the exchange of views and arguments, the input of ideas and the stimulation to try something new.

So what are you waiting for? Get together and get reading!

10

Attending and participating in conferences

I had been putting it off for years, but now it was going to happen. I didn't sleep too well the night before. Come to think of it, I hadn't slept well for the previous week or so. Part of me hoped that something would 'happen' and the whole event would be cancelled. Was it too late to back out? Never before had I hoped to wake up with full-blown 'I can't possibly go to work today' influenza. However, the day dawned. Nothing had 'happened'. I didn't develop flu overnight. I knew I had no choice. It was time for me to do my first ever conference presentation. What made it even worse was that it was on a Friday late afternoon, spoiling my 'happy Friday' anticipation of the weekend, so I had to somehow concentrate on work for the rest of the morning with 'the talk' always on my mind. If ever there was a case of getting out of your comfort zone, this was it, but it was an important step for me to take in my own development.

Speaking at a conference

At the time of this anxious Friday, I was working as a middle manager in a large school and had been in the profession for around 25 years. I knew my strengths and shortcomings – and I knew of a few things in my professional life that I had still not done (i.e.

skilfully avoided over many years) but deep down believed I should tackle. One of these was speaking at a conference.

Now, I would love to say that I volunteered and put my name down to speak, that I had been brave and taken this big step all by myself. Alas, it wasn't quite like that. Instead, I was approached by the organizer of an annual modern language conference to speak as a guest presenter. Those attending would be coming from all over the world for this three-day conference and I would be delivering my presentation twice, first to one audience and then to another.

I knew my fate was sealed when I realized that my upcoming 'I'm out of the country and unavailable' holiday wasn't due to begin until a week after the conference. I had no legitimate excuse left. I knew it was the right thing to do. And besides, it was 12 weeks away at that point; surely something would happen before then to get me out of having to do it.

In spite of my reluctance, I knew this was the right thing to do; I knew that it was important to force myself out of my career comfort zone. Trying something new and different is important for everyone, even if you do it only once. And besides, how could I encourage others to speak at a conference if I had never done it myself? No, this was important for me and would definitely be professional development. So I said, 'OK, I'll do it,' and now the day had finally dawned.

Preparation

As a conference speaker you would ideally want to choose the topic yourself, but this is not always possible. I did not choose my own topic but I was asked to speak about 'Communicative language learning' for about an hour, to two audiences each of up to 70 people. It was still an interesting and motivating topic for me but I had to spend weeks preparing my talk, taking a few hours here and a few hours there. I started with an outline of what I wanted to say, then framed a skeleton plan of how I would stage the talk, then prepared PowerPoint slides to introduce each section, and finally thought of what precisely I wanted to say and where I wanted to end up.

For me, the main challenge was to deliver a talk that wasn't yet another history of the topic with all the familiar points being churned out again. I decided instead to present a personal viewpoint and to relate communicative learning to communication in life generally. Once I knew where I wanted to go with the talk, the rest fell into place easily.

The second main challenge was timing. As a teacher I am used to lessons where I put my students into groups, ask them questions, and involve them as much as possible. This, though, would be different. I had to talk for around 55 minutes and allow a few minutes for questions at the end.

I am not someone who likes a script, or even notes. You may feel safer with notes to refer to, and it is important to use whatever method works best for you. I have given many speeches over the years for staff members leaving for a new job and I knew from that experience that I prefer to have a framework in my head and thoughts of what I want to say, but otherwise to speak without notes of any kind. I still had the uncertainty of the timing, though, and with no opportunity to try out the talk beforehand in front of an audience, I was left with no option but to deliver the talk to myself at home, to get an idea of the length. It felt very odd, of course, but it was essential to do this. Fortunately, my years of practice in planning my lessons so that they finish on time proved invaluable, and my dry run at home was just the right length.

PREPARING STEP BY STEP

If you are going to give a talk for the first time, take the following steps:

1 Consult with any colleague who has talked before at a conference for advice, tips and practical help

2 Choose your topic carefully (see the following experience of Fiona Johnston for more on this)

3 Plan carefully and thoroughly. Know the aim of your talk and what you want to say

4 Know your audience – who are they and what are they expecting?

5 Where appropriate, include examples of what you're talking about and avoid it being too theoretical. A bit of humour always helps, too!

6 Try to do a dry run beforehand (again, read Fiona's comments on this), not least to check that you have timed it properly

Presenting and CPD

On the day itself I did my presentation twice. The first audience was around 70 and the second about 40. The timing was perfect, and once I got going I was fine and I enjoyed it. I had some good feedback, which was welcome, and despite all the anxiety leading up to the event, I was very pleased to have done it.

How did it help my own development?

- I challenged myself to do something I had always previously avoided. Even if you don't do something a second time, just doing it once is good
- I now have more understanding of what is involved in doing a talk and can therefore empathize more with colleagues doing talks
- I can have more credibility in recommending this opportunity, and am better able to help and advise a first-time speaker especially
- I have a broader appreciation of the topic I spoke about, due to my planning, those teachers I spoke to about it when preparing, and the comments of those who attended
- Although I had already had plenty of previous experience of public speaking, I had never before spoken to such a large gathering, or had to gear a talk to very experienced colleagues from around the world. This has made me more confident and better equipped to do the same thing again

Tip

Don't feel intimidated by your audience – they have chosen to be there, which means that they are interested in your topic and will be keen to hear what you have to say. They may not agree with everything you say, but that doesn't mean they won't be inspired by your talk. Just to get people thinking, questioning, or re-evaluating their views or experience is worthwhile.

My experience: Fiona Johnston

At the 2014 IATEFL Conference, Fiona Johnston gave a presentation called 'Write here, Write now'. In 2013 she had done her first ever conference presentation and she was sufficiently inspired to want to return the following year. I tracked her journey before, during and after her 2014 conference talk to gauge how the experience helped her own professional development journey, and how doing the talk has helped her own teaching.

The conference is in a few months' time. What are your early thoughts and feelings?

The talk I'm doing this year is about written fluency – something which has interested me for a while. I did a teacher development session at my school ('Writing in the communicative classroom'), which is now a session I include on teacher training courses. It involves a couple of activities which I also use in class (the written discussion on flipchart-size paper, with coloured pens, and the reducing silent dialogue) and the more I've done it, the more I've realized that writing is no longer as synchronous as it used to be. There is a new genre/skill which isn't exactly speaking and isn't exactly writing but somewhere in between, and it is a skill that's increasingly useful with the rise of social media: for chatrooms, for Facebook chat, for chat boxes that appear during webinars (not just at universities but also other areas of training) and for computer games that have a chat function, nearly always in English.

I worked backwards from the activities I had, since synchronous written communication is something that course books don't really address. The idea also grew out of the blog work I do with classes, when we go to the computer room and I encourage the students to post, responding to each other's postings in real time. Some students really struggle with this instant kind of response.

The problem now is that I've got a general idea, and my abstract says that I have done research into this genre, whereas I haven't done any research yet. I'm making several assumptions based on what I've seen. I now need to do some more 'scientific' research.

What made you decide to do your first talk last year?

The reason I did the first talk last year was largely to push myself out of my comfort zone. Not only did it mean standing up in front of a large group of people, many of whom had probably been teaching for much longer than me, but the talk was about technology, not something I would normally pride myself on. I had recently finished the Trinity Tech course and was quite keen to share the main thing I learned on the course and in my subsequent adventures in blogging. The subheading 'A technophobe's adventures in blogging' is what I think drew so many people, as many members of the audience had heard about blogging but had not used it in class. It was so reassuring for me to find out that I was not the complete fossil I thought I was! Working where I do, among so many colleagues for whom tech stuff is as instinctive as breathing (as well as being brilliant teachers), had given me the impression that I was about to get left behind.

Many teachers I met at this first conference said that they, too, were rather afraid of technology in the classroom but, like me, didn't want to turn into a dinosaur. I guess I should feel more confident second time around, but I'm just as nervous as before, and I think it may be because the first one was about my personal journey and the huge part that tech-savvy students played in it, whereas this one will need a bit more background work. It is definitely an incentive to continue developing as a teacher as I might not do this amount of work on something so scary if I didn't have the incentive of the conference to keep my nose to the grindstone. You can't keep procrastinating as the conference date gets closer!

The 2014 conference is now just a few days away, and yesterday you did a dry run of your talk in front of colleagues at your school. How did it go?

I think it went OK. It reassured me that some bits flowed quite well but feedback flagged up some good points about how I could improve it or rearrange some parts or present some information differently or more interestingly. For example, one suggestion was to move student comments to after the presentation of the data rather than before, and one of my grids looked too dense, so it was really nice to get the feedback that that would be more interesting presented in a different way.

It's great to do a dry run for a number of reasons. One is to get the timing right, because initially I thought that I wouldn't have enough for half an hour, then I realized I had actually got too much and then I got it down to what I think will be 25 minutes plus five minutes for questions, and it was just right, so that was an enormous relief. I actually felt more nervous doing it in front of colleagues, I think because the people who were there know me and I would be more afraid of embarrassing myself in front of my colleagues than people who have never seen me before and who will probably never see me again, but it also felt very supportive because I knew that anything they said would be to help me make it better rather than to dent my confidence, and this gave me great encouragement.

To help with nerves, you must get completely familiar with your presentation, down to knowing which slide comes after which. Also, being confident knowing that you have done the research and also realize that, for a lot of people in the room, what might seem obvious common sense to you might not to them. There will be some people in the room who will take something away from it. It's important either to have a run-through of the session in front of a group of people, or at least to run it past somebody.

With one week to go I'm nervous! Last night, after the dry run, I felt a sense of slight anti-climax because I'd been working on it up to two in the morning and cutting up bits of paper but feeling relief knowing that it went OK. Quite a few people said they came away from it with a couple of new activities or a new way of thinking about something and that means a lot.

The other thing was I've been doing a lot of background reading and research for it and had developed various activities to find stuff out for the talk but in fact a lot of them have gone down so well in class I'm going to use them again. All my background reading has definitely informed my teaching and it's made me feel quite excited about teaching writing.

The conference was a few days ago. How did your presentation go?

It went very well. I was very, very nervous before I set off. Once I actually got to the conference, though, it was reassuring because there were so many like-minded people. It was a really useful experience to be surrounded by people who were as positive about teaching as I was. It was also a chance to catch up with friends and colleagues, as well as former students who had been on teacher training courses.

I was very pleased that so many people came. The immediate impact of that day was that once I got going it just felt very natural because I felt so rooted in the research I had done and talking about activities I use every day that it just felt like I was sharing experiences rather than 'giving a presentation'.

What was really nice as well was that I got really positive feedback from people who did come, and a number said that they hadn't thought of doing writing in that way before, particularly, I think, teachers who don't usually teach in this country (the UK). Non-native teachers told me that they tend to shy away from writing because they don't feel that writing and marking essays is very relevant. My conference focus was on developing written fluency skills and the feedback I got from some of the teachers confirmed my belief that what we need to do is develop students' online written fluency, because that is grounded more in the real world, rather than an artificial classroom situation – although it is different, of course, when teaching exam classes.

How did doing the presentation contribute to your professional development?

Where I've felt writing is most beneficial to their everyday lives is practising this idea of communicating in real time in writing. All my research and the feedback I got confirmed that this is something that isn't adequately covered. So, doing this talk and the whole process of it has not only contributed to my own continuous professional development, but also to that of the people who attended.

Doing a talk enables you to focus on a particular area of interest to you and I think if it's of interest to you then you are going to have the passion to enthuse about it and the audience will be with you. I chose a topic that was very definitely linked to classroom experience and I focused on students and the benefits to students and to teachers, so I'd say that for someone starting off, connect your talk to your own real-life experience because no one can argue with what you have done with your own students. My talk this year has led to an invitation from Russia to write a 600-word article on computer-assisted language learning.

The benefits of attending

Not everyone will feel willing or able to speak at a conference (there may be a limit to how far out of your comfort zone you want to go) and, for most people, the greatest benefit of conferences is attending them. The chance to hear talks on a wide variety of topics is one to be grabbed if the opportunity arises. This is becoming easier with the rising popularity of online conferences. As Fiona said, the chance to meet old and new colleagues from around the world is invaluable, especially for those whose working context is remote.

According to Fiona, there are many benefits – in terms of CPD – of attending a conference and listening to speakers:

- It pushes your boundaries by exposing you to new ideas
- It gives you a chance to network and create new contacts as well as meeting up with former colleagues

- It allows you to consider the needs of students in a particular area and identify needs that are difficult to put into a course book
- It will inspire you to come up with new activities to try out with students, will confirm whether or not your current ones are still relevant, and prompt you to repurpose activities that you currently use

If you want to get a taster of giving a talk, after attending a conference you can return to your school and give a summary of a session or sessions that you attended and in so doing your colleagues will benefit, and you will benefit from having attended the conference and then cascaded back to the advantage of your colleagues. What's more, you might then be inspired to present at a conference yourself next time.

In North America, the TESOL convention is held annually in a different city in the USA or Canada each year and is attended by 6,000 participants as well as publishers. Special interest sections include Adult Education, Bilingual Education, EFL, ESP, Materials and Writers. Affiliates hold conventions and organize other events in places including Saudi, Brazil and South Korea.

TESOL also offers online courses for teachers and managers (e.g. Fundamentals of TESOL, Teaching & Assessing Adult Learners).

Conference topics

Big and small conferences occur worldwide throughout the year and people come back from them enriched with new ideas, stimulating discussion, or raging with indignation at something they have heard. You may choose from a range of talks on a variety of topics, according to what interests you and what you want to find out more about.

Here are just a few examples of the hundreds of talks given at IATEFL 2014:

- 'Initiating students to poetry: a task-based approach'
- 'Teaching English via computer games'
- 'Taking tablets in the classroom – a remedy for everyone?'
- 'Critical thinking and creative thinking skills for exam preparation'

- 'Play to learn: practical and fun games for language learners'
- 'The joys of IELTS marking'

> ## Tip
>
> Many of the talks given at conferences are available to view later online, so you don't even have to attend to benefit. Visit the IATEFL website: www.iatefl.org.englishuk.com-conferences

An example of an online conference, the International House Teachers Online Conference (IH TOC) of 2014 contained numerous ten-minute talks on a wide variety of topics, available to anyone with the equipment and time to dip in and out (www.ihtocmay2014.blogspot.co.uk). Talks included:

- 'No more boring drills for young learners'
- 'Progress – shall we talk about it?'
- 'From teacher to enabler: stimulating acquisition outside the classroom'
- 'Writing without a pen'
- 'Class notes in 1–1 sessions'

Check out the IH World website (www.ihworld.com) for details of the next IH TOC. And ask your manager for information about any other forthcoming conferences that you might be able to attend – or even talk at!

The views of a manager colleague

Attendance at conferences

'Obviously there is a financial aspect to this, but just "getting away" can be enormously refreshing for anyone. Many schools will sponsor someone to go to a conference on the understanding that they keep clear notes and either write these up for all staff on return, or deliver a staff meeting to discuss the topics and their relevance to your local context. Ensure that the conferences are widely publicized in the school and ask for interested parties to apply – but don't forget that you can also ask people if they would like to go, depending on their interests. Don't always ask the same people, though…'

Giving talks at conferences

'Intimidating? Yes, it can be – but enormously rewarding for the speaker and good publicity for the school, too. Remember that speaking in front of your peers is nerve-wracking – so give help and support for new speakers, and perhaps the chance to give their talk as a "dry run" for a staff group in your school, or at a local teacher training college/university/teachers' centre.'

CPD TASK

Option A

Do one of the following if you have never given a talk or attended a talk at a conference.

- Find out from your line manager about any forthcoming conferences in your area and whether it would be possible for you to attend (or perhaps even give a talk). If you are able to attend a session, come back from it and share what you learned with your colleagues – perhaps by leading an INSETT or teacher development session. Otherwise, reflect yourself on what you learned and how it might benefit you in your current role.

- If it is not possible for you to attend a conference, choose a topic of particular interest to you and do some further research. If possible, take this one step further and deliver an INSETT session on it for your colleagues. This might also give you the confidence to speak at a later conference.

- Alternatively, set up an informal discussion group with colleagues who are interested in the same topic.

Option B

Do one of the following if you *have* talked at or attended a conference.

- Reflect on the experience and make a list of points to summarize how you benefited from it. How did the conference develop you professionally? What is the evidence for this? Maybe it helped you in your current role (as a teacher) or more generally as an employee.
- Deliver an INSETT or teacher development session at your school, to share what you have learned with colleagues and let them find out more about the topic. Alternatively, write a summary and distribute this to your colleagues.
- Encourage others to attend or give a talk at a conference.

Summary

Conferences, big and small, take place all the year round in many different countries. These conferences may take the form of a major event attended by hundreds of delegates over several days, or just be a one-day workshop attended by a couple of dozen participants. The event may be local or further afield. It may be an online conference, which means that you can 'attend' it from your home. Sessions may be interactive or be simply a talk. There may be one topic or session or a choice of many. You may like or agree with what is being said, or you might disagree – but you'll have a reaction of some sort.

You might want to go one step further and deliver a talk and research a topic, share it with others, exchange views and ideas, and in so doing raise your own profile. Whatever the type, whatever your role, being involved in conferences will open the door to ideas and discussion, to tips and suggestions, to agreement and to controversy. You will come back all the richer for the experience.

11

Writing

'The Adventures of Johnny Redway' was a set of stories I wrote for my own amusement as a child. I followed this up with 'The Crimefighters', but Johnny Redway was always my favourite (and I still think it's a great name). And then there was a national newspaper's short-story-writing competition, which I entered when I was 12. I'm glad that I no longer have these great works of literature in my possession because, if I read them today, I am sure I would be acutely embarrassed by them. But yes, I fancied myself as a writer when I was a child (as well as a radio DJ, a train driver and a super-hero) but I eventually settled for being a teacher, resisting the temptation to change my name legally to Johnny Redway.

Eventually I ended up doing 'grown-up writing' with a book about becoming an EFL teacher, and now here I am again working on my own professional development by writing a book about... professional development. Writing, though, doesn't only have to be about writing a book, and in this chapter we will look at some different types of writing and discover how writing in one form or another can contribute to our professional development.

Types of writing for CPD

Writing can involve a number of different possibilities, such as:

- writing new course materials for use in class (materials development)

- writing blogs (for more on this, see Fiona's Johnston's interview in Chapter 10)
- writing a review of a new work-related book (such as a course book), either for your own organization or for a publisher
- writing an article of professional interest, either for your organization (perhaps to be read by colleagues as part of an INSETT session) or for publication
- writing a book, either a course book or some other work-related book

My experience: Jacqueline Douglas

I asked teacher and trainer Jacqueline Douglas to tell me about how she got into writing, her writing experiences to date and how the experience has helped her in her professional development.

How did you get into writing?

I suppose it falls into three categories:
- Writing for my own lessons because I love making my own materials and adapting materials. I'm currently teaching an advanced class and this is my favourite because I'm not using a course book and trying to make it work but instead I am using authentic materials and creating my own materials.
- Materials development for other courses.
- Professional articles in professional ELT publications; I've done a few of these.

In my articles for publication I've written about something I really got into a few years ago, which is the idea of 'live listening' in the classroom and inviting guests into your classroom. If you are teaching in a non-English-speaking country, your students have less exposure to English than they need so, if you do have a visitor who comes to see you, as my mother did, drag her into your classroom because everybody really benefits, including the visitor. My mum was really happy to meet some locals and chat with them and the students love it that they have an English-speaking visitor in their class and they can ask her questions. I wrote about different ideas for live listening and I've also written about CLIL (Content and Language Integrated Learning), and other topics that I was already interested in and wanted to develop.

I approached journals that I thought might be a good 'fit' for what I wanted to write about, so I pitched to them based on my knowledge of what is usually in those journals. I went to *English Teaching Professional* and they accepted my proposal. That's a really good message for other people who are considering writing – that if you contact editors with what sounds like a reasonably organized pitch and you've got something to say, they are likely to accept and commission you. That's the good news. The bad news is that they won't pay you very much for 2,000–3,000 words, but you're not doing it for the money.

How has writing helped you professionally?

It's a good thing to have on your CV, so that by the time you've written your article you've got a writing section for your CV, which is a good thing, especially if you want to do more writing.

It gives me a better chance to do some more writing. If people see that I have written some articles, someone might ask me to do more.

I am better equipped to do materials development.

I have been able to deepen my knowledge and appreciation of topics that interest me.

Being published has increased my confidence as a teacher and trainer. (Sometimes someone will say they saw an article of mine in a journal or I see that I've been quoted in someone's DELTA assignment, which is strange but nice.)

Being published led to a conference talk I gave at IATEFL, further raising my profile and increasing my experience.

The idea of writing a book has crossed my mind, although I'm a teacher, not a writer, and I'm not sure I will get beyond rejection letters for a book. Doing my MA, doing materials development, writing articles for a publication, has encouraged me a little bit more each time so I can now actually see a possibility where a book could happen.

For someone interested in a particular topic or just wanting to develop their knowledge and awareness of a topic, writing about it would definitely help to inform and improve their teaching. For me, writing about CLIL in that journal and just consolidating my thoughts from the course I had previously run really helped me to continue developing rather than having all these thoughts just scrambling about inside my head. It was nice to have them all down in a 3,000-word piece that I could go back to and see as the sum of my progress. I could use that as a starting point for the next courses I worked on.

There is potential, too, for someone who would like to write an article but can't find a publisher or who doesn't actually want to be published, to research an area they are interested in and to write an article for themselves. Colleagues could then read it for an INSETT session at the school, where the content could be discussed and explored further and linked to classroom practice. Teachers are interested in their own development and sometimes they just need a nudge in the right direction, so if someone said, 'Wednesday 4 p.m., let's have an INSETT session about what someone has written', that would get a positive response.

Writing for development

As we have seen, 'writing' does not necessarily mean writing a book. Doing materials development, either for your own purposes or for your organization as a whole, is a very good way to get started and, as well as giving you that first step, it can also enhance the effectiveness and freshness of your lessons.

Writing an article would also be an excellent step, especially on a particular topic in your work that you are interested in or want to explore further. Initially, you could write an article as a springboard for a reading group session (see Chapter 9) or even a school INSETT session (see Chapter 6). Alternatively, you could try to get an industry publication to publish it. Two such publications are *Modern English Teacher* and the *International House Journal of Education and Development* (*IH Journal*).

Here are three comments from managers in different organizations about the usefulness of writing as development.

WRITING FOR PUBLICATION

'If you can encourage staff to write for a specialist journal or an ELT publication, you are endorsing them as members of a professional community. It can be very daunting and many people feel they have nothing to say – but if some interesting ideas have come out of observations or action research, this is a logical next step. You may need to provide help and support at the beginning, but it's worth it – and it's also a useful marketing tool.'

WRITING COURSE MATERIALS

'Writing course materials can be very useful, particularly where the teacher has specialist knowledge that can be deployed for the organizational benefit. It will not be seen as INSETT, however, unless a) time is made available for it and b) resources are made available for it (such as computer access) and the resulting materials are stored and indexed professionally. If these aspects are ignored, it will stop being developmental and become another chore which the management is placing on the shoulders of their already overworked staff.'

WRITING A BOOK REVIEW

'Writing a review of a course book allows a teacher to form and articulate their professional judgement. The review can then be shared at a teachers' meeting. Be careful, though: if you ask a teacher to review a course book that you have already committed your organization to using and the review is damning, what are you going to do? Reviewing materials is also a useful way for newer teachers to familiarize themselves with the wealth of published resources available. It can also be interesting to ask for two reviews of the same thing: one from a new teacher and one from a more experienced staff member. Their perspectives on the usefulness of the material can vary greatly. Asking a more experienced member of staff to review a very up-to-date course book is also a subtle way of raising their awareness of changes in methodology and approach which they may be unaware of.'

Journal guidelines for writers

Here are the guidelines for potential contributors to *IH Journal* as an example to potential writers.

'The *International House Journal of Education and Development* was founded by Charles Lowe (then director of IH London) and Matthew Barnard, in 1996. The original intention was to provide a forum for debate, a platform for creating new ideas and refloating old ones, debunking myths and generally generating a sense of adventure for people teaching TEFL or teaching English as a Second Language.

'The new digital *IH Journal* is published twice a year, in autumn and spring, and aims to include some of the best and most stimulating thinking in EFL teaching. We hope to be readable but serious, though always with room to be light-hearted as well. We are always on the lookout for new materials ideas, papers, photos and articles. We always want profiles and pictures of your school and its teachers, so get on to the computer and start writing! It might be the start of something big – who knows, maybe you will be the next Ruth Gairns or Michael Lewis!

'Writing for the *IH Journal*

'If you are an ELT expert, teacher trainer or teacher from within the IH network or beyond and would like to contribute to the *IH Journal*, we would be delighted to hear from you.

'If you have an idea for an article, please don't hesitate to contact us. All submissions will be carefully considered and the editor will select the most suitable content for each issue. We apologize, but we cannot guarantee that every submission that we receive will be published.

'Articles are generally 1,000 to 1,500 words in length and submitted by email only. We also ask IH staff to review online and printed resource material and course books. If you are interested in doing a review, please get in touch.'

(Reproduced with permission from *IH Journal* (www.ihjournal.com))

Writing a book

Maybe, though, what you really want to do is to write a book and get it published. This might be a course book or a reference book such as this one. I never planned to get into writing but I was lucky enough to be approached by a publisher in 2000 about writing a book on becoming an EFL teacher. As well as that and this current book, I have written a number of book reviews, both for publications, such as those mentioned in this chapter, and directly for publishers.

THE BENEFITS OF WRITING A BOOK

My writing experience has benefited my own development in many ways:

- My first book helped me embark on a period of reflection about my own teaching and training
- This in turn resulted in my re-evaluating and adapting some of my approaches and previously held beliefs to the benefit, I hope, of my students and trainee teachers
- With this current book, interviewing so many people in the profession opened my eyes to professional development opportunities that I hadn't previously considered, and to different views on CPD. This is always a topic I have been interested in, but now even more so
- I now feel better able to advise teachers and trainers at different stages of their careers on professional development possibilities
- By talking to school directors and managers (see Chapters 20 and 21), I have become much more aware of the organizational and developmental needs of middle and senior managers and this has helped my understanding of how organizations need to grow and how they do grow
- By having my name on publications, I have received further offers of writing work
- Like Jacqueline, I have never quite got used to seeing my name quoted in assignments and even in exam papers. Although it feels a bit embarrassing, I do also see it as evidence of having achieved something and producing work that others have read (even if they haven't liked it!)

Maybe, though, your ambition is to write a course book. Is this so impossible? Read the following case study to find out.

My experience: Dave Rea

Dave Rea is one of the authors* of a very popular and well-received series of General English course books for adult language students at all levels, *English Unlimited* (Cambridge University Press, CUP). I asked him how he got involved in writing and how it has helped his development, and for advice to prospective authors.

How did you get involved in writing?

Before working on these books, the only other writing I had done was on my own materials. I had always been interested in materials writing and then CUP asked for submissions. They asked to see sample material and for a statement of my beliefs as a teacher in terms of what should underpin the material, and for a kind of syllabus. So I submitted all that and from that CUP selected four of us from all those who had submitted and sent us forward to develop a course book series. So the process was very 'publisher-led'; publishers will do a lot of research to have a sense of where the market is going and what people want. They ask people to submit proposals and, if it is in line with where they're going in the next five to ten years, they'll ask you to talk to them and hopefully then develop the idea together.

What was the process like?

For the next year the four of us spent weekends at Cambridge developing ideas and material for four levels of books and coming up with a syllabus for each level. We then put together a formal proposal that was submitted to different markets, which gave feedback, and then it got final approval as a project and we signed contracts and started! The process involved lots of writing and rewriting, and consultants came in and talked to us – lots of stuff like that.

---

*The other authors of this series of course books are Theresa Clementson, Alex Tilbury, Leslie Anne Hendra, Adrian Doff and Ben Goldstein.

To write the actual books took about four years – that was four books, of course. All four of us worked on one or two of them at the same time and those had multiple drafts. After a couple of years they commissioned books at two more levels, and for those books we broke into pairs because by then we knew what we were doing more.

There were many challenges but one of the biggest learning curves for me was working on a syllabus for each book because I had never had to do this before. Most course books have a multi-strand syllabus – a grammar syllabus, a lexis syllabus, etc. – and we based the book around communicative goals with about eight different strands to each syllabus. They all had to marry up and fit together and it could be mind-bendingly complicated.

What qualities do you think are needed for writers of course books?

I think anyone could write a course book – as long as you're a good planner. One of the things my publisher said at the start was that they were looking for people who were very creative and very nice and I think those two things are very important. You've got to be able to constantly come up with new ideas because you're always having to change what you've originally come up with; this can be a relentless process. And you need to have a good relationship with your editors in your writing partnership and everyone we worked with was really nice. Because writing is nowadays more publisher-led, the best way in is to be able and willing to develop ideas that a publisher has planned.

What advice would you give someone who would like to write a course book?

One thing to do is to submit material or even a proposal (a syllabus, sample material, a statement of how that fits in with the competition, and a statement of your teaching beliefs). If the publisher has a project in the pipeline and your proposal fits in with that, they might ask you to come in for a chat and maybe they'll say that your proposal is in line with what they want to do and ask you to help them with that project.

Also, many people get into writing books through reviewing them. If you send your CV to a publisher and tell them what context you are working in and say that you are really interested in reviewing any material, that helps you form a relationship with an editor who will send you material for you to review. Part of this reviewing process is that, while you are commenting on and critiquing the material, you are coming up with ideas yourself. The editor then gets to know what you can do and what you can produce and whether you can meet deadlines. Later they might need a writer and, because they know you and what you can do, they might approach you to help them produce some work. It's about getting your foot in the door.

How did writing the course books contribute to your professional development?

I learned about the importance of a syllabus, how to construct one, and how every strand of it fits in with everything else.

I learned a lot about meetings and how to put forward ideas and to work with others in a team and to negotiate. All of this was completely new to me and I learned a lot of meetings-related skills.

I used a corpus for the first time, which was very exciting.

I learned a lot about lexis and grammar by doing plenty of research.

Because we wanted the book to have an international feel, this opened my eyes to how non-native speakers use English and to intercultural strands, and I read a lot about intercultural training.

I'm certainly better at writing material for my own classes now!

I'm much more confident about language now because my own knowledge has increased so much.

CPD TASK

This task is for you if you want to become involved in writing but haven't yet done any. Choose one of the options below:

- **Materials development**

  Find out whether your school has any opportunities for materials development that you could be involved in. If not, do what Jacqueline did and develop some materials for your own lessons.

- **Writing an article**

  Decide on a topic related to the profession that you are especially interested in or have particular views about and pitch your idea to a publication such as *IH Journal* or *Modern English Teacher* to see whether they would be interested in publishing it. Alternatively, why not go ahead with the article anyway and use it as the basis of a reading group session at your school?

- **Writing a book**

  If you have always wanted to write a book, maybe now is the time to try. Start by preparing a full proposal and a sample chapter and submit it to publishers for consideration. Even if you don't initially get accepted, just doing the proposal and the sample chapter will have given you valuable writing experience. Indeed, you could even go ahead and write the book anyway. If you don't feel ready to do this by yourself yet, maybe you have a colleague who is also interested and you could work on the book idea together.

  Whatever option you chose, spend time afterwards reflecting on the experience and how it informed your teaching or training, furthered your knowledge on a particular issue, or increased your confidence and desire to do more.

THINKING TASK

If you have done some writing, whatever form that writing took, reflect on how it has helped your development. How has it informed your teaching or training, furthered your knowledge on a particular issue, or increased your confidence and desire to do even more? Has your own profile within the profession or within your organization increased? Do you think your writing may open up further career opportunities later? What would you like to do next?

Summary

Whether it is materials development, a blog, an article, a book, or something else, doing some professional writing can have a positive impact on your teaching, your training, your profile in your organization (and that of the organization itself) and even on your opportunities to do more writing in the future. You can write for yourself or for others and in so doing you can add to your expertise and experience. And, of course, depending on what you write about, your students – the learners or the trainee teachers – might also benefit.

So what are you waiting for? Get writing!

12

Action research

'Action research' is a term that seems reassuringly self-explanatory – you do some research and you take action. Of course, it's not quite as straightforward as that but it will do as a starting point. The research can be something very practical and simple; it doesn't have to be a huge project on some theoretical subject. In this chapter we will explore what form such research might take and what you might do research in, and we will look at a typical process for action research. We will also read an account of research undertaken by a teacher and discover how the research done and the action taken helped that teacher's development and in turn helped his learners.

THINKING TASK 1

Think of and write down five things that you believe describe action research or, alternatively, five questions about it that you would like answered. Do this task before reading the rest of the chapter.

My experience: Jan Madakbas

Jan Madakbas has worked in various countries as an academic manager, CELTA and DELTA trainer, teacher, assessor and examiner. Jan spoke to me about action research generally, and in particular about one piece of action research he did. Given Jan's background and experience, you might be surprised by the nature of the action research he undertook – trying to improve his board work. Here's what Jan had to say.

What is action research?

It's something many teachers and professionals in other areas do. It's an approach to professional enquiry. If, for example, you've got some kind of problem or there's something you want to learn or know more about – basically, if you want to understand your work better and maybe improve it – then you carry out what we call action research. Sometimes it's called 'classroom research' when it takes place in the classroom.

What action research have you done?

Very often it's personal, so it's about what I do and why I do it and whether it has any effect on my learners. Action research can be a project of any size, but it works best when it's of a size you can easily manage and that doesn't require too much data collection. One of the things I did was a mini-project to find out more about my board work – I'm an experienced teacher and board work is a pretty basic area and it was something I felt I was taking for granted. The board is a record of learning, as in you write something up on the board and the students copy it, or you use it to write on it things that come up in the lesson such as emerging language. So I wanted to evaluate how effective my board work was, and to do that I planned my board work in advance (experienced teachers wouldn't normally make lengthy lesson plans).

What were the stages of the action research you undertook?

Action research usually begins by identifying what it is you want to investigate – in my case board work. Then you go on to explore the issue and decide how to do this. So I talked with colleagues and made some enquiries and looked at other teachers' boards. After this, I devised some actions for myself. So the first stages are *identify*, *explore*, *plan*. I took in my camera and I took pictures of my board work to see how effective and useful it was and how I might be able to make it more effective and useful for my learners. Other options could have been conducting a survey of students' opinions or getting observers in to provide some feedback.

The next stage was *investigation*, when I looked at my board work and took photographs of it at various stages of the lesson. Then I'd compare my board with other boards I had seen and taken photographs of, as teachers often leave their board work unwiped, which was quite handy!

After this came the next stages, which are usually *analysis*, *action* and *review*. So, basically you start with identifying, then exploring, then planning to do something about this, then you'd investigate, analyse, take action and review, and then you might start the process all over again if you're still not happy with a particular aspect.

What were your conclusions on your action research on your board work?

Well, my conclusions, unfortunately, were that my board work was all right on the whole! The only issue was with neatness and layout. I had identified this as an area to investigate and, when I looked at other teachers' boards, I noticed, for example, how other people used colour and how they marked phonological or grammatical features. I realized that I was doing all of that already, so that was OK, but at times my board work was a bit all over the place. Other boards I saw were organized much more neatly, with columns, for example.

I also realized that a lot of what went on my board was student-generated in response to their questions, and that I was writing meaningful fragments much more to do with the lexical approach style of teaching, and other people weren't, so I was quite pleased with what I was doing in that regard. Not much of my board work was teacher-led grammar presentation, but was mostly student-led. So, overall, I was quite pleased but I decided I needed to work on the neatness and organization of my board work. I still take pictures of my board work to this day, actually.

One other thing that came out of it was having a record of my board work from the photographs even after I had cleaned the board. I could get my camera out, look at the photograph of the previous lesson's board work and the next day have a revision activity based on what I had put on the board the day before. It meant that the action research produced this additional benefit; it made my board work a more meaningful part of the learning process as I could recycle what I had written on the board in previous lessons.

How long did your action research process last?

Well, it's ongoing. I'm still taking photos of boards and I suppose this is one of the things that has changed the way I teach – I have my phone in class, it's on silent, I take photos of my board, and the students don't mind and it's a reminder for me of what went on in previous lessons.

What other types of topic do people do action research on?

People do this type of thing with various degrees of formality or informality. One example is looking at the use of music during fluency activities. It's the smallest of things but the questions to ask are whether it helps students speak more loudly or speak more in their groups, and whether they feel safer because of the background noise. These are things you can observe and write a diary about, and you could even make class recordings and have a survey of what students felt as well. It shows that action research doesn't have to be about big topics. A survey of what students think about something is a very common way of finding out information as part of your research.

Error correction analysis is another topic: how many errors do I correct in class and what kinds of errors do I tend to correct? Which errors am I drawn to? If you record yourself, you may discover, for example, that you are more interested in grammatical errors and ignoring meaning errors or pronunciation errors. And what sorts of correction technique do I use? Do I only use a range of two or three techniques? Recording yourself or getting an observer in can give you useful feedback on these areas, as can looking at a photo of your board after the lesson.

Teacher talking time is another one. How much does the teacher talk and how much do the students talk? That's another important area that could be investigated.

Translation and the effect of translation on learning is another topic worth looking at. Do students appreciate the use of translation or would they prefer the class to be all in English? How much time does the teacher spend reiterating instructions again and again, as opposed to making it clear first time in their own language, for example?

Another one is the effect of different types of task and how much useful language they produce and how much they help students with their fluency.

Types of written error can be analysed from homework – the research doesn't always have to come from the lessons – and you can assess the effectiveness of your teaching in a particular area by analysing what students have written: 'Oh, I obviously didn't teach this very well.' So all sorts of things can be researched and action taken.

You said earlier that as a result of your research into your board work you concluded that yours was all right. How did you go about measuring and assessing the effectiveness of your board work?

I entered the process with certain beliefs and principles about what was good board work – for example, writing up meaningful fragments rather than single words. I wanted to check that what I was doing followed these beliefs and principles and to compare what I was doing with what other teachers were doing. I was pleased with the large amount of student-generated work on my board. Regarding the neatness of the board, I could see from my photos, for example, that I was increasingly using more colour.

Could you summarize the benefits of this process to you and your students? How did the process contribute to your professional development?

The biggest benefit was realizing that I could use my camera to take photographs of my board work and two or three weeks down the line I could just produce examples to help students remember and revise what they had learned. That was something I took away from the process that I use all the time now. I'm also focusing on greater use of colour, more neatness, using columns, and making sure the fragments 'line up' in an organized way.

The quality of my board work with the improvements I have made has resulted in students copying down what I've written in a similarly neat and organized way, and this helps them remember what they have studied and learned.

Finally, what prompts people to start doing action research?

Well, for me it was just something that was niggling me and I thought, 'This is easy to do something about so why don't I just do it?' And doing the research kept me fresh.

If you're going to give a talk or write an article, it's good to do some action research to collect relevant data.

It's good for the organization because organizations like to have staff carry out research projects – for example, where I work we have a lot of non-native trainee teachers and if we could produce some findings into research into native vs non-native teachers and get that published or be a talk at a conference, then that gives the organization some prestige.

And if you feel you have some kind of problem – for example, with teaching grammar to very high-level teachers and thinking 'Should I be teaching them more grammar?' or 'Is the grammar I am teaching them actually useful for them?' – then doing some action research can be really eye-opening for any level of teacher.

THINKING TASK 2

Having read the interview with Jan, refer back to your task at the start of this chapter. Which of your questions are answered? Which of your statements can be confirmed as true or false? Did Jan answer your questions or help you establish whether your predictions or assumptions about action research were true? If you have any gaps, try to find a colleague who has done some action research to see whether they can fill those gaps.

Topics for action research

Jan gave a number of examples of possible action research topics for the classroom in addition to the one he chose to do. Here is a reminder of his list:

- Board work
- Error correction analysis
- Background music as an aid to increased fluency and confidence
- The use and effectiveness of translation
- Teacher talking time vs student talking time
- The effectiveness of different types of task
- Analysing the effectiveness of teaching based on students' written work

THINKING TASK 3

Think about an action research project related to areas in the classroom that could be investigated and in which you have a particular interest. Alternatively, choose a topic from Jan's list that you would like to research.

Now go back to Jan's interview. What were the principal stages that he followed during his action research project?

How to conduct research: an informal investigation

If you don't want to do a full-blown action research project at this stage, limit yourself to some informal investigation – maybe a survey of your students or discussions with colleagues – in order to collate some useful information, feedback and ideas around your chosen topic. For example, if Jan's board work project was an area of interest to you but you didn't want to do a full action research project, you could do a classroom survey, perhaps as part of a lesson on effective learning, and elicit the views and opinions of students about what helps them about their teacher's board work. Depending on the level and age of your learners, you could simply ask them to answer a series of questions, such as:

- How important is classroom board work to you?
- Do you usually copy what's on the board?
- What do you like about my board work?
- What do you not like?
- Do you think it is neat?
- Do you think it is organized?
- Do I use different colours well?
- What would you like me to do differently when I use the board?

Of course, you can ask other questions and provide a choice of possible answers for them to select from (making it easier for you to collate and analyse your results). You could also ask a number of different classes over a period of time for more comprehensive data: the more students you ask, the more useful and reliable the answers will be. You can then review your use of the board according to the answers.

Another possibility would be to ask your students to give you feedback during a particular lesson. 'Have a look at my board. What's good about it and what's bad about it? Is it useful to you? How could I improve it?' You could even give students mini-whiteboards or some flipchart paper, and ask them to reconstruct your board and then erase and redo your actual board work and tell you why they have done it in that way.

How to conduct research: a full research project

You could do a full action research project on your chosen topic over a much longer period of time. The stages Jan followed were as follows:

1 **Planning** – including identifying the question and doing initial exploration into it

2 **Investigation** – including data collection

3 **Analysis** – analysing the results, reflecting on them and drawing conclusions

4 **Follow-up** – using your findings, which you have analysed and reflected upon, to take action to improve the chosen aspect of

your classroom work and help you as a teacher to help your students be more effective learners

5 **Review** – finding out later whether the changes you made have been effective and, if necessary, repeating the process in order to make further adjustments based on the feedback you have received on your actions

Making a research plan

One of the topics Jan mentioned as a potential area for investigation was the use of background music to promote confidence and fluency during speaking activities. This is a topic close to my heart because for as long as I can remember I have used music in this way in my classrooms and always assumed that it is a good thing to do. I have never previously done any research into this activity but (as an example of how one person's experience can inspire another) Jan's interview with me has motivated me to do my own action research the next time I have a class to teach.

Until I have the time and opportunity to carry out this research, I can think about why I use music and what I believe the effects of it are. And I can begin to think about how I might conduct my research.

The music I use is usually classical or soft jazz and I have it on at low volume during student-centred tasks, especially freer-speaking activities – and I also have it on before the lesson begins to create a more welcoming environment. Almost any time a trainee teacher comes in to observe one of my lessons they ask me about the music, and many students have told me how much they like it. But does this prove anything? My assumptions are that:

- students feel more inclined to talk to their partner or group if there is some quiet music on in the background – in particular, shy students or those working in small classes
- music playing makes the students feel relaxed and comfortable
- the music indicates when an activity should begin and when it should end (switching off the music usually results in students stopping the task)
- music encourages students to speak more, which will ultimately help them become more fluent

The fact that over the years I have never had any student comment negatively on the music has suggested to me that they find it a positive aspect of the learning process, and when some students and observers have given positive feedback, I feel more convinced of the value of the music – but I can't be sure of this, of course.

THE STAGES OF RESEARCH

So what can I do when I do my action research? Following Jan's model, I am thinking of doing the following:

1 Planning

I will find out how many other teachers, if any, also use music. I will find out what kind of music they use, at what stages of the lesson, and for what reasons. I will also ask them whether any students or observers have ever commented on their use of music.

2 Investigation

First, I will stop using the music over a one-week period to see whether I perceive any differences in students' involvement in speaking tasks, and whether there is any reaction. After this process, I will also ask students whether they preferred doing tasks without the music. Second, I will prepare a questionnaire to collect data for me to analyse and act upon.

3 Analysis

I will assess and analyse the results and draw conclusions.

4 Action

Depending on the results, I will either continue as before (if the data results encourage me to do so) or take action and make changes. The changes might be to stop the music altogether, change the type of music or vary it more, or use it at different stages (fewer or more activities with the background music). I will then monitor the changes over a period of time, including asking observers for feedback.

5 Review

After a period of time I will review my actions and respond accordingly, perhaps repeating the process with variations in order to try something different again.

If you are also a 'music playing teacher', you could do this research as well, thinking carefully about the most effective form of data collection for your context. Otherwise, choose a suitable topic for investigation and follow this procedure stage by stage. Of course, the whole point of development is that the research you do and the actions you take (which may include not changing what you do) will help you do something more effectively and in turn help your students learn more effectively. And if the results of your investigation show that you don't need to make any changes, then that is good, too, as it confirms the validity and effectiveness of what you already do. Of course, I am hoping that I don't get the message 'Turn off the music!'

So go ahead. Do some action research of your own, either on the limited scale of an informal investigation or a more comprehensive piece of research.

Tip

If you want to read more on the topic with further examples, there is plenty of reading out there that a simple Internet search will discover. Look also at the professional development section on the British Council site: www.teachingenglish.org.uk/article/action-research

Summary

Identify a problem or an area of interest, investigate it, collect data on it, analyse the results, reflect on them, take action, review the process and repeat the process again if you want to take it further. As we said right at the start, do some research and take some action. Action research is an excellent way to improve some aspect of your classroom practice in order to help you help your learners, or even just to confirm that what you are already doing is just fine, and now you know it with the backing of data.

Action research can be on almost any aspect of what you do; it really is your choice. And it doesn't have to focus on a perceived problem – it can just as easily be on a topic you want to explore further and find out more about. Whatever you do, and however you do it, undertaking action research is an excellent form of professional development. If you have never before thought about doing it, then maybe the time has come.

13

Being a student again

'Bonjour. Comment allez-vous?'

'Très bien, merci. Et vous?'

It's 1971, at St Anselm's School (as it was then) in the delightful UK city of Canterbury, in Room 12 if I remember correctly, and my French teacher was Mrs Norris. My French lessons were conducted mostly in French, and they began with standard phrases for beginners such as the ones above and most of which I can still remember now, though my ability to have a conversation in French long ago left me. As I recall, I was good at remembering words and phrases but started to feel a bit at sea once we got into grammar. To be honest, I wasn't a very good language learner at school. Little did I think that I would end up teaching a language.

I have worked in many private language schools during my career, as well as a further education college, and in most of them the Director of Studies or equivalent would do some teaching as part of their timetable. One benefit of this is that the DOS can continue to relate first-hand to the teachers they manage and support as well as to the students they look after. It is important to have that empathy, that understanding, in order to remember and appreciate the work teachers do and the issues they face. In the same way, it is good for teachers from time to time to go back to being a student again, whatever the course of study, in order to empathize with their students and to let that process of being a student again inform their teaching beliefs and approaches.

Developing through learning

As a teacher of English to students who have a different first language, I always emphasize the need to be able to relate to learner difficulties, and this is something I talk a lot about when I am training new teachers. I have certain beliefs about language learning issues but, although I am convinced of them, the fact is that I have not done any language learning of my own since those 1970s days in my French classroom. So what better way for me to engage in a bit of my own professional development than to go back to being a student, and particularly a language student, to test my beliefs?

In no particular order I find myself making the following assertions, and others, on a regular basis, especially when I am working with trainee teachers on pre-service courses:

1 Learners forget a lot of what they have learned and it needs reinforcing.

2 Learners cannot digest too much new language at one time.

3 Learners get tired and frustrated.

4 Learners need to hear new language many times before having the confidence to repeat it accurately.

5 Learners need lots of practice of what they have learned.

6 Learners need encouragement.

7 Learners need correction.

8 Learners need emerging language to be focused on.

9 Learners need to see and acknowledge progress.

10 Learners need to see mistakes as part of the learning process.

11 Learners need to be able to ask questions and to be curious about language.

12 Learners need to be motivated.

13 Learners need to see new language in its written form.

14 Learners need to have basic rules and patterns to follow.

15 Learners need to know what parts of language are called.

16 Learners need to write things down and to keep a record of their learning.

17 Learners need a variety of teaching methods.

18 Learners need constant recycling and revision.

19 Learners need context that is relevant and useful and recognizable.

20 Learners need to take some responsibility for their learning.

I wanted to find out to what extent my statements above were true for me and what additionally I could learn as a teacher from going back to being a student. How could this experience help me develop as a teacher? I wanted to confirm to myself that all those assumptions I continue to make based on learning a language a long time ago are really true.

Learning a new language

For the first time since my schooldays I decided to embark on a language course. I also decided that I should set myself a real challenge and take on a difficult language from scratch. Given that I am a frequent traveller to South East Asia, and scheduled at the time of writing to go again in a few months' time, I chose Mandarin with the ultimate aim of using what I learned during my upcoming visit.

Due to time constraints, I decided to do a combination of an audio-book 'self-learning' course and having a native speaker as my one-to-one teacher for one or two hours per week. Given my previous doubts about audio self-learning courses, I was also interested to see how effective – or not – my experience with this would be. I was both excited and a bit nervous as I prepared to start, given that I don't consider myself to be a natural language learner.

LESSON ONE

In the first lesson I learned ways of greeting people – greetings for individuals and pairs/groups, both formally and informally, including the more formal 'Good morning' and 'Good evening'. I learned how to respond to the question 'How are you?' with 'I'm very well thank you, and you?' And I had my first introduction to the nightmare of different tones. For example, I had to learn to say 'ma' in four different tones to mean four quite different things. I was really going to struggle with that. In addition, the way each item of language is spelled (below) bears almost no relation at all to how you say it, which quickly confirmed my teacher view that students need to hear language spoken over and over again and to practise saying it. In particular, for me, the spelling of '*xiexie*' ('thank you') gave me no clue at all about the pronunciation and I had great difficulty getting the tone right with '*si*' ('yes'). I just could not seem to reproduce that particular sound accurately.

Here are a few other examples of my first language lesson:

- *ni hao / nin hao / nimen hao / ni hao ma? / nin hao ma?* = various greetings
- *wo hen hao / mamahuhu* = responses to greetings
- *xiexie... nine?* = 'thank you, and you?'
- *zaoshang hao* = 'good morning'
- *wangshang hao* = 'good evening'

I also learned phrases for 'see you later/tomorrow' and 'goodbye'.

After the lesson I recorded my reactions to the first lesson:

> 'It felt like I had learned a lot of new language but I actually learned very little, although I was reminded of a great deal about what it's like to be a learner. It is incredibly frustrating, struggling to hear the pronunciation and not being able to replicate the pronunciation models I am given, and of course the complete difference between the spelling and the pronunciation. And just forgetting the tiny, tiny, tiny amount that I have learned almost straight away and having to go over it over and over again, so when my teacher said, 'Let's go on,' there was no way I could do it. I have got to really practise, practise, practise and it reminded me of my low-level students and how unbelievably frustrating it can be and how slow the learning process is and almost how daft you feel not being able to remember what you've learned and not being readily able to produce what you've learned, especially when your native-speaker teacher obviously finds it easy and you can't keep up.

> 'The other thing is I had to write down everything I learned, even though it was written in the book. I need to write it down to help me remember and then to keep going over the dialogue, and I need to master that first lesson before moving on to lesson two.'

The next morning I had forgotten some of what I had learned, so I went over it again, and again the next day until I felt I had retained everything and could use it. Although I hadn't learned that much of the language in my first lesson, I felt I had made progress and that was both my reward and my motivation. It felt good, even though I partly wished I had stuck to the easier option of improving my schoolboy French! The real reward was a day or two later when I went to a Malaysian restaurant and tried out a bit of what I'd learned on the waiters and was told by one 'Your pronunciation is very good.' That little bit of praise was very rewarding and motivating – and I always remind training teachers to do this for that very reason.

SUBSEQUENT LESSONS

I continued my lessons with increasing enthusiasm and repeated frustration. It helped me to have a routine to my learning and to be flexible in terms of how much I could learn in any new lesson. And this was another important lesson for me in this process because, if I had been part of a class with other students, the level of difficulty I already faced would have been multiplied many times over. Of course, there would have been advantages, too, such as the chance to practise with others and have some pressure reduced, but I would have felt increased pressure at other times such as when the teacher would ask me to answer a question or repeat some new language with other students listening. And I would have lost my ability to dictate the amount of new language to be learned at any given time.

On the other hand, I was to an extent re-evaluating my views on the audio 'teach yourself' method. It gave me the chance to 'replay' any lesson as many times as I wanted. However, that in itself would have had little, if any, value to me without the support of my teacher. I really appreciated the fact that my teacher was a native speaker. All in all, it was good to be a student again.

Slowly (very slowly), I learned more and more and practised as much as I could and increased my confidence in using my new bits of language. As I write, I am eagerly looking forward to my trip to Malaysia to try it all out. How well will I be understood? Will I be able to understand responses spoken at what will surely sound like the speed of light? I will report back later in this chapter...

Reviewing assumptions

Already, I can begin to consider how this is experience is helping my development as a teacher. I can now go back to the assumptions I stated earlier and see to what extent they applied to me, and whether I need to add any that I didn't think of before. My initial conclusions were not especially surprising:

1 **Learners forget a lot of what they have learned and it needs reinforcing.**

   True for me: I forgot language I had learned a short time before and I needed to go over it many times and to use it several times before it 'stuck'. Teachers need to provide lots of revision and recycling activities as well as progress tests.

2 **Learners cannot digest too much new language at one time.**

   True for me: I could only deal with small chunks at any one time. Teachers should not overload learners, especially low-level ones, with too much new language.

3 **Learners get tired and frustrated.**

   True for me: I became especially frustrated at what I felt was slow progress and forgetting so much so quickly. Teachers need to be aware of this and be sensitive to it in what they plan to do in their lessons.

4 **Learners need to hear new language many times before having the confidence to repeat it accurately.**

   True for me – many, many times, in fact: I often heard myself saying to my teacher 'Say it slowly, please.' I needed that security of hearing accurate models as often as I could. Teachers need to give clear, accurate and natural models of new language and to break down each component of a word, phrase or sentence.

5 **Learners need lots of practice of what they have learned.**

   True for me, and that included 'real-life' practice with native speakers whenever possible. Teachers need to provide lots of varied practice and give feedback afterwards.

6 **Learners need encouragement.**

   Surprisingly true for me: receiving any kind of praise for my efforts really motivated me. Teachers need to say things such as 'Good', 'Well done', 'Yes, that's right', 'You're doing very well', etc.

7 **Learners need correction.**

True for me – and an obvious one because without that correction you won't improve. Teachers need to correct (sensitively) key mistakes in order to help their learners become more accurate and more confident.

8 **Learners need emerging language to be focused on.**

True for me, especially through me asking questions such as 'And how do you say…?' Teachers need to respond to what naturally emerges in a lesson and to immediate learner needs.

9 **Learners need to see and acknowledge progress.**

True for me, and very much linked to point 6.

10 **Learners need to see mistakes as part of the learning process.**

True for me: I wasn't concerned that I had made mistakes; I knew that was part of the process, but I did want to be corrected.

11 **Learners need to be able to ask questions and to be curious about language.**

True for me: the more motivated I felt, the greater the interest I took. Teachers need to welcome relevant questions and to respond to them. Questions are to be welcomed, not feared.

12 **Learners need to be motivated.**

True for me: I had a motive – to use the language on my upcoming trip as well as to develop myself by being a student again and re-affirming my previous assumptions. Teachers need to find out the different motivations of their learners – why do they want to learn/improve their English?

13 **Learners need to see new language in its written form.**

True for me, although I needed to hear and say new language before I saw its written form. Teachers need to provide learners with a clear record of the written form and how it is constructed, as well as practice of its pronunciation.

14 **Learners need to have basic rules and patterns to follow.**

Less true for me, but teachers do need to provide them when appropriate (e.g. 'In English, when a verb follows a preposition, then the verb will be in its -ing form' is a basic rule that can be followed).

15 **Learners need to know what parts of language are called.**

Not true for me: for example, I didn't need to know that the word I learned for 'hungry' was an adjective because I already understood this. Perhaps I need to re-evaluate the importance I place on this when teaching.

16 **Learners need to write things down and keep a record of their learning.**

True for me: once I had learned words, phrases and sentences, I studied the written form in the book but still felt the need to copy everything into my learning notebook to help me remember what I had learned. Teachers need to encourage their learners to keep lexical notebooks and to structure them in a way that will help them revise and remember what they have learned. I know I'm very bad at this, but as a teacher I can use this weakness of mine as I know it hinders me and I don't want my learners to have the same weakness in their note-taking.

17 **Learners need a variety of teaching methods.**

Not true for me personally with the kind of lessons I had undertaken, but in a class setting with other students and more and longer lessons, I am sure it would be true. Teachers need to plan for variety and to cater for different learning styles and needs.

18 **Learners need constant recycling and revision.**

Absolutely true for me: teachers need to cater for this in their lesson planning.

19 **Learners need context that is relevant, useful and recognizable.**

Absolutely true for me: you have to have a context for the language you are learning. Teachers must provide a clear and relevant context to help learners understand the meaning and use of what they are learning.

20 **Learners need to take some responsibility for their learning.**

Yes, and this reminded me of the immense discipline and focus required in undertaking any kind of course, especially when done alongside work. Teachers need to encourage this in the lessons and homework they plan and show learners how they can continue to learn and improve outside the classroom.

Obviously, everyone has their own preferred ways of learning and for any student the context of their studies is a major factor. My experience did not throw up any real surprises, though a few of my previous beliefs proved less significant for me, mainly due to the context of my learning. There is a big difference between learning with a private teacher at your own pace and learning in a classroom with fixed lessons. Beginner students where I work study for a minimum of three hours a day, five days a week, with homework and private study on top of that. Such a learning context would have provided me with many more challenges than those I faced.

How did I get on during my trip to Malaysia when I tried to use some of the language I had been learning for the previous six months or so? It wasn't much, and I certainly was not at the level, or anywhere near the level, of being able to have any kind of conversation beyond the very basic types, but I was able to surprise locals with my (less than convincing) Mandarin phrases and expressions. They certainly appreciated my efforts and my biggest reward was those occasions when they understood what I said! Although my level remains basic, I was able to use what I had learned among locals in an Asian country, and this was my equivalent of passing an exam.

Language learning for CPD

The experience of language learning has aided my ongoing professional development in the following ways:

- To varying extents, my previous beliefs about language learning have been confirmed and that will give my training of new teachers greater validity when I comment on learner difficulties and needs.
- With much more recent language-learning experience than before, I will be able – to an even greater extent than before – to relate to my learners when I am teaching, and especially low-level learners, in terms of their needs and difficulties.
- In particular, I have learned that I had actually underestimated how frustrating and slow it can be to learn a language, and had also understated the need for continual encouragement and motivation from the teacher. I always knew these were important factors, but I had not appreciated just how important. Now I will empathize more with students regarding how it feels.

- I have also been reminded by my own teacher of how important both encouragement and patience are. I knew this already, but the extent to which they can help a learner was really underlined. As a result of this process, I am now going to ask to teach an elementary class (A1/A2), which I haven't done for a long time, in order to see how my own experience can benefit my teaching of learners at that level.

This is a colleague's view of the value of teachers going back to being a language student:

'It's an excellent way of reminding yourself what it's like to be a student struggling with unfamiliar concepts. It also helps you identify which features of methodology you do or don't respond well to, which can lead to interesting discussions on learning styles, approaches in the classroom, etc. The most obvious way to do this is to offer lessons in the language of the country for your newer staff – perhaps taught by a local teacher or by an experienced teacher who has a good level in the local language. If you have a staff body that is comfortable in the local language, you can always offer language classes in another language, which one of your staff can teach.'

My experience: Danny Norrington-Davies

As a different example of becoming a student again, I spoke to Danny about his experience of studying for an MA and how this has been a development opportunity for him. Danny talks about the personal benefits this has brought him, specifically in relation to particular classroom activities he does.

How have your studies benefited your professional development?

I did an MA in ELT and Applied Linguistics and I did it for myself because I wanted to learn a bit more about language, and my dissertation was about something I use a lot of in the classroom but never really thought much about how it worked. What the MA did for me was to really make me question what I do and to understand what I do in the classroom.

I use visualization activities a lot and I've talked about them at a conference as well. I've said that such activities are really good at helping students remember a text very well, and how it generates lots of language, and students like doing them, but the MA made me study it and I discovered that they truly are remembering things better from doing visualization activities and so it really taught me to be sitting in a class and thinking, 'Why is this working?' or 'Why is this not working?' or 'Why is this really boring?' So it was great to be really able to have someone really backing up my ideas, so that if someone came up to me and said, 'This is a very odd thing to do' or 'I'm not sure this is very helpful', I can say, 'Well, studies have shown that...' One student in particular said, after we'd done it in class, 'Now, if I don't see pictures, I don't understand the text.'

So doing a course like this:

- has helped me as a trainer and as a teacher
- has helped my students to remember more effectively
- has taught me to really question what I do and why I do it
- has helped me with a particular activity in the classroom because I can say why we are doing it.

Doing a course such as the one Danny did can also improve your prospects of getting internal promotion or a different job elsewhere with new challenges and new rewards. Such career progression is also very important in terms of CPD.

For many teachers who have the CELTA or equivalent, the obvious next step to going back to being a student is to take the DELTA course which, as well as deepening your knowledge and awareness of theory and practice in teaching will, assuming you pass, also improve your career prospects and opportunities to go into non-teaching areas such as training and management. If you do not have the DELTA yet and are thinking about taking it, find out more about it by going to www.cambridgeenglish.org and by talking to colleagues to have done it, especially any who have done it more recently. The website details other teaching courses as well.

In North America holders of CELTA, etc., get language school teaching or part-time ESOL teaching jobs in community colleges and the DELTA is not so useful. An MA in a related field is essential for university teaching and for virtually all full-time TESOL positions in community colleges.

The USA has fewer private language schools than in some other parts of the world. There is a huge number of volunteer TESL opportunities for immigrants offered by churches, refugee organizations, public libraries and others. Most opportunities are in community colleges, but faculty positions are rare and most instructors teach part-time, have no job security and receive no benefits (sick pay, health insurance, paid holidays/vacations). To get a full-time job, you virtually always need a Masters degree and significant experience.

CPD TASK

The obvious task would be for you to take some kind of course, even a very short one. You could even limit yourself to doing what I did and get a self-study audio course and find a friendly native speaker to supplement it and then test either the beliefs that I stated at the start, or others that you have. You could even just ask a student to spend a couple of hours trying to teach you some of the local language and see what difficulties you encounter, and also what rewards the experience brings.

If none of this is possible, why not do a survey among your students about their language-learning experience and see what issues they identify?

Whatever you do, at the end of the process make a list of what you have learned from the experience and what conclusions you have drawn. How has the process helped you develop as a teacher? And, if you have actually attended classes, what did you think of the teaching? For whatever reason, did that teacher's approach make you re-evaluate your own teaching in any way?

Summary

It is very easy after a while to forget what it is like to be a student, and especially a language student. To go back to the other side of the desk can be a very helpful and illuminating reminder of what it is like and that, in turn, can re-affirm previously held beliefs, change those beliefs or add new ones. All of this can help to inform the way you teach and to increase the empathy you need to have for your learners.

14

Becoming a trainer

I have become convinced over the years that development opportunities can be as much about being in the right place at the right time as they can be about planning targets to achieve over the coming year, although sometimes I wonder about all the times that I wasn't in a particular place at a certain time and what opportunities I missed out on without realizing it! If you work at a centre that offers teacher training and certification courses such as the CELTA, you might at some point get the chance of becoming a teacher trainer on them, or you might move to a different organization that offers the same possibility. However, we should not restrict talk of 'training' only to such pre-service training courses of which CELTA in its various forms is the oldest of its kind. As well as CELTA (Cambridge) (www.cambridgeenglish.org/teaching-english/teaching-qualifications/celta/) and CertTESOL (Trinity) (www.trinitycollege.com/site/?id=263), there are many other training possibilities including online courses.

Pre-service courses

I was definitely in the right place at the right time when the school I was working at needed a new teacher trainer to work on what are today called CELTA courses and I was asked to take on the role, despite having been an English language teacher for only three years at that time. Accepting that role proved to be hugely significant in my own development.

To gain a place on a CELTA or CertTESOL training course to become an approved trainer, you need to be offered the opportunity by your organization, to be suitably qualified, to have sufficient experience, and to be trained up according to Trinity or Cambridge requirements. And you have to be sure that this so what you want to do and think you will be good at doing. 'Suitably qualified' would usually mean having the DELTA or equivalent qualification. Sufficient experience would typically involve several years' experience, preferably in at least two different contexts. And, of course, such a developmental opportunity will only be possible if you work for or seek out an organization that offers these courses and which might have an opportunity for you at some point to become part of the training team.

In North America, additionally, there are training opportunities in private organizations offering certificated courses and there are some in colleges and universities offering certificate or Masters programmes, but a Masters in TESOL or a related field is needed.

CELTA is a pre-service course intended primarily for people starting out in English language teaching who have little or no teaching experience. As part of the course, they have to do a total of six hours' teaching practice as well as completing written assignments and observations. It is an intensive course and it can become a bit stressful at times. The full-time version of the course lasts four weeks but the course is also available part-time, either face to face or a combination of face to face and online.

THINKING TASK 1

- If you are already a CELTA (or equivalent) trainer yourself, make your own list first of how the course has aided your professional development. Then read my list below to see how our lists overlap and what points are different. See if you can come up with five to ten specific examples of how being a trainer of this sort has developed you in any way.

- If you have never worked on such courses, speak to a colleague about the above task. If there is no one to ask, consider how you think training people to become teachers could help you as a teacher in any respect.

Training courses and CPD

Working on CELTA courses has helped my teaching (and in so doing helped my trainees and my students) and it has opened up many other opportunities. Trainers on initial training courses worldwide will have similar tales to tell, as well as going into training on other courses such as DELTA.

More than a quarter of a century of working as a trainer on CELTA courses, or their equivalent, has aided my development in many ways, as follows:

- It has made me constantly assess and reflect on how I teach.
- It has made me always think of the learning aims of every lesson I teach and every stage of that lesson.
- In the early days especially, it taught me the importance of thorough analysis of language and of anticipating the problems students might have with it and possible solutions to those problems.
- It instilled in me the need to be organized in all respects.
- In dealing with many hundreds of trainees over the years, I have developed many people skills, including dealing with those under stress or those who are 'difficult' in some way. Helping people stay calm, positive and motivated has also been a vital skill I have developed.
- Working on these courses has ensured that I stay up to date with current methodology and thinking, and this has benefited both my training and my teaching.
- Other training possibilities have arisen from this experience.
- It enabled me later on to become an assessor of CELTA courses around the world, giving me invaluable insight into how organizations and trainers in other countries run their courses.
- In my case, as a consequence of my work, I also had and took the opportunity to run standardization meetings for more than 50 trainers and assessors worldwide at a time, which gave me experience in addressing and running meetings for very large groups. This also gave me the confidence to do a conference talk.

- With this experience, I have been able to move into tutoring various online courses for teachers and managers and this, in turn, has greatly developed my confidence in using technology.

THINKING TASK 2

Read the second part of my experiences below, and also the interview that follows with Martin. What do you think will be some of the differences between working with pre-service candidates on a CELTA course and working with a group of experienced teachers from the same country and organization who want to update their methodology?

NON-CERTIFICATION COURSES

My own training path and the development opportunities it has provided started with that offer to become a trainer at the school I was at in 1987. I have also worked with closed or non-certification groups of teachers seeking further development themselves, most recently a closed group of Korean teachers. 'Closed groups' will often be a group of practising teachers from a particular school and maybe from a different country whose course has been organized by their employers or by their government. Such courses are normally designed to improve the participants' training skills and knowledge of current trends and methodology, especially if they work in a context where further training opportunities are limited. Only some organizations offer such courses and therefore provide opportunities for this kind of training.

The two types of training are completely different, with different aspects of development as well as shared ones. Working with closed groups of trainers from a particular country can also be a rewarding experience and perhaps one more easily attainable for some teachers wanting to get into training. This can often be an excellent first step into training, making your suitability as a CELTA trainer in the future that much greater.

My most recent experience of working with Korean teachers was hugely enjoyable, with additional developmental aspects:

- I learned a great deal about how English is taught in South Korea and how culture affects the approaches taken. As the school I work at has many Korean students, this will help me understand their needs and learning styles.

- When I am training, I will be able to use that experience and understanding when discussing different approaches and different learning styles, and especially if I come across anyone wanting to work there.
- By sharing the teaching part of the course, the teachers could observe me teach and I could observe them teach, which is beneficial to both of us in terms of being exposed to different approaches and styles.

My experience: Martin Oetegenn

I spoke to Martin Oetegenn about his training experiences, not just his work on CELTA but also his time in Peru and in China, where he provided further training for experienced and practising teachers. These teachers were mostly looking for more ideas about methodology to incorporate into their lessons. The courses took place in the teachers' normal place of work.

Why did you apply to become a CELTA trainer?

I saw it as a kind of career progression, so it was a way of moving forward and developing and having a new experience in this kind of context, so that was part of my motivation. I'd also been inspired by some of my previous trainers, so I wanted to do what they had done and have the same sort of impact that they had had on me.

When you first started training on CELTA, what was it like?

It was quite daunting at first because you feel a big sense of responsibility – people pay large sums of money to do the course and they are often at a turning point in their lives, maybe doing a career change or something like that, so there's a lot riding on it for them. I definitely felt that pressure to do them justice and to bring out the best for them. Obviously it's a stressful time for them, so dealing with that was a new factor. It wasn't something I'd really had to deal with when teaching students, so that was something that I had to learn, from watching how my colleagues dealt with it and asking people's advice. It was quite a challenge at first but after a while you find you can manage people through that stress and that can be very satisfying.

What do you enjoy most about it?

I just enjoy the people and it's really nice when people enjoy the course and enjoy teaching. When they finish and you know that they're going out there to start their teaching career, it is a big deal for them, so it's very satisfying when you get them through it and you've helped people to develop.

It's definitely informed my teaching. At first it was quite a useful reminder of how you're supposed to teach, all those little techniques that you have been taught yourself and then kind of forget about, but I think it goes both ways because the teaching also informs the training and it helps you to have a realistic expectation of what trainees can do.

Tell me about the training you did recently with practising teachers in Peru and China.

This was a hugely different experience from doing CELTA. The motivation on a career level was that it was a great opportunity to experience a different context and I hoped that it would inform the way I trained as well. The experience itself, in Peru especially, was of a school that was fantastically well organized and with great opportunities for development and training. The people I trained were very keen and had loads of ideas and the sessions were very well received, so that was lovely.

It was quite a different context in China. They hadn't really had much training before so, whereas going to Peru was like preaching to the converted, in China the teachers had to cope with a huge change in teaching methodology. It was challenging but really interesting and on a selfish level it was really useful for me because now I feel I've got a much greater understanding of the students we get who come from China and the occasional CELTA trainees from there. I've got so much more respect for them now – I did anyway, but even more so now – just to see how much they have to adapt to our style of teaching.

So would you recommend training?

I think if you're planning on staying on in the industry and you don't have plans to do anything different, I'd say go for it if you have the opportunity to do so. It definitely helps with motivation and with development. It is possible to get jaded in this industry; you just reach a certain point with your development and it can be rejuvenating to do something completely new, so I would certainly recommend considering it. It wouldn't necessarily be a great career path for everybody, though – with CELTA you need to be good at dealing with stress and with other people on the course who are stressed out. And you need to be organized. Those are the fundamental considerations.

How would you summarize how being a trainer in different contexts has helped you develop professionally?

I've learned a lot about diplomacy and thinking carefully about what to say and how to say it. You need to be clear about the message you want to get across, but you have to really work out the best way of getting that message across according to who you are speaking to and this can be different for each person you speak to. I'm the sort of person who can be quite rash and talk without thinking first, but I have noticed a change in me in that regard because you realize how much more effectively you can communicate if you just think about it first.

As it did for Martin, the training experience can teach you:
- better organizational skills
- about different contexts and to have a better understanding of students and trainees from those contexts
- about dealing with people, especially those under stress, which will help you in every aspect of your work
- skills to inform your teaching, as teaching will inform your training

All this will make you both a better teacher and trainer.

As a teacher or trainer, you can participate in many professional development courses and workshops (both face to face and online) for your own development. Of course, trainers are needed for these courses and for the thousands like them that take place worldwide, and so they all represent training possibilities. For example, International House in London offers a number of courses for experienced teachers, with each course run by a trainer who might be an experienced teacher wishing to become involved in CELTA training later, or already a CELTA or DELTA trainer. These are some of their courses:

- 'Life in Britain – bringing culture into the classroom'
- 'CLIL' (Content and Language Integrated Learning)
- 'Classroom Skills for Primary Teachers'
- 'Language Development and Teaching Skills'
- 'Current Trends – Theory and Practice'

Recent courses for closed groups have focused on groups of teachers from Peru, China, South Korea, China and Albania, among others.

All these courses have provided training opportunities leading to significant professional development for trainers and senior teachers. Many organizations around the world offer similar courses and opportunities. As you read the personal experiences reported here, ask yourself whether this is something you would like to do.

My experience: Ifthaquar Jamil

Ifthaquar, like Martin, has worked around the world on training courses for experienced teachers.

Tell me about your experiences and how working on these courses is different from working on CELTA.

I've worked in the UK on 'Language Development and Teaching Skills', 'Current Trends', and various closed groups with Basque teachers and Korean teachers, as well as courses in Peru. Working on these courses, compared with CELTA, gives you more scope in terms of ideas and you can explore the material much more because there's no assessment. You find out initially what their working context is and then work out how to exploit materials to make life easier for them in their teaching. I started my training career working on these courses and later progressed to becoming a CELTA trainer and later a DELTA trainer. I personally think that the best people to run these kinds of closed-group courses for teachers are people pretty much straight off their DELTA. They've got all the terminology and they're enthusiastic and they're still experimenting, so I think the quality of the dialogue is better and you can have more of a discussion, whereas someone with huge experience runs the risk of 'talking down' to them a bit, maybe. You certainly don't need to be a CELTA or DELTA trainer to work on teacher courses.

How has working on these courses helped you in terms of your own professional development?

It has helped me to:

- understand different teaching and working contexts better
- be more aware and more sensitive when I do work on CELTA and give feedback that the people I am training will in some cases go to work in very different contexts from the one I am in. A lot of what I do in my school may not be applicable in their context – it makes me have a more open mind and to be less critical in my feedback
- be a much better teacher because it helps me understand the theory better and why I'm planning my lessons and my teaching in a particular way to help my students
- consolidate everything I did on my DELTA because of all the principles you learn. I think 'Ah, that's why I'm doing that' and it helps me with exam classes as well. By telling other people how and why we do certain things, such as task-based learning, you understand more about the theories and the approaches and become aware of where your own knowledge may be lacking. I've refined it through doing these teacher courses and I think it is fantastic for someone post-DELTA to do

As mentioned earlier, increasingly now there are opportunities to work on courses online. For a number of years I have tutored on 'Educational Management' courses such as 'Effective Communication', 'INSETT', 'Managing Change', and 'Observation and Feedback' as part of the International House online CPD programme (see the IH London website: www.ihlondon.com). These courses attract experienced teachers who have moved into management and, as well as developing my skills in using technology to manage these courses, I have learned a huge amount about the different contexts that teachers work in around the world and the different challenges they face. By working together, not only am I able to help them, but they are also able to help me by giving me an invaluable insight to working contexts elsewhere, and I have picked up a lot of good ideas. As Ifthaquar said before, it is a dialogue that both sides benefit from. For those participating on these courses, there is a great opportunity for development in their roles as managers.

The benefits of training

If you're still not entirely sure whether training teachers is for you, or of how it might benefit your development, I asked a variety of different kinds of trainer what they enjoy most about doing it, and how it has made them better teachers. This is what they had to say.

'WHAT DO YOU ENJOY MOST ABOUT BEING A TRAINER?'

- 'I like the purposeful nature of training, with its clear goals.'
- 'I like the responsibility – it makes me feel slightly more worthwhile in the scheme of things.'
- 'With CELTA you often meet people on the cusp of a big change in their lives, and I get vicarious pleasure from that, given I'm in such a rut. With some trainees it's a real pleasure to see their excitement about starting in a 'new' work area. Some discover a real joy in being in the classroom and I really like watching them and helping them develop.'

- 'Helping people to achieve their goals is always a positive experience. After all these years, I still like watching TP!'
- 'I like the opportunity to work with lots of different colleagues. Sometimes in GE you work alone, so it can be fun (and sometimes challenging!) to work in a team.'
- 'I like making materials and tweaking them. I always think I can improve.'
- 'I like seeing trainees put into practice what I've shown them.'
- 'I like meeting people years later who have gone on to have a successful career in teaching.'
- 'I enjoy learning about the nature of what we do as language teachers.'
- 'I enjoy the challenge of helping trainees understand.'

'HOW HAS TRAINING MADE YOU A BETTER TEACHER?'

Trainers said that training had improved their teaching by:
- 'helping me understand what works and what doesn't'
- 'seeing the limitations of what's possible in the class'
- 'having to show trainees what we mean in terms of best practice (demonstrating in feedback)'
- 'keeping up to date and making me reflect on what I do. (Sometimes it confirms my beliefs, sometimes it makes me question them.)'
- 'forcing me to read a little and keep up (on a superficial level!) with current ideas'
- 'always changing materials'
- 'learning from teachers from other contexts – different ideas and different ways of doing things'
- 'learning from other teachers that their different approaches and methodologies also work; this has made me reflect more on my own practice and re-evaluate my teaching'

Summary

Some people enter this profession because they want to supplement their existing income with teaching. Others enter it in order to have a few years working in a new country before going on to do something different. Most, though, enter the TEFL profession and remain within it for their entire career and for those people there comes a time when they want to branch out and do something in addition to teaching, and training is one of the most common directions they take. Training is not just about working on CELTA and DELTA courses, or equivalent, but includes working with experienced teachers and helping them develop their skills and broaden their knowledge. You may work with such groups in the country where you are working, or by travelling to where they are working, and courses may be face to face or online. You don't have to be a CELTA or DELTA trainer to work on these types of course.

Alternatively or additionally, you may seek out the opportunity of becoming a CELTA trainer, and later a CELTA assessor of other courses, and later a DELTA trainer. Any kind of training will not only give you the opportunity to help others in their professional development but also help you with yours. You will add or develop many skills and qualities to your own teaching; you will learn a great deal about other contexts and this will influence your own teaching and training; and you will consequently have more opportunities available for yourself in your future career progression.

In short, the developmental opportunities are considerable and wide-ranging, and the satisfaction of sharing your own experience and expertise with other teachers, or helping those starting out in the profession, is immeasurable. That combination of teaching and training is one that will keep you developing as a teacher and as a trainer. Each benefits the other.

15

Professional groups and journals

Teaching, and managing for that matter, can be seen as a lonely job at times. There aren't many jobs where, for much of the day, you have no contact with your colleagues. If you work in an office, a shop, a hotel, a restaurant or a bank, you are working with colleagues for most of your day. Working as a teacher, you may be in a classroom with your students and no colleagues for up to six or more hours a day. Just as a bus driver spends the day driving the bus and looking after passengers, with no contact with other drivers or managers, so a teacher will spend much of her day looking after her class and her learners, with no contact with other teachers or managers. In many ways this is often a liberating and exciting part of the job, but it can also result in a degree of isolation at times.

Fortunately, you have a worldwide professional community to be part of, to supplement the times you do get to share with your own colleagues. In addition to all the online resources we read about in Chapter 7, you can also take advantage of professional bodies, communities and journals, both online and in person. Alongside the various websites that allow you to converse with like-minded colleagues from around the world, you can join professional bodies, sometimes for an annual membership fee, which open up more doors and more avenues. They allow you to develop through being part of a group and sharing ideas as well as reducing that element of professional loneliness you may sometimes feel.

THINKING TASK

Test your knowledge by answering the following questions.

1 Do you know what 'IATEFL' stands for and what it offers its members?

2 Have you heard of TESOL International and what members gain from joining it?

3 What other professional bodies are you aware of that you can join and be part of?

4 Do you remember what a SIG is and do you know of any examples?

5 How many ELT journals are you aware of? How many have you actually read in the last 12 months?

If you struggled to answer any of the above, what follows will fill those gaps in your knowledge.

IATEFL

IATEFL (www.iatefl.org) is the International Association of Teachers of English as a Foreign Language. A worldwide community of around 4,000 members, IATEFL describes its mission as 'to link, develop and support English language teaching professionals worldwide'. It does this through:

- regular publications, including their own magazine *IATEFL Voices* and a free conference selections publication
- an annual conference with an extensive programme of talks and workshops, which attracts over 2,500 delegates
- 15 special interest groups (SIGs) to help teachers develop their own lines of interest
- reduced rates on professional journals
- funding support for attendance at the annual conference, SIG events and online courses
- links with teachers' associations in other countries
- assistance in helping groups establish their own local teachers' association

If your organization doesn't already have institutional membership, you can join as an individual member.

THE BENEFITS OF IATEFL MEMBERSHIP

Chapter 10 focused on the value of attending and participating in conferences. Every year thousands of ELT professionals from more than 100 countries around the world attend the IATEFL conference, held at a different UK venue each time.

IATEFL also has a number of special interest groups, which we have already read about in earlier chapters. Their SIGs in 2014 had the following titles:

Business English	Learning Technologies
ESOL	Materials Writing
English for Specific Purposes	Pronunciation
Global Issues	Research
Learner Autonomy	Teacher Development
Leadership and Management	Testing, Evaluation and Assessment
Literature, Media and Cultural Studies	Teacher Training and Education

For more information, go to: www.iatefl.org/special-interest-groups/sig-list

IATEFL also offers you the chance to view webinars and SIG webinars, free to both members and non-members.

CPD TASK 1

Go to the IATEFL website (www.iatefl.org) and find out about:

- **the next IATEFL conference.** When and where will it be held? If the programme of events is already on the site, check this out, too. If you are unable to attend, consider asking a colleague who will be attending to go to a session that looks interesting, and give you their feedback on their return. Alternatively, many sessions are available to view online
- **funding arrangements.** Depending on your context, you may be eligible to apply for an IATEFL scholarship giving you free attendance at the conference
- **what each SIG has to offer.** Consider joining one or two groups of particular interest to you or even starting a SIG within your own organization. This is a great way to develop in a particular

area that interests you and could lead to you becoming a specialist in that area
- **when the next webinar is scheduled;** and keep an eye out for future webinars

GROUPS IN OTHER COUNTRIES

There are teacher associations throughout the world to keep you in contact with professionals in your country. The table lists some of them:

Country	Association
Australia	Australian Council of Tesol Associations
Austria	TEA (Teachers of English in Austria)
Brazil	BRAZTesol
Canada	Tesol Canada
Croatia	HUPE-Iatefl
Egypt	EgyptTesol
Germany	ELTAS (English Language Teachers' Association Stuttgart) HELTA e.V. (Hamburg English Language Teaching Association)
Greece	Tesol Greece Tesol Macedonia-Thrace
Hungary	Iatefl Hungary
India and South Asia	British Council ELTECS India and South Asia ELTAI (English Language Teachers' Association of India)
Israel	ETAI (English Teachers' Association of Israel)
Japan	Japan Association for Language Teaching
Nepal	Nelta (Nepal English Language Teachers' Association)
New Zealand	TesolANZ
Poland	Iatefl Poland
Republic of Korea	Korea Association of Teachers of English Korea Tesol (KOTesol)
Slovenia	Iatefl Slovenia
Spain	Tesol Spain
Switzerland	ETAS (English Teachers' Association of Switzerland)
United Arab Emirates	Tesol Arabia
United Kingdom	British Association of Lecturers in English for Academic Purposes
Uruguay	URUTesol
USA	EnglishUSA Tesol

CPD TASK 2

Wherever you are in the world, check out your local professional body and see what it has to offer. It may be one from the above list or a different one.

TESOL International Association

TESOL International Association (www.tesol.org), like IATEFL, has interest groups, 21 at the time of writing. You can register your particular professional interests to make it easier to link up with others who share them. TESOL also has a community, an ideal opportunity to get chatting with like-minded colleagues around the world, and well over 6,000 professionals attend its annual convention.

CPD TASK 3

1 Go to the interests section of the TESOL International Association site (www.tesol.org/connect/interest-sections) and compare the interest groups to IATEFL's SIGs. What additional areas are offered with TESOL, and are there any you might be interested in joining?

2 Now have a look at the 'Attend & Learn' section of the site (www.tesol.org/attend-and-learn) and find out about virtual seminars, online courses, the TESOL Resource Center and several other options. What can you find that might be of interest to you and that could add to your ongoing development?

LinkedIn

LinkedIn (www.linkedin.com) also has a community for ELT professionals that you can be part of. This community, which is free to join, offers you the chance to participate in online discussions with colleagues across the globe.

Topic areas discussed have included the following:

- How important is pronunciation?
- Are adult learners really more motivated?

- Is it the teacher's job to take care of the emotional needs of students?
- Action research. Name your topic.
- Are native speakers better teachers?
- Students learn best when...
- Unannounced teaching observations. Good or bad?
- What methods do you use to ensure vocabulary retention post study?
- English teachers need to be trained – agree or disagree?
- The Common European Framework (CEFR)
- A student has their head down, sleeping in class. I would...
- What should we focus on if we got 30 hours to train teachers (speakers of other languages)? How to make it effective
- Teaching functional language
- I'm in the process of developing a new method of teaching language for adults.
- First day of classes...
- What books or articles have most influenced your teaching?
- If you could change one thing about ELT, what would it be?
- Having a physical relationship with a consenting adult student
- Is phonics necessary to teach pronunciation?
- How many sounds are there in English?
- Should all teachers have a TEFL certificate?
- What's the best way to use pop songs?
- What qualities should an ideal foreign language teacher have?
- What will happen if a teacher is more of a comedian than a teacher?
- Lifeless teaching and a lifeless class – what to do?
- Students learn best when...

If you are looking at the site today, these particular topics may no longer be available, but there will be others. The list above, though, gives a good idea of the range and flavour of discussions that take place – a rich mixture indeed.

CPD TASK 4

Choose one or more of the above topic areas that people might have different views on and get a discussion going in your own staffroom (e.g. 'How important is pronunciation?').

Alternatively, pick a topic that you would like to understand better (e.g. 'The Common European Framework') or one that you'd like to collate information and ideas about (e.g. 'What books or articles have most influenced your teaching?'), or even something you would really appreciate help with yourself (e.g. 'Lifeless teaching and a lifeless class – what to do?').

Then you could go to the LinkedIn site (www.linkedin.com), find a current topic of interest and join in yourself. After any such discussion, ask yourself what you got out of it and how it helped you or might help you in your work.

Publications and journals

Many professional journals are published regularly and you can read them as part of your professional development. They offer a huge range of articles and features on matters relating to all areas of the ELT world, along with book reviews, special features, news, blogs and conference news. Most are available online as well as in hard copy form. Here, in no particular order, are nine examples:

- *EL Gazette*
- *Modern English Teacher*
- *The Teacher Trainer*
- *English Teaching Professional*
- *ELT Journal*
- *Internet TESL Journal*
- *IH Journal*
- *IATEFL Voices*
- *TESOL Quarterly*

It would not be realistic to subscribe to all the journals listed here but, if you are new to this area of your development, the information that follows should help you see which journals would most appeal to you. Subscribing to just one will allow you to broaden your context and experience and offer possibilities for development referred to in previous chapters. For example, you could:

- set up a reading group (see Chapter 9) and use articles from journals for your discussions
- submit an article of your own for possible publication, if you are interested in getting into writing (see Chapter 11)
- lead or suggest an INSETT session at your school, based on a topic you have read about in a journal (see Chapter 6)

One idea, one experience, can lead to another.

CPD TASK 5

How many of these journals have you seen before? Find out which ones – including others not on this list – your organization subscribes to.

EL GAZETTE

The *EL Gazette* will give you access to the monthly digital version of this journal for members of the industry as well as links to professional associations. It includes the following sections:

Language News	EL People
Higher Education News	Materials
EL Policy	Themed Issues
EL Accreditation	Listings
EL Association News	Awards
EL Prospects	Supplements
Reviews	Conference Specials

Link: www.elgazette.com

MODERN ENGLISH TEACHER

The website of this quarterly publication promises 'great articles and features, practical advice for translators and language professionals and reviews of the latest dictionaries, reference books and software'. As an example, the July 2014 edition contained the following features:

Practical Ideas

Exam Preparation

The View From Here (spotlight
on ELT in Turkey)

Professional Development

Technology Matters

It Made Me Think – about

blended learning

English for Academic Purposes

Teaching Teenagers

English for Specific Purposes

Materials Writing

Reviews

Link: www.modernenglishteacher.com

THE TEACHER TRAINER

The Teacher Trainer describes itself as 'a practical journal for those who train, mentor and educate TESOL teachers'. As well as the current issue, you can also access and download previous editions. Archived content includes numerous articles in these categories as well as many others:

Book and video reviews

Classroom practice

Conferences and workshops

Content and integrated language
learning (CLIL)

Current research

Different schools of thought and
feeder fields

E-Matters – and 'It's a wired
world'

Games for use in teacher training

Have you read…?

In-service training and
development

Interviews with…

Language matters

Meet a colleague

Observation and feedback

Pre-service training

Training around the world

Link: www.tttjournal.co.uk

ENGLISH TEACHING PROFESSIONAL

English Teaching Professional also has richly diverse content, including blogs, available both online and in hard copy six times a year. You can subscribe at a cheaper rate to the website only, which gives you full access to the articles on the website.

As an example of the kind of content the site offers to help teachers of young learners, the section called 'Young learners' has an article called 'Bring on the sheep choir!' (4 August 2014) by Samuel

Barbour, in which he 'writes his own songs, poems and plays to make language learning fun and meaningful'. Other articles in this section included those on content, pronunciation, literacy, games, enduring activities, and the challenge of teaching very young learners.

The cover of one edition of the journal advertised featured articles on self-directed language learning, creativity, gap-fills and 'ludicrous language' – plenty to read and find out about.

Link: www.etprofessional.com

ELT JOURNAL

If you go to the website of this quarterly publication, you can access free articles covering a range of professional topics. One edition of the magazine (July 2014) has a special focus on young learners and includes articles on future directions in teaching English, primary English teacher education in Europe, online games for young learners, using songs in the classroom to enhance learning and many more. Another recent regular edition (October 2014) includes articles on the authenticity of course-book topics, changing students' writing skills and perceptions and summer English courses. Each edition of the magazine also has book reviews, news about IATEFL and reader responses to previous articles.

Link: www.eltj.oxfordjournals.org

Tip

Subscribing to even one of these publications, or accessing it online if available, will open doors to learning and sharing, to ideas and thoughts and to inspiration and arguments.

INTERNET TESL JOURNAL

This exclusively online journal has more than 800 free-to-read articles going all the way back to 1995, along with other features such as lessons, activities for both teachers and students, and links. Among the range of articles you can read and learn from, five recently posted were on:

- keeping computer lab sessions focused
- numerically assessing young learners without tests

- frameworking in Business English classes
- digging deeper into songs for writing activities
- using personal photographs for narrative writing

Go and have a look and choose an article that you think will interest you, just to see what the site has to offer. It's free; it's easy; it's there.

Link: iteslj.org

IH JOURNAL

International House has schools around the world and it has its own journal. The website is particularly user-friendly and you certainly don't have to be working for International House to use it – it is for all teachers, anywhere in the world. Go to the website to view editions of the journal from the past 20 years. A recent edition included articles in the following areas:

- Classroom matters
- Management matters
- Young learners
- Quality
- Modern languages
- Special-interest columns
- Reviews

See Chapter 11 for more on this journal and for the opportunity to submit articles for possible publication.

Link: www.ihjournal.com

CPD TASK 6

Go to the *IH Journal* website (www.ihjournal.com) and select an article to read that looks particularly interesting.

IATEFL VOICES

One of the benefits of membership of IATEFL is receiving its publication *IATEFL Voices* (along with its various SIG publications). Published six times a year online, every issue contains:

- articles on all aspects of English language teaching
- regular columns
- ELT materials

- reviews
- practical activities
- IATEFL and ELT news

Link: www.iatefl.org

> ## Tip
>
> If your organization has institutional membership of IATEFL, you should be able to access *IATEFL Voices* as well as some of the SIG publications. Find out whether your school is a member.

TESOL QUARTERLY

You can read one online edition of *TESOL Quarterly* for free before deciding whether you want to subscribe for regular future editions. As with the other publications described in this chapter, each edition contains numerous articles, special features and reviews.

Link: http://www.tesol.org/read-and-publish/journals/tesol-quarterly

CPD TASK 7

If you haven't yet read any of the journals listed above, or any other, choose one that you have particularly liked from this chapter and become a regular reader and user of it. Don't just read it but take something from it. Let the content inform the way you teach or manage and let that in turn benefit the students you teach or the people you manage. Discuss the content with your colleagues and try out the ideas given. Explore ideas you have read about but haven't previously considered. Keep up to date with current thinking. Contribute. And enjoy!

Summary

In this chapter we have looked at some of the professional organizations and groups you can be part of, if you aren't already. Remember that your teaching centre may have institutional membership from which you as a staff member can benefit.

The journals described here are just a few of the many available. Some come with online editions, some are free and others are hard copy only, but they all bring ELT professionals together from across the world and provide hundreds upon hundreds of industry-related articles for you to read, learn from, respond to and be inspired or enraged by. Any or all of them will help you think and develop. And then there are the letters, the book reviews, the special features, the blogs...

It all comes down to one obvious conclusion: you don't have to be or feel isolated. If you can't get to face-to-face conferences or meet colleagues from other schools, you can do it all virtually, from the comfort of your home. You can share with and learn from like-minded professionals everywhere and you can read professionally stimulating articles on just about any topic you can imagine. And from all this you can continue to climb those professional stairs of yours as you benefit from these organizations and journals, whatever your role might be.

16

Taking a sabbatical

'Close your eyes. You're on a beach. The weather is sunny and hot. You have a cold drink next to you and a good book. The beach is very quiet. The smell of good, local food surrounds you as you think about dinner later. You don't have a care in the world. You don't have to go back to work for another six months. Life is good.'

I think most of us who have worked as teachers have done this kind of activity in class, either to introduce particular language or to introduce a topic. Unfortunately, of course, when the time comes to open your eyes again, you realize it is raining, you are at work, all you can smell is the polluted air coming through the open window, and all you have to look forward to for dinner is a cheese sandwich.

Taking a few months to a year off work to 'do other things' may seem as fanciful as that beach and that scenario, and for many people taking time off work is sadly not possible, either because your organization doesn't allow it or because you can't afford such a long time away from work unpaid (unless you are doing paid work elsewhere). Therefore, this chapter may be equivalent to you closing your eyes and dreaming. Nonetheless, for others it really is possible and an opportunity that many are able to take and to benefit from. It doesn't have to be a year, or even six months, but the chance to do something different and to do it somewhere different is a development opportunity that cannot be ignored, even if it is a possibility open only to some.

What is a sabbatical?

A sabbatical is usually an extended period of leave from an employer, perhaps involving doing something different from but related to your work. This might be working in a different organization, perhaps in a different country, or travelling to new places. It could also mean staying at home but learning something new, such as doing one-to-one tuition, writing a book, taking a course or learning how to play a musical instrument. Whatever you do and wherever you do it, a sabbatical means that you are not going to your regular place of work for quite a long time. Keep your eyes closed: maybe you could make it happen!

THINKING TASK

Imagine that you really could take a year off to do other things. Consider your answers to the following questions and make some notes before reading on.

- At what point in your career might you feel you want to take a sabbatical?
- What would some of your reasons be for doing so?
- How might a period of extended travel help you on your return to work?
- How might doing the same kind of work that you are used to, but in a very different context, develop you professionally and make you better or more confident at what you do?
- What do you think it would be like to return to work after a year away?

Now read the following experiences of two people, Will and Jacqueline, who were able to take a sabbatical and see which of these questions they answer, and whether they answered them in the same way. Will was away for around ten months, and Jacqueline, with her husband and work colleague, was away for a full year. Will's sabbatical was work-focused while Jacqueline spent nine months travelling and three months working. I interviewed each of them a few months after they had returned to work.

My experience: William Morrow

Why did you take a sabbatical?

Well, it came about by chance. I'd been working at the same school for about four years and I had been involved in some different positions and then I had gone for a teacher training position and not got it and I was feeling a bit demotivated. Then I overheard a conversation with another colleague about an opportunity to train abroad and I weighed up the pros and cons and I thought, if I wanted to develop and progress in my career, then this would be a good way to do it, rather than perhaps having to wait a long time to get another chance at it in the place where I was working. So, with that in mind, I asked for a sabbatical, knowing that my school encouraged staff to take sabbaticals. So it really stemmed from a chance conversation with a colleague.

I knew what I was going to be doing and where I'd be going, so I asked for the sabbatical with the position already confirmed. It was going to be in Ecuador where I would train to be a CELTA tutor. My school was very encouraging; they thought it was a good idea for me to go out and develop and experience new things.

During my time away, I started by shadowing one CELTA course as a trainer in training and during that first month I built up a portfolio of work. Once that initial month of training was done, one of the tutors left and I slotted into his position for the following five courses, so I was just developing and developing and getting used to things all the time as an assistant course tutor. After five courses I took on the role of main course tutor for the first time, so it was a very rounded training programme.

How was the experience of being in a different school in a different country and with a different culture?

It was a very good experience because where I work there is a 'house-style', which in a way is good, because you get to work with so many different trainers and there is so much help and assistance, but I just think it was nice to step outside that 'bubble' and realize that there are other ways of doing things and these ways are valid and these ways work. I think, if you are working in the same place for a long time, you tend to think that is the only way you can do things and you just aren't exposed to other possibilities and other approaches – you're in that school and that's what you do and that's how you do it.

I've always tried to put myself in the students' shoes as often as possible. Every year I try and I fail miserably to learn a language, just to keep my empathy levels up, because it's easy for that empathy to just disappear – you can forget what a huge task it is to learn another language, just how difficult it is. So going to Ecuador and seeing these lovely and highly motivated students really made me want to go that extra mile for them. It was a nice experience.

To anyone who might have the opportunity of taking time off and working elsewhere, what would you say?

I'd recommend it. As I said before, I think it's very good to step outside your comfort level and realize that the world doesn't stop in the institution that you currently work for and that there are far more opportunities and scope to work in different ways. I came back from my time away excited to train.

How would you sum up how this sabbatical has developed you professionally?

Developing ways to interact and converse with the trainees was much more complex than I thought it was going to be. What I really developed most was my ability to be gentler in my interaction with trainees who were often under a lot of stress. So 'people skills' – especially dealing with people's stress and anxiety and the sometimes overwhelming nature of the course – will be useful generally at work, not only on training courses.

My teaching now is stronger and more developed. My lessons structurally work much more efficiently and I think that the students get way more out of them and they can better see the progression through a whole lesson in terms of clarity of aims. My training has made me a better teacher.

My experience: Jacqueline Douglas

Why did you take a sabbatical?

In our industry I think we are not very well paid as teachers but we do sometimes get the chance to take a sabbatical, so it just seems that we ought to grab that chance. It's a luxury that other people in other professions on the same salaries don't have, so I thought of it as an opportunity that I wanted to take while I could, after some years doing the same job. That was the 'push'; the 'pull' factor was fulfilling a travelling dream of mine and my husband's to travel around the world without flying, so it meant we could do that. The travelling took up about nine months of the year, and I then worked in a couple of places – in Cambridge in the UK and in Russia.

Starting with the travel, what did you get out of that experience?

When we look back in our old age, we can say, 'We did it', which is better than never having taken the opportunity to do it. That's the overall feeling I'm left with. Day by day, it was just wonderful that it went on for so long that it became our life. That was one of the things I was really looking forward to, and it happened – it wasn't a holiday. We got to the end of a month and rather than going back to work, it just carried on and so it became our lifestyle and it was absolutely brilliant and such a privilege to be able to do it.

Did that experience have any effect on your teaching or training?

I wouldn't say it's had a direct follow-on into the classroom beyond sharing my experience with the students and using that as a basis for a lesson, but the work aspect has, and we'll get on to that.

How difficult was it to come back to work after such a long time away?

(much laughter...) I suppose, because you know your date, you're sort of preparing yourself. We had a fairly easy transition because we came back home about three months before returning to work, so it wasn't the whole transition of coming back home and straight back to work, and I'd recommend that staggered return to anyone able to take such a long time off.

Did you come back refreshed and eager, or did you have other feelings?

Definitely refreshed and eager, especially as by the time we came back we were already looking ahead to our next big project, so that made it easier. But we certainly felt refreshed and eager to work, so the sabbatical had that very positive effect.

Let's get on to work, which you said has had a more tangible effect on your own development. What did you do in Russia and Cambridge?

We were asked to run a CELTA course at a university in Russia because, to meet the training needs, they had to get the department 'skilled up' to a greater degree. That was really good because we got the feeling that you could arrive with your rucksack and run a course – and it worked. This was very confidence-boosting in terms of being able to do that again in the future when possibly working freelance at some point, so it all felt like real professional development to us and made us see other possibilities and realize that we could do this kind of freelance work anywhere in the world.

The structure of CELTA there and the whole context we were in was entirely different from what we were used to. We were in a university rather than a private language school, and the course participants were all people whose first language was not English, i.e. Russian speakers, and all with prior experience – something else that was very different for us. In addition, most of them worked in the university so it was an exclusively internal course and they didn't need lots of language development because they knew all the grammar. What they needed was help conveying meaning without translation and help with responding to content, which was something they had never come across before, so overall their needs were quite different from what 'normal' CELTA trainee needs would be.

In Cambridge I worked on CLIL (Content and Language Integrated Learning) courses because I had built up my CLIL skills here at my school. I transferred those skills and that knowledge to the school I worked at in Cambridge.

Taking the sabbatical as a whole, but particularly with regard to the work you did, what do you feel you got out of it in terms of your professional development?

Taking a sabbatical gives you a chance to breathe, whatever that means to you. You're not on the treadmill, working until you drop; you do feel that you can cut loose. It's good for your mental well-being. Working in any new place, and particularly in a different country, influences the way you work and broadens your skills and approaches as well as your understanding. The first time I took a break to work elsewhere (in Thailand), I benefited from being exposed to a different working context because until then I had only worked in one place and needed to see that there are other ways to do things – and I wanted, and got, that development.

The benefits of a sabbatical

Will found the following benefits of his training sabbatical in terms of his professional development:
- Increased productivity in the classroom
- Enhanced ability to diagnose problems that the students or trainees are having
- Increased ability to help teachers with their planning and awareness of aims
- Increased empathy with students; just living in a different country with a different language has helped with this

- Exposure to new and different ideas and approaches, which helps with all aspects of the job

Jacqueline found the following benefits of her sabbatical in terms of her professional development:

- She learned a lot about how it is possible to adapt the Cambridge course to meet the needs of trainees in other contexts, while still meeting all its requirements and rubric. This will help her in the future if she works on other CELTA courses around the world.
- She made good contacts that might be part of a network that could help her get work in the future.
- She hopes that, when organizations see her CV, they'll realize that she can 'turn up and train'

Questions about sabbaticals

Let's go back to the questions listed in the task above, with reference to Will's and Jacqueline's experiences.

1 **At what point in your career might you feel you want to take a sabbatical?**

In Will's case it was after he had worked in the same school for four years. In Jacqueline's case it was after a much longer period of work. No point would be the same for everyone; it really comes down to the individual feeling that the time is right, along with an opportunity existing at that time, in most cases after many years in a job.

2 **What would some of the reasons be for doing so?**

In Jacqueline's and her husband's case, the primary motive was to fulfil a long-held travel dream coupled with wanting to work in a different place for a while. In Will's case it was the opportunity to train as a CELTA tutor and to do so in a completely new context. Almost everyone I know wants, as their primary reason for taking a sabbatical, to experience similar work in a completely different context and to broaden their experience and approaches and exposure to different working patterns and different countries and cultures. As a side effect, having this additional experience can further your prospects of career development, either where you work or elsewhere. For others, the main reason, whether travelling or not, is simply to 'have a break' and a good rest from their job so that they can return to it fully refreshed and recharged.

3 **How might a period of extended travel help you on your return to work?**

In Will's case it was clear. He came back an approved CELTA trainer, which not only enhanced his prospects of a permanent training position in the future but also informed his own teaching approaches and beliefs. Indeed, soon after he returned, he secured a teacher training position, so the outcome of his sabbatical was measurably successful.

With Jacqueline, with her travelling adventure, she came back feeling refreshed and excited. Her world travel, coupled with her additional work, especially in Russia, gave her priceless experience of other contexts and cultures and other ways of working.

4 **How might doing the same kind of work that you are used to, but in a very different context, develop you professionally and make you better or more confident at what you do?**

Both Will and Jacqueline spoke a lot about the benefits of doing this. Will spoke of stepping outside the familiar 'bubble', experiencing a very different culture and realizing that there are other valid ways of doing things that work just as well as what you are used to. They both felt that working in the same place for a long time could lead you to think that this way is the only way of doing things. Being exposed to other possibilities and other approaches showed them that this was not true and broadened their outlook. They both developed professionally from seeing that there were other ways to do things.

> Tip
>
> It is easy to become 'institutionalized' and either forget or be unaware that schools, courses, teachers and trainers can operate equally well but in a different way in other organizations and other countries. Having the opportunity to work elsewhere for a while can broaden your outlook and, if you can't do this, just talking to colleagues elsewhere (e.g. at conferences) can offer a similar benefit, albeit to a lesser extent.

5   **What do you think it is like returning to work after a year away?**

The longer you are away, the harder it might be, but Jacqueline gave some good advice on this when she talked about a 'staggered return'. But after the initial shock of returning to your own place of work, a successful sabbatical should mean that you feel refreshed and full of new ideas that you have picked up along the way. Not only do you and your students benefit from these ideas, but you could also share what you have learned with colleagues, maybe in an INSETT session, and such a domino effect can only be good for the organization as a whole.

Points to remember

If you are in a position to consider applying for a sabbatical (and an online search on this subject can produce many useful articles and tips), you do need to bear in mind some important points.

IS THIS THE RIGHT TIME?

Don't make a rash decision, but think it over carefully for some time, and don't make a decision based on a current period of tiredness or lack of motivation that may pass in a few weeks. Is this the right time in your career? Sabbaticals are really for people who have already been working for many years. I even read one article suggesting that no one under 38 should need one! Quite what happens to us at 38 I don't know (and, in my case, can't remember). You also have to be sure that you are able to survive a lengthy period without your regular salary.

Taking a sabbatical does not mean that you have 'left' your employer. You remain employed by them and subject to all the conditions of your contract. If you are planning to work elsewhere during a sabbatical, you should ensure that your employer permits this.

WHO WILL BENEFIT?

A sabbatical should ultimately not just be for your own benefit, or that of your students or other clients, but also for the benefit of your organization as a whole. In asking for a sabbatical, show your employer why it would be a good idea for them for you to go away. Maybe, for example, your plan is to take a further course, which will enhance your overall profile in your school. In other words, don't think of this extended break as being just for you.

WHAT FORM WILL IT TAKE?

If you are planning a sabbatical in order to further your own professional development, you need to do something specific rather than just taking time off. Whether that something is working elsewhere, doing a course, researching a career-related topic or something else, there does need to be 'something'.

It is best to have a desired outcome from your sabbatical. What do you want to do and achieve during the time away? What is the best way to achieve this? Have a plan at the outset and start on this plan well in advance. When you return to work afterwards, take time to reflect on whether the sabbatical met your objectives and whether it benefited you and your work. What was the outcome and was it worth it?

> ## Tip
>
>
> Find out whether your organization considers applications for a sabbatical and what the process is. If they don't, then you can't go any further.

Summary

I have never taken a long sabbatical but I have taken some short periods of unpaid leave, partly for writing and partly to 'have a break'. If I got the chance to take a year to do other things, though, I would – and I still hope to do so some time!

Keep in mind the difference between 'time off' and taking time to do other things to further your development, which is the focus of this book. Not everyone needs or even wants a sabbatical, and only a tiny percentage of people are ever able to take one. However, if you are in that tiny percentage, then plan it in advance, have a goal, achieve that goal, and use what you have done to be a better teacher or trainer when you come back.

And if a sabbatical is simply not possible for whatever reason, you could always try closing your eyes...

17

Going into management

As a child, any ambitions I had of going into management were limited to managing Arsenal football club, an ambition yet to be fully extinguished. Even when I went into teaching, it never occurred to me (why would it?) that I might one day occupy a management position in a school, but development opportunities often 'happen' rather than being planned and such was the case with me. I will expand later on my own management experience and how it has helped my own professional development, but first we need to establish a context and to define what we mean by 'management'.

Management roles

Teachers seeking promotion to a management role are most likely to get the opportunity to become part of what is referred to as 'middle management' (as opposed to 'senior management'). Unfortunately (as it can cause confusion), different organizations sometimes use different terms to describe similar jobs or roles within 'middle management'. In a private language school the middle management would include a person usually referred to as a 'Director of Studies' (DOS) and maybe an 'Assistant Director of Studies' (ADOS). The DOS and ADOS would have a multitude of roles including teacher support and development, staffing and timetabling, curriculum development, students' academic welfare, and all the day-to-day issues involved in making sure classes run smoothly in all respects.

What might surprise those with no experience of school management is just how much of the manager's job involves administrative tasks such as making sure student reports have been completed by teachers, checking that registers have all been filled in correctly, and ensuring that staffing spreadsheets are accurate and up to date.

On top of this, more time than you might expect is spent on 'troubleshooting' (dealing with issues as they come up). This 'troubleshooting' part of the job can sometimes be frustrating in the way that it stops a manager from doing what they set out to do at the start of the day! No two days are ever the same, and rarely does a day go by exactly as it was intended to.

Depending on the size of the operation, senior managers might include the Sales Director, the Finance Director and the owner or Director of the School. Their side of the operation focuses much more on the business aspect, making sure that the organization makes a profit, is promoted in the marketplace in order to gain new clients and enhance its reputation, and plans ahead in terms of strategy and vision to make sure it remains competitive. Sometimes in such schools there is weekly enrolment and sometimes enrolment is for a longer period. Middle managers in schools with weekly enrolment will have to deal much more, for example, with changes to the numbers and levels of classes and the recruitment of teachers to deal with rising and falling numbers.

In universities and colleges enrolment would normally be for at least one academic year and the managerial structure will be bigger, usually with 'department heads', as will the organization as a whole, often making communication more difficult. Communication will be that much more difficult for any organization that has more than one site and maybe several in different locations. It is generally felt by teachers who have worked in both the private and public sector that there is a lot more administration involved not only for them as teachers but also for all managerial staff.

THE DIRECTOR OF STUDIES (DOS)

The role of the DOS is to:

- support the teachers
- look after the students
- provide academic guidance and professional development
- ensure that all classes have a room and a teacher

- deal with the unexpected (often 'troubleshooting')
- bridge the gap between teachers and senior managers
- line-manage staff
- observe classes

This is a simplified list: the role covers everything connected to the smooth day-to-day running of the classes: the teachers, the students, all the administration of classes, understanding and applying effectively all the systems and procedures of the organization, and liaising appropriately with other staff and other departments.

This is just the start of the description of what a DOS does; knowing when to finish is quite different! When I was DOS at a small school, I found myself changing the light bulbs, doing the vacuuming, ordering board pens, and most other things that needed doing on top of what you might expect a DOS to be doing. When I held a managerial position in a much bigger organization, there were many departments and I could concentrate much more on the academic side of the job. I once had a job description for my role, but once in the job I felt it was several pages too short as a true reflection of what I did. And let's not forget that most DOSs also teach for a few hours a week.

This may all sound quite daunting, but it's also exciting and challenging and blissfully unpredictable. No two days are ever the same and you can never be quite sure what lies ahead as you arrive at work for a new day.

Below are two tales of teachers who went into management for a fixed period and then returned to the classroom.

My experience: Chris Milnes

I spoke to Chris as he came to the end of a one-year contract as an Assistant Director of Studies of General English, just before his return to the classroom.

Why did you apply for this one-year management position?

I hadn't had any management experience before and I thought it would be a good experience. It had always appealed to me, especially line-managing people and helping them with their job and passing on the benefits of my experience.

What have been the most rewarding aspects of the job?

As well as helping the teachers, it has been seeing students from a different angle. As a teacher you view students in a different way. If they're in your class, you just see them from one angle and, if you hear that one of them has gone to speak to a DOS about your class, you might take it quite personally, but now I've got a more rounded view of the students. When I go back into the classroom, I'll see them more as people rather than just students. I'll be more aware that they've got different needs that I can meet better, both individually and as a group, which I've always tried to do before, but I think now I'll see them in a different light.

It's interesting to step back from teaching. I think, having dipped my toes into management, that I've got a more rounded view of the school because before I saw things only from the teachers' point of view. Now I can see things from a middle manager's point of view as well, and I've also seen how senior management works.

What else have you learned?

I've learned a lot about timetabling. I can see better from both sides now how this works and why hours are allocated as they are, and who gets which classes and why. It's a very complex and sensitive area, with many issues affecting how classes and teachers are timetabled.

I have learned that you can't deal with everyone in the same way. You have to adapt your approach, especially in terms of people's personalities. For example, if you need to speak to someone face to face, you might need to do it quickly but you have to wait until the right moment and show sensitivity, if they appear busy or stressed, for example.

In general, I have learned a lot about dealing with people. I always thought I was good at this anyway, but putting me in this different situation and in a new role has definitely developed that.

Any other comments?

I know my colleagues who work in management much better than I did before and I appreciate them and what they do much more. Just seeing how well people work – something as a teacher I wasn't able to appreciate – they are unsung heroes! Sometimes you do have to tread on eggshells and sometimes you get caught in the middle between teachers and senior managers. I'm looking forward to going back into the classroom because I can use what I've learned with my more rounded view of the job. I don't think management would suit anybody, but you wouldn't apply for it if it wasn't your sort of thing.

So in summary, how has going into management developed you professionally?

- I have been given an invaluable insight into middle management and can now see things from a different point of view.
- It will help me deal better with people at all levels within the organization.
- It will help me as a teacher as I have a much more rounded view of students now.
- I have a better understanding and appreciation of how systems and procedures work and why certain decisions are taken.
- My own capabilities and skills have increased.

My experience: Clare Webster

Clare also took up a temporary position as a middle manager and spent 18 months as Assistant Director of Studies for Teacher Training. Here is what she had to say shortly before coming to the end of her time as a middle manager.

Why did you apply for this position?

The position came up and I had previously thought I might be interested. I was curious because as a teacher and a trainer you see one side of the school, so I thought it would be really interesting to find out more about other departments and about running a huge school and managing all the teachers and trainers. So I wanted to see that different side of the school and to be exposed to managerial areas in terms of both the running of the school and the development of teachers. I didn't really know if I would have much to offer, although I suppose everyone can offer something. So I just wanted to see the school from a different perspective, and especially from the client's perspective – you have a lot more exposure to clients before they sign up; I've heard it called the 'customer journey', from the initial enquiry to them booking and then actually finishing a course. People who call up or come in off the street for a chat about what we can offer – that was new to me.

It's really interesting to find out how all the different departments tie in, and to find out how decisions are made and who makes them, and sometimes to have some influence in the decision-making process, and how the decisions have an impact on the people who actually deliver the courses.

What have been the main challenges?

One of the main challenges has been battling between the administration that needs to be done and helping and supporting the teachers and trainers. I can see that the admin is important, and it's interesting to see how processes and systems work and to understand them, but a frustrating day can be doing mindless admin tasks and feeling you're not making any progress. Some days you feel you're fighting fires. It can be a very reactive and responsive job and this took me a while to get used to. People can come in needing something right away and you have to drop what you're doing, and I found that quite tricky in the beginning because I was thinking to myself, 'But I'm in the middle of doing something.' But I quickly realized that people come first because that's what we're here for and you have to fit in all your other tasks around this.

I have learned that, if you need to concentrate on something, like writing up an observation report, it's best to do it at home or find a quiet room and leave the office for half an hour or so. So that's been a challenge in terms of managing time and managing the different roles, and something that has been a real area of development for me.

Working as part of a team, I've learned that communication is everything because it's very easy to miss things – little things can be left or forgotten and these can have a knock-on effect on other departments. When you are working as part of a team, it's really important that everyone communicates well, especially as there's a lot of cross-over between departments.

How has being a teacher and a trainer helped you in your management role?

I think it's invaluable. You need to know where the teachers and trainers are coming from and the questions and the queries they have are ones you can relate to. I don't see how managers can support and develop teachers and trainers without having had that experience themselves. Teachers need and deserve development and you've got to be able to see things from their point of view. It's been great to be able to observe teachers' classes and to give constructive feedback and ideas for development and, being a teacher myself, I have been able to do this.

Do you think that any teacher could be a manager?

I guess not, or at least not well. You do need to be able to empathize with your teachers and see things from their point of view. You've got to be able to recognize strengths and to put yourself in their shoes in order to develop them. I've also learned that no one knows all the answers. I think when you're a teacher you think there's this management team and they know everything, but that's not the case and no one can be an expert in everything.

In summary, then, how has this position developed you professionally?

- I've been challenged and pushed and I've learned not to be afraid of a challenge.
- I've learned that no problem is unsolvable or the end of the world. You think about it, you ask your team and you find a solution.
- I've learned a lot about dealing with people and listening to them and showing a genuine interest, even something as simple as saying 'How are you?' to a teacher who's been off sick.
- I've learned that people are different and react to things in different ways, so you need to be tentative in how you approach people and sensitive about when and where you speak to individuals.
- I've learned much more about what people in other departments do and how the organization works. As a teacher, you've no idea about this. Now I can see people's roles and purpose within the organization and this will make me a more understanding teacher.
- I've learned that everybody needs a bit of praise sometimes; they need praise to stay motivated. It's important to be able to tell people what they're doing well in addition to what they can improve on.
- I've learned a lot about the organization's systems and procedures, and how to use online systems, spreadsheets, etc.
- When I go back into the classroom and training room, all these areas will make me a more confident teacher and more aware and appreciative of how everything works, so all in all it's been a terrific developmental opportunity for me and I would recommend it to anyone interested in pursuing a similar opportunity. Above all, it's a great career-development challenge.

Management and CPD

Here's how going into management helped my own development.

I had been a teacher for only three years when I was given the opportunity to become a teacher trainer, working on what is today called the CELTA course. Four years later (and I still don't quite understand how this happened so early in my career), I applied for and was given the position of Director of Teacher Training in a different school. I did this for about three years before moving on. A few years later I became the Director of Studies at a small school, a job I also did for about three years. And some time later I was the ADOS at a very much larger organization, again for around three years. Between each position I returned to the classroom to both teach and train. Today, I still do some management work from time to time as well as teaching and training, face to face and online.

The fact that I spent around three years in each of the management roles probably says a lot about me and why I applied for these various posts. I like variety. I like a challenge. I like to be stretched. I like to find out what I do and don't enjoy and what I am good at and not so good at. I like to move on and do new things. Management provided me with that challenge, that variety, that voyage of personal and professional discovery. It also taught me a lot about the skills, qualities and demands of a management position and which of those I possessed and which of those I was lacking – allowing me to focus on areas where I could develop.

In no particular order, the following are my top six examples of how I feel occupying management positions has helped my own CPD journey. There are others, but six will do.

1 It taught me invaluable lessons about dealing with the unexpected and staying calm and looking for a solution. 'Stuff happens' in a management job, and often you have to put your plans and schedule on hold to deal with a situation. Dealing with solutions rather than problems is the key, and this has helped me in other aspects of my work.

2 Understanding the roles and responsibilities of other people and other departments in the organization helped me understand and appreciate better how an organization works from top to bottom, and how each person's role contributes to the successful running of a school. As a teacher I inevitably had a much narrower understanding and vision of what goes on in a school every day, but thanks to my management work this has changed. In particular, I can recognize more clearly now every aspect of the 'client's journey'. I also have sympathy for anyone who has to do timetabling of classes and allocation of teachers and hours.

This is a complex, time-consuming and sensitive task, which I had never really appreciated as a teacher. This has allowed me to help other teachers and clients who have queries or complaints about any aspect of timetabling. I can now usually answer any timetabling question beginning along the lines of 'But why...?'

3 I am more equipped to deal with difficult situations and unhappy clients or staff. It is important to try to understand why someone is unhappy and then give them your time and attention, even if you can't give them what they want (e.g. a student wanting a refund or a teacher wanting more teaching hours when none is available). I also became much better at reading feelings and personalities and trying to adjust my approach and tone depending on who I was speaking to. For me, this is fundamentally a job about people and supporting and guiding them, but also sometimes alerting them to a problem in the right way and then trying to help them with that problem (e.g. dealing with a complaint a teacher has had from a student, or chasing someone up because they have forgotten to do something). It's not just *what* you do, but *how* you do it.

4 My understanding of all the systems and procedures in place has expanded immeasurably – why we have them, how they work, and the problems and time involved. My general skillset in this area and in related computer work has grown enormously and helped me subsequently, giving me the confidence later to enter the wonderful world of online tuition.

5 Working as part of a team is a vital part of the job, along with liaising with those in different but related positions. I have worked alongside co-managers with hugely differing personalities and approaches; adjusting to each one and establishing harmonious teamwork and achieving things together has been an enlightening process. Realizing that people work in different ways and achieve results in different ways has shown me the value of being flexible in my approach and expectations.

6 Prioritizing tasks and keeping to deadlines is something I was always OK at doing, but I now have an even keener awareness of the importance of this, and of being flexible when 'stuff happens'. This has continued to help me in all aspects of my work. Linked to this is the need for good time management, something I am also much better at now than before.

Of course, I discovered areas that I wasn't so good at, which I have therefore identified as further areas for development. These include personal ones (I work better in the mornings but need to learn how to perform equally effectively later in the day) and professional ones (sometimes it takes me longer than it should to master new computer systems and applications).

THINKING TASK

It could well be that you have never considered going into management, or simply don't want to, or don't see the possibility of any such opportunity presenting itself. With that in mind you have a choice of three tasks. Do the first one if you would like the opportunity of middle management ELT experience if the opportunity arose. Do the second if you have no desire or expectation of dipping your toes into the management pool. And do the third if you currently or have ever previously held a management position in ELT.

Option 1   You have never had any kind of managerial experience within this profession but, given the opportunity, you would like to one day.

A Why would you like to be a manager? Are your reasons similar to those of Chris and Clare, or different in some way? Make a list of these reasons and how you would expect or hope such an experience might help you develop professionally and/or personally.

B If possible, speak to one of your current managers, someone who has previously taught, and discuss your reasons for wanting to get into management and what you would hope to get out of it. How different were their reasons, and to what extent have their hopes been fulfilled? What advice would they give you?

This will help you consider ways that becoming a manager might provide professional development and whether it is a role that you could be comfortable in. If so, maybe it's time to start looking...

Option 2   You have no desire or expectation of getting into management. That's not unusual; it's not for everyone. Choose between these two tasks.

A What do you think are the principal skills and qualities needed by an ELT middle manager? Which of these do you believe you do or do not possess (some of the ones on your list may not be exclusive to managers). Do you think that, by having some managerial experience, you might develop these skills or qualities – or could you develop them in other ways?

This will help you consider those necessary skills and qualities a manager needs to have and prompt you to see whether you could develop in any of them (not necessarily by having a management role).

B Think of someone in your organization who holds a management position and make a list of everything you think that person does in the role. Then find some time to speak to this person and ask them to discuss your list and to add anything you haven't thought of.

This will help you gain a better understanding of a manager's role and responsibilities.

Option 3 You are currently a manager or have previously been one.

A Make a list of how the job helped you develop, and the challenges you had (and whether or not you overcame them). What do/did you like best about the job? Does your list contain anything not mentioned by Clare and Chris?

This will help you reflect on areas where you have developed from being in management, and maybe highlight areas where you feel you need to continue your development.

Summary

Taking up a management position may not be every teacher's cup of tea, and such a position may not be easily forthcoming, but if it is something that interests you and is a possibility, it is a fantastic opportunity for career development in many areas, both professional and personal.

It's not an easy or a predictable job: people can be difficult and situations can be difficult. However, it can be exciting, rewarding, challenging and full of variety. You will learn a lot about people and about yourself. You will learn skills and develop qualities. You will develop a much greater understanding of how things work and how decisions are made. You will make your own decisions and play a part in others. You will help and support and develop teachers. You will learn time-management skills and how to prioritize tasks and to be flexible according to events. And you will be able to teach your students with your increased knowledge, awareness and people skills, and also to be more confident in yourself.

18

Get SMART

You will have seen by now that a theme of this book is that, whether you are a teacher, a trainer or a manager (or any combination thereof), you are always developing in one way or another, almost without realizing it. So far you have read about the many different things you can do to further your own professional development. Some have been 'big' ideas, such as 'becoming a trainer' or 'writing a book', and many others have been much smaller but no less significant, such as reading an article or trying out a new type of lesson.

In the final chapter we will come back to this theme as we explore the importance of reflection, but for now we want to consider how we can formalize our development in some way – how we can make it SMART.

THINKING TASK 1

If you don't know what a 'SMART' target is, try to find out before reading on. And if you do, try to recall a SMART target of your own that you have achieved recently. Did it meet the SMART criteria?

Setting SMART objectives

The first known use of the term 'SMART criteria' was in the November 1981 issue of *Management Review* by George T. Doran and they are also often attributed to Peter Drucker's management by objectives concept. SMART objectives have the advantage of being easy to understand and do, and they make success in achieving them easy to measure.

Normally in any teaching centre, all staff members have an annual appraisal or professional development interview (PDI), in which the staff member's performance over the previous year is reviewed and discussed and where performance targets for the following year are agreed. In my experience, the onus is very much on the staff member to suggest areas they wish to develop in and for the manager to help turn these suggestions into something more tangible. Thus we have SMART targets.

You can always set yourself SMART targets at different times – you don't need to go through the process of a formal appraisal or PDI to do this. Similarly, throughout this book we have looked at different ways of developing yourself, and in most cases you could turn these ideas into SMART targets so that you can be more focused and better able to measure and track your own development.

WHAT IS SMART?

Each letter in the acronym refers to a different criterion for judging objectives:

S – **specific** (also significant and stretching)

M – **measurable** (also meaningful and motivational)

A – **achievable** (also agreed upon and acceptable)

R – **realistic** (also relevant and rewarding)

T – **time-bound** (also tangible and trackable)

'I want to improve my teaching' may be a worthy ambition, but it is not SMART in any way. It is general, not specific. It is not measurable at all. Because it is not measurable it cannot be achieved. It is not realisitic because it is too general. And it is not time-bound because it is left completely open.

Let's look at each SMART component in turn.

S – specific

There is a big difference between 'I want to improve my teaching' and 'I want to improve the quality of my board work in order to provide students with a better record of what we have done in class.' The latter is much more specific than the former. 'I want to do better pronunciation work' is also somewhat general, especially when compared with 'I want to incorporate more use of phonemes when recording pronunciation on the board to help students longer term with their pronunciation of individual sounds.' It will not be possible to measure targets if they are not specific to begin with.

'Significant' and 'stretching' are two more terms used when looking at the 'S'. Obviously, you would want any achieved target to be significant to what you do, and if it stretches you in any way then there is that element of challenge and accomplishment. The concept of stepping out of your comfort zone could be linked to this idea of stretching yourself.

THINKING TASK 2

Which of these would you describe as more specific in their wording?

1 To attend at least five teacher development sessions
2 To improve my language work in class
3 To incorporate more video work in my teaching
4 To improve the clarity and appearance of my class handouts

- The first one is specific. Replace 'five' with 'some' and it would be less so
- The second is less specific. What aspect of your language work? Why and how?
- The third is more specific than 2 but still could be better. For what reason? How will this help your learners in lessons or improve the overall quality of your lessons?
- The fourth is specific, especially if the teacher can identify what aspects they are referring to (by 'clarity', are they referring to layout, including spacing, font size or handwriting?)

M – measurable

You cannot measure something that is not specific in the first place, nor can you measure something that does not produce evidence of progress or achievement. 'To attend at least five teacher development sessions' is easily measurable – the person either did this or didn't. Of course, merely attending the sessions doesn't necessarily result in improved performance, so there is an argument that the target needs to be extended to include this aspect, but the target as it stands is both specific and measurable.

'To improve the clarity and appearance of my class handouts' is also measurable because the visible evidence of improvement is there and, if you have learners who have seen the before and the after, they can confirm that there has been an improvement.

'Meaningful' and 'motivational' can be added to 'measurable'. There is no point in setting a target for the sake of it – and I have heard colleagues emerging from an appraisal expressing this very reaction ('I couldn't think of anything so I just said something so we could "tick the box" and finish.'). Targets need to come out of previous performance, and one aspect of performance review is observation reports and from those observation reports it becomes possible to look at areas that have been identified as developmental needs. Targets should emerge naturally from the performance review discussion so, even if the staff member begins the appraisal discussion not sure of possible targets, the discussion should lead them towards thinking of areas that could be made SMART.

By the end of a performance review, therefore, whatever targets are set should be meaningful to the staff member and should motivate them. Knowing that any target is measurable will further motivate them because, if all goes well, they will see the progress they have made.

THINKING TASK 3

Start thinking now of a target that would motivate you and be meaningful to you. Make it specific and make it measurable. Be very clear in your own mind about how the achievement of this task will be measured or evidenced. This task will be built upon throughout the rest of this chapter.

A – achievable

If a task is achievable, it means you can answer the question 'How can the goal be accomplished?' and, for that matter, 'Can it be accomplished?' Even if your target is specific and measurable, there is no guarantee that it can be achieved in the context you are in. There is no point having as a target 'to become a CELTA trainer by the end of the year' if your centre does not run CELTA courses, unless you are planning to change your place of work. What's more, any target you propose must be *agreed upon* and *accepted* by your line manager.

'I want to teach an IELTS class for the first time by the end of the year' is specific, measurable and achievable if you are experienced and if your school runs IELTS classes and likes to give teachers the opportunity of teaching IELTS classes when they haven't done so before. However, there is another aspect to consider here if a target is to be agreed upon as being achievable and that is whether any training or support needs to be given, and whether that training or support will be available.

So, if your objective is to teach an IELTS class for the first time, to achieve this you will need:

- the opportunity to observe a current IELTS teacher
- support from your line manager
- someone to do an early observation of you teaching IELTS to diagnose any areas you need help with.

If you are a manager, your target might be to attend a particular management conference in the year ahead. This is certainly specific and measurable but is only achievable if the school agrees to it and is willing to fund it (unless you are paying) and if it is not going to be at a difficult time operationally ('We can't let you go because two other managers will already be away at that time.').

THINKING TASK 4

If you have thought of a possible target for yourself that is both specific and measurable, do you think it is achievable in your context and do you think it would be acceptable? If not, you will need to think again. Try to make sure that you have a target now that meets the three criteria we have looked at so far.

R – realistic

You can have a target that is specific, that is measurable and that is achievable – but is it realistic as well? 'Realistic' is not quite the same as 'achievable' because a target could be achievable in theory but in practice not actually realistic. A goal has to represent an objective towards which you and your line manager or organization are both *willing* and *able* to work.

The target must also be relevant: this means relevant either to you or to your organization, or both. Anyone can come up with a target, but if it has no relevance to you or to your organization, it's a non-starter.

The 'rewarding' element links to the motivational aspect mentioned under 'S'. A simple way to exemplify this is to refer back to the situation of the teacher in an appraisal who forces herself to come up with a SMART target because the box on the form has to be ticked. If this person will not find this target rewarding and will not really commit to it, then it is not realistic to expect this goal to be achieved, even though it is achievable.

Tip

Always make sure that targets set are ones that arise from the staff member herself – things that that person really wants to do and will commit wholeheartedly to.

THINKING TASK 5

Review the target you have been building towards during the course of this chapter. Is it realistic? Will you find it rewarding? Would you really commit to it? If your answer to any of these questions is no, you will have to begin the process again.

T – time-bound

Is your target time-bound or timely, and is that deadline for the completion of the target a realistic one and one where progress can be tracked? Without a realistic time frame, you may well find yourself losing sight of your goal and allowing it to drift and be forgotten, especially if your line manager is not following up on it and checking with you and supporting you. Tasks need deadlines to maximize the likelihood of them being achieved, but it has to be a manageable time frame. Ask yourself, 'Is it realistic for me to achieve this goal by the date given?'

THINKING TASK 6

Assuming that you have now chosen a target that is specific, measurable, achievable and realistic, decide on a sensible time frame for the achievement of this target.

If you have followed the tasks through, you will have set yourself a SMART target which can now become a CPD task.

The performance review

Whatever your role, be it teacher, trainer or manager, the chances are that you will be asked to a regular professional development interview (PDI), perhaps annually, at which your previous performance is reviewed and targets are set for the year ahead. In my experience the typical process for this has three parts and is as follows:

1 Preparation

Your line manager will approach you to agree on a date and time for your PDI and may give you a form or some questions to consider in advance, to make sure the interview remains focused. The line manager may ask other managers whether they have any comments or suggestions that they would like fed into the discussion. The line manager will review the staff member's previous PDI report and observation reports as well, in order to prepare.

2 Interview

Your interview with your line manager may start with a discussion of general matters before moving on to looking back at your role and contribution since your last PDI and the quality of your performance in that role. This can often be an acknowledgement of a good job done but may also address any issues that have arisen (such as needing to improve at admin tasks). It will also refer to feedback from other managers and comments in observation reports.

The line manager will then ask you to suggest areas you would like to focus on in the year ahead that will add to your ongoing development. You will go on to discuss whether these are feasible and what, if any, training or support would be needed. These ideas, if agreed to, are then turned into SMART targets (you would usually have up to three for the year ahead). The conclusions and outcomes of the meeting, including targets, are subsequently written up into formal record of the PDI.

3 Follow-up

After the report is written up, signed by both parties and put on record, your line manager should check in from time to time with you to ensure that you are on track with your targets and are getting whatever support or training has been agreed. Ideally, after six months or so there should be an informal 'catch-up' meeting to review progress since the PDI. At the next PDI the targets set at the previous one can be reviewed and recorded.

PDI documentation

Below are typical examples of the types of form used at a school for the 'before' and 'at' stages of an appraisal and in them you will recognize the stages discussed above.

Preparation Form

Please use this preparation form to help you prepare for your PDI. This form was designed to give you an idea of the topics that will be covered in your PDI. It is for your use only and is not retained as part of the interview.

General overview of previous year

1 In which areas do you feel you have performed particularly well? Why were these successful?

2 In which areas do you feel you could perform more effectively? How could you do this?

3 What have you found rewarding/less rewarding?

4 In what ways do you feel your role might be developed to be more relevant/useful/ productive for the organization?

5 Are there aspects of your job that you feel are not relevant/ useful/productive for the organization?

6 To what extent do you feel you have met the general targets/objectives that you set last year? What evidence do you have that supports your conclusions?

Discussion of teaching/training practice and development

1 What type of development have you undertaken – e.g. background reading, attending TD sessions?

2 Did you complete any action research projects as a result of your observation(s)?

3 Were there any problems or difficulties that prevented you from achieving something that was agreed as a learning outcome from your last PDI?

4 What aspects of your classroom practice do you feel have been successful? Why were these successful?

5 In what ways do you feel that your classroom practice could be improved? How could you do this?

Targets relating to teaching/training practice

1 What targets and standards do you want to set over the next year for your classroom practice?

2 How can the department/organization help you achieve them?

General targets

1 How would you like to develop outside your classroom practice?

2 In what way(s) do you think you can contribute to the goals of the GE/TT department and/or the organization?

3 What are your longer-term goals?

4 How would you like to see your job developing?

5 What skills/practices do you wish to develop during the coming year?

Training needs

1 What training will you require over the next 12 months to enable you to achieve your targets?

2 What other training would you like to discuss with your line manager, e.g. doing the DELTA?

PDI Meeting Record

Name	
Position	

Department	
Date of meeting	
Interviewed by	

Section 1 – General overview of performance

Section 2 – Review of teacher/training skills and development

Section 3 – Targets relating to teaching/training practice

Target (specific)	Measurable (success criteria)	Achievable (resources)	Timed

Section 4 – Targets relating to departmental/organizational objectives

Target (specific)	Measurable (success criteria)	Achievable (resources)	Relevant (linked)	Timed

Date for interim PDI review		
Signature: Line manager		Date
Signature Staff member		Date

Section 4 refers to targets relating to organizational objectives; see Chapters 20 and 21 for more on this.

Types of target

Below are some real examples of a variety of types of SMART target. They are from appraisals of a teacher, a CELTA trainer, an online management tutor and a line manager over a period of a few years. The 'realistic' element has not been recorded since that is assumed from the presence of all the other components, as well from the real commitment of the staff member and the organization.

Target (specific)	Measurable	Achievable (support or training required)	Timed
Run a teacher-development session on reducing stress on CELTA courses	Successful meeting and feedback	No training needed	March 2009
Revise the teacher-training interview form	Positive feedback from interviewers and CELTA tutors	DOS support	January 2009

Develop teacher-training materials for CELTA courses	Successful use of materials on courses and positive feedback from trainees	None	December 2011
Attend a management course	Researching and attending a course and giving feedback	None	December 2011
Build next-level course in Moodle	Ability to (for example) build different question types and quizzes	e-Learning support	July 2013
Learn to use raptivity software	Ability to build in raptivity	e-Learning support	July 2013
Develop and extend theoretical knowledge of management theories and applications	Ability to refer online course participants to relevant literature on a range of topics	Programme Manager support	ongoing
Attend ELT management conference	Conference attendance in 2013–14	None	2014
Learn to use Skype	Use of Skype on courses	Training from IT department	March 2012
Run General English teacher-development session	Positive feedback from attendees	None	December 2012
Teach a four-week IELTS course	Good results and positive feedback	DOS and peer support and opportunity to observe classes first	May 2008
Incorporate use of IWB in lessons	Positive feedback from students and observations	DOS/peer support	End of the year

Summary

As professionals, we are doing things on an almost daily basis that make us better or more confident at what we do, that increase our knowledge on a subject or that allow us to discuss issues relating to what we do. But, just as our students want to see evidence of their progress as learners, so we as professionals need to see evidence of our progress, and for our own managers to see that progress, too. Making SMART targets, either just for ourselves or as part of an annual PDI, is one clear way of doing this, and so is being able to review, consolidate and further that progress or that achievement. By getting SMART we are formalizing and focusing on our professional goals and forcing ourselves to do so. The longer you stay in one organization and the longer you stay in the profession, the more you can achieve and see that you have achieved. So if you haven't had the opportunity to do so before, now is the time to 'get SMART'.

19

Get ahead

During the course of this book so far you have read about a number of different ways to further your professional development, some of which you will have been familiar with and done yourself, and others that maybe you haven't done / had the opportunity to do / considered. Along the way I have given you mini tasks, some of which were reflective, some predictive and some reactive following an interview. In however small a way, these tasks were intended to get you thinking and to give you a nudge towards expanding your knowledge on a subject, or reflecting on previous knowledge and experience, or actually getting you to do something yourself to help you continue your professional journey.

In the previous chapter we discovered more about using SMART targets to plan ways of developing over a period of time and to measure that development, and that is beneficial for all staff, whatever their role. But development goes way beyond annual SMART targets for your appraisal. As we have seen throughout this book, your progress as a working professional follows a similar course to the progress of learners in a classroom: it is continuous and can involve doing what might seem the smallest thing. So asking a colleague to point you to a resource book that will help you find practice activities for weather-related lexis is as useful a piece of added knowledge as teaching a Cambridge CAE class for the first time is useful as a new skill that you have acquired. Whether you are using a new course book for the first time or becoming a DELTA trainer, you are doing something that will take you out of that professional comfort zone and stretch you in some way so that you are not doing the same thing in the same way as you do day after day and month after month.

In upcoming chapters these points are discussed by senior managers in terms of how any kind of development can help the organization as a whole as well as individuals because it is important to see that 'bigger picture'. It is important to recognize how even the smallest thing can make you do your job better, and in so doing help your learners, or your trainees, or your staff.

In this chapter, then, I will provide a series of further ideas to supplement what you have already done and these will revisit some of the chapters that you have read. In most cases they are just 'small things', some perhaps very obvious, but along the way I hope you will think, 'Ah, I've never thought of doing that. I'll give it a go'.

We will also revisit the British Council and Eaquals websites that were referred to in Chapter 7 and these, in combination with the additional tasks, will provide you with more opportunities not only to do small developmental tasks but also to make longer-term plans which are SMART. And if you think that this will be the end of the tasks, well not quite. In the final chapter we will look further at the importance of reflection and of the value of reflective tasks.

Self-assessment and planning

The principal purpose of this book has been to give you ideas for new things to try or to suggest that your staff do, and also to hear from those who have done those things in order to provide further encouragement and ideas. The two websites we visited in Chapter 7 help more with longer-term professional assessment and planning and it is important to link whatever you do to your longer-term professional plan and development.

So, to go from one point to another point on your professional journey, what kinds of developmental activities should you be considering? Don't just do a series of isolated activities, but 'join the dots' and recognize the purpose of everything that you do. Where are the activities taking you and how are they helping you to do your job better and to help those you work with do better themselves? With that in mind, let's go back to two websites we visited before.

EAQUALS

When you go to the Eaquals site (http://eaquals.org/pages/7104) and follow the links, you have the opportunity to self-assess your level of development (and where there is room for further development) in a number of key areas including 'lesson and course planning', 'language awareness', 'digital media' and 'professional conduct'. For each area there are development phases ranging from '1.1' to '3.2' where you can indicate what you have done or are doing and what you haven't done. When I did this self-assessment myself, I wasn't surprised to discover that digital media is an area where I need further development.

So make this your first task. Go to the site and start a new assessment. This may confirm some aspects of which you are already aware, but it may also reveal areas you hadn't previously considered.

BRITISH COUNCIL

Additionally, find time to return to the British Council website (www.britishcouncil.org) and to spend time here. By going to 'British Council for you' and following the links to 'continuous professional development', you will discover various options depending on the stage of your career you identify yourself as being at. These include 'starting out' and 'developing' – whatever stage you think you are at, there is a checklist to confirm this. From there you can click on a self-assessment in a number of areas such as 'evaluating and assessing learning'. You can then go to 'planning your development', which also has links to articles, blogs and other links.

Either of these sites, then, offers a huge range of options in terms of self-assessment, identification of areas where further development is now needed, and concrete examples of how to make this progress. The ideas and first-hand accounts given in this book should give you more ideas of what some of these suggestions entail and what other teachers have gained from taking these next steps.

Additional ideas

Let's now return to some of the areas already covered in the book and look at some additional ideas. If you have done a fuller self-assessment on one of the websites above and if you have identified areas that you would like to focus on, see if any of these tasks fit into your broader plan to get ahead. Refer back to any SMART targets you set yourself as part of Chapter 18 or ongoing SMART targets you have set yourself at work.

STARTING OUT

If you are currently teaching, set yourself a simple target for the next week or month. Choose from the following suggestions:

- Find a piece of authentic material (e.g. a newspaper article) that would be suitable for use with a class you are currently teaching and devise a skills and language-focus lesson around it. Establish clear learning outcomes and, after the lesson, reflect on how successful the lesson was and on how it could have been made more effective. What did you learn from this lesson about using authentic material with your classes?
- If your school has a library or staffroom resources, find a resource book that you haven't previously looked at to give you ideas for activities that you haven't tried before.
- Reflect on the last week or month. In what areas, big or small, have you developed as a teacher? What do you know now that you didn't know before, or can do better than you did before, or understand better than you did before?
- Think of any piece of advice about teaching that you think would help you in any way and ask a more experienced colleague for that advice.
- Look at a course book that you are not familiar with but at a similar level to the one you are using now. What are the main differences in its format and approach to language and skills? If you were an English learner yourself, what do you think would be the positive and negative aspects of the book? As a teacher, how do you think you would need to adapt and exploit it? Overall, do you prefer your existing book or this alternative?

BEING OBSERVED

The next time you are observed, identify aspects of your teaching or of your class where informed feedback would be beneficial to you. Ask whoever is observing you to give feedback in these areas and then try to implement their ideas and feedback into your teaching.

OBSERVING OTHERS

Try to arrange to observe a lesson taught by a colleague who you feel would be useful to watch in relation to a specific aspect of your teaching that you have identified as in need of developing. Tell that teacher what it is you are particularly hoping to see in the lesson and, if it is possible, have a brief chat with the teacher afterwards. What did you gain from the experience?

DAY-TO-DAY DEVELOPMENT IN THE STAFFROOM

Think of a question you want answered. It could be about some grammar you have to teach but are unconfident about, or the best way to teach a particular piece of language, or something you heard a teacher talking about before that you want to know more about. Go and ask! Make this a regular event – it is such a good way of finding out information and about different ways to do things.

TAKING PART IN INSETT SESSIONS

The next time you are able to attend a session, decide on what it is you hope or expect to get from the session. Afterwards, consider to what extent the session delivered what you hoped it would. Did you learn/find useful aspects that you hadn't anticipated? Overall, how do you hope this session will improve your classroom practice?

USING ONLINE RESOURCES

In Chapter 7 you were referred to a number of different websites for both teachers and learners. Here are some suggestions for using those sites:

- Decide on three or four useful sites that would be good to recommend to your students for self-study.
- Explore a site from that chapter in more detail in order to discover something new, or to further your knowledge or understanding of an issue of interest.
- Compile a survey among colleagues and draw up a list of your teachers' favourite sites.
- Try out a different kind of lesson material from one of the sites and reflect on its value.

- Search for a site that you haven't come across before and decide whether the content is of sufficient interest and usefulness to your ongoing development to add to your list of favourite sites.
- Help a colleague by recommending a really great site that you know.

TEACHING EXAM CLASSES

If you are in a position to teach an exam class that you haven't taught before, then consider doing that. Or you could research an exam that is taught at your school but which you don't know much about so you will be more knowledgeable in your answer if students ever ask you about it. And if you are asked to teach that class in the future, you will already know something about it.

Alternatively, ask if you could observe an exam class lesson. Set yourself a list of objectives such as:

- I want to see how different the teaching approach is to a General English class.
- I want to observe how different the motivation and commitment of the learners are.
- I want to notice how activities are linked to the exam.
- I want to discover a bit more about the exam itself.
- I want to assess the level of the exam based on what I see.

After, you could discuss these objectives with the teacher and ask any other questions you might have – if the teacher is willing!

READING GROUPS

In Chapter 9 you read about the idea of setting up a reading group to discuss articles or books of interest and in that chapter there was a blog article about dogme vs course books to trigger a discussion among a group of teachers.

Below is a further article, a summary of a conference talk, reproduced with the kind permission of the speakers at the conference and the writers of this article – Melissa Lamb and Richard Chinn. This article resulted from a talk given at the Brasshouse Conference in Birmingham in 2014. I hope it will stimulate discussion, either in an actual group session, or informally in the staffroom.

IH London teachers Melissa and Richard stress the importance of listening to learners as their language develops in order to provide useful feedback.

What's your starting point in a lesson? Fluency or accuracy? If you begin with fluency, then this provides opportunities to give learners feedback on how they have completed a task and on how they could do it better; thus upgrading their current linguistic abilities.

This kind of language is often called 'emergent language,' but for our purposes we'll be using the gerund form of the word, as we feel it embodies the dynamic nature of how language 'emerges' in class.

- *What is emerging language?*
- Emerging language is unplanned and emerges in a lesson due to the learners' need for linguistic input in order to communicate an idea.
- *What is reformulation?*
- Reformulation is when a more knowledgeable other (teacher or peer) remodels what the learner is trying to say into a more natural form. This could be dependent on a gap in lexical knowledge, grammatical accuracy, pragmatic appropriacy or generally moving the learner on in terms of their development.
- *What is the process the learner goes through in order to develop their linguistic knowledge and abilities?*
- Noticing: the learner becomes aware of the difference in their own language use and the natural features of the target language. Input becomes intake – moving from explicit knowledge to implicit knowledge.

Implications for class

- Training learners in 'noticing' language and what features to concentrate on
- The teacher's duty is to focus on meaning and re-encode the message by making silent the appropriate form
- Giving learners what they need at their point of need

- There are two main areas of exploration with emerging language: horizontal (syntagmatic/structure or pattern) and vertical (paradigmatic: meaning)
- Drawing attention to form from function (syntagmatic exploration)

Hearing learner language

This is an important skill to develop, particularly because it's easy to grab at something the learner says and reformulate it inaccurately, not conveying the essence of the learners meaning.

Here are some strategies to help with this:
- Practise noting down learner language. Focus on the key messages the learner is trying to put across word for word and whether this communication is successful or not
- Look at this after class and write down what you would say. Where you are not sure what the learner is trying to say, cross it out
- When you become practised at this, while monitoring or in open class feedback, you can practise 'recasting'. If you're not sure what the learner is trying to say, negotiate meaning before you recast
- When you feel comfortable with this, start boarding your 'recasts' and focus the learners on the reformulated chunk
- Once you've got this down, try some of the below

Reformulated learner language

Instead of focusing purely on errors, ask yourself how natural the student's utterance is and what exactly they're trying to say.

It's key to really negotiate what the learner means and provide them with a more target-like form.

Here are some examples from an intermediate class and a pre advanced class. See if you can tell which is which.

I collect my children every day from school at 3:00

I pick my kids up every day from school at 3:00

When I young I argued with my younger sister for not eating her dinner

When I was young I used to tell my younger sister off for not eating her dinner

using her computer all the time

being late

playing with the cooker

(My boss used to tell me off for +ing)

I don't like the taste when I eat mushrooms

I don't like the taste of mushroom

(I hate / can't stand / can't bear)

He's got no feelings

He's got a heart of stone / He's so hard hearted

I don't feel relaxed here because I'm not similar to everyone else

I feel like I don't fit in

Don't tell anyone my secret

Don't tell a soul / say a word to anyone

Who did you elect in your country?

Who did you vote for? I voted for X

Focusing on emerging language

So, what do we focus on exactly?

Vertical extension
(Paradigmatic)

I feel like I don't | fit in
belong

I don't like the taste of mushrooms
taste+ of+ noun phrase
Horizontal extension (Syntagmatic)

Exploring Language

Recording language on the board

As you are monitoring you can select language for the feedback stage. In some ways this language is going to 'feed forward' to another task or for learners to take with them.

Remember that you still have to be systematic when dealing with language, and learners need appropriate information with sufficient depth in terms of meaning (e.g. questioning), highlighting form and phonology (connected speech, prominence etc.).

You should also be selective about the language you highlight in response to learner needs.

Further ideas for focusing on, consolidating and recycling emerging language:

- Delayed or on the spot (delayed avoids interrupting learners on task – on the spot is more immediately important)
- Say something similar
- Count the words you hear (focus on recognition and phonology)
- Progressive deletion

- Create a poster summarising/categorising what you have learnt
- Create a dialogue, tutor reformulates and learners compare to their original text
- Silent drilling and shadow repetition
- Which would you say? Which would I say? (comparing on cards). Listen to the learners on task and write up what they said on cards and what you would say on other cards. The learners match them up and then you look at features of the language
- Students select the phrases they feel are useful and design a practice activity for other students or vice versa (mini whiteboards)
- Recycling cards and recall activities (see Nick Bilbrough's book *Memory Activities* published by CUP for more ideas on this)
- Task repetition
- Flash the chunk up for a few seconds and then learners write what they remember
- Number the sentences and the learners throw dice. The leaner who throws the dice needs to recall the sentence and then the group need to put it into a meaningful context. The teacher checks and reformulates individually or delayed
- Dictionary/corpus work to find other patterns and collocations

What are your thoughts on these activities? Are there any of these you'd like to know more about?

10 Reasons for focusing on emerging language

1 The learner – Psychological validity (Johnson 1988 in Thornbury 1997): Learners are more predisposed to notice features relevant to the task they have performed

2 Theory of learning: 'Matching' (Klein 1986 in Thornbury 1997) or rather 'noticing the gap' in their current stage of interlanguage. Ellis (1995 in Thornbury 1997) uses the term 'cognitive comparison', as learners compare what is similar to the target form as well as what is different

ATTENDING AND PARTICIPATING IN CONFERENCES

Check the IATEFL website referred to in Chapter 10 (www.iatefl. org) and ask your line manager as well to see if there are any conferences that you might be able to attend. If not, go to 'web events' on the IATEFL site to find out about online events that you can 'attend' remotely. You can actually take part in a conference from the comfort of your home and still get all the benefits from the talks. And you can access summaries of talks given and even view recordings of talks from previous conferences.

Whether you attend face-to-face or online, or view a filmed session from the past, or just read the summary of a session, you should choose a topic of interest to you for whatever reason. For example:

• I don't know what that is and I want to find out.

• I know a little about this but I want to find out more.

• I'm really interested in this topic and I want to see what other people have to say about it.

- I'm sceptical about this area but let's see if my views can be changed.
- This is an area of my work that I need ideas on.

Whatever your objective – whether one of the above or something quite different – after your conference event, reflect on the extent to which your objective was met. Maybe it has spurred you on to wanting to explore the topic even more, and maybe to run an INSETT session at your school about it.

WRITING

For most teachers the most useful form of development is to do materials development – writing or designing new material for your learners. Others, as we read in Chapter 11, may want to try to get into writing an article for a professional publication, but for now think about materials development.

- You could find some authentic material and design a lesson around it for your current group of learners.
- You could re-design material from a unit in your course book that you don't feel works very well as it stands and make it more suitable for who you are teaching.
- You could design a skills and language lesson from scratch around a topic that your learners have expressed an interest in.

Writing your own material and then using that material in class and evaluating it for future use and amendments can be a very satisfying process. If this is something you like doing from time to time and feel that you are good at it, you might seek out opportunities in the longer term to contribute to course book writing. As Dave Rea said in the Chapter 11, one thing can lead to another...

ACTION RESEARCH

As we saw in Chapter 12, action research doesn't have to be 'big'. If this is something you would like to do but remain a bit unsure about, refer again to the British Council website (www. britishcouncil.org) and follow the links to action research. Or you could ask around your staffroom to see if any of your colleagues have done some research of their own.

Carrying out action research as a shared project can make it even more rewarding. You could find out if a colleague shares with you an interest in a topic that they would like to do some research in followed by classroom action and reflection, and you could work on it together. And, even if you have done some action research already (perhaps as a result of reading Chapter 12), doing a joint project on a different area would be a good way to develop your experience.

BEING A STUDENT AGAIN

Embarking on a course, either for a further qualification such as DELTA or for your own interest such as learning a new language, would be a valuable process of development for you. However, for whatever reason it might not be possible, so you might consider an alternative idea to put you back into the learners' frame of mind. What you do could be an action research project, and we had examples of these in Chapter 12. Or, more simply, just attending a training workshop can be an illuminating experience and remind you of some of the frustrations of being a learner.

Some years ago I had such an experience when my colleagues and I attended a training session on how to use interactive whiteboards, at that time a very new and innovative piece of technology. I (and others) left the session frustrated and no more confident than I was at the start of the session owing to the form of presentation – basically it was a lecture with demonstrations but no 'hands-on' practice. Whenever I tell trainee teachers to avoid 'lecturing' and to involve their learners in the learning process, such experiences as that IWB lecture reassure me that such advice is valid.

So 'becoming a student again' doesn't have to mean signing up for a course. In my experience teachers who have attended courses / lessons / training sessions almost inevitably emerge from them commenting on 'the teacher' (or trainer) and all such experiences inform our own teaching from the point of view of what helps learners to learn. So take any opportunity you can to be a student, and take something from that session that will be beneficial to your teaching and to your students' learning.

BECOMING A TRAINER

Here, too, you might not be in a position to become a trainer at this stage but that doesn't mean that you cannot benefit from your training colleagues. If, for example, you work at a CELTA or DELTA centre, maybe you could ask if you can observe a session during the course, especially if you think you would like to become a trainer at a later date. From the title of the session predict what you expect the content to include and the type of delivery from the trainer. So, for example, for a CELTA session called 'Selecting and Clarifying Lexis' at this pre-service level what and how much would you expect to be covered? What do you think the extent of trainer-led input will be? What do you think are the key points that are likely to be covered?

If you are already a CELTA trainer, you could observe a DELTA session along the same lines – not all CELTA trainers necessarily go on to or want to go on to DELTA training and this is one way to get a flavour of how different it is and whether it might appeal to you.

And if you are already a DELTA-level trainer, why not observe a colleague doing a DELTA session to see how differently they do it compared to you. What can you learn from watching other trainers and how might this help your own development as a trainer?

Whatever the type of training we are talking about, including online training, you should consider ways of learning about both the content and type of delivery of such courses to inform you more about training and to see for yourself how it can contribute to development. Observing sessions delivered by colleagues or changing some of your materials and sessions is one way that will contribute to on-going development.

BEING PART OF PROFESSIONAL GROUPS

Just do it! There are countless groups online that you can join to share and discuss ideas relating to teaching, training, management, or numerous special interests such as pronunciation, writing, technology and many more. In Chapters 7 and 15 you were introduced to many different websites and groups, so find a group or two of interest to you that you feel will help you in your overall development or your development in a particular area, and get involved. It is like being part of a massive international virtual staffroom and sharing with colleagues across the world is a very easy and very positive form of development.

GOING INTO MANAGEMENT

Just 24 hours before writing this I was asked to visit a group of DELTA candidates to answer questions about being in academic management. Among the questions I was asked were:

- 'Management always seems to be a thankless task to me. Is it?'
- 'How do managers deal with issues such as disruptive students, students who always come late, teachers who don't do their admin duties, etc.?'
- 'What are the most rewarding aspects of being a manager?'

If, like the candidates I spoke to, you have no previous managerial experience, what do you think are the possible answers to these questions? Once you have thought about this, try to ask one of your academic managers to see what they say. It can really help an organization as a whole if staff in one department have a greater understanding of what staff in other departments do. This is especially true of teachers and managers benefiting from teachers knowing better what managers do, why they do them, and the challenges they face.

If you are an academic manager already, how well do you think your teachers understand your role? If, like me, you feel that it is valuable for teachers to have a better awareness of your role, then why not do something to raise their awareness. Ways of doing this could include:

- Devise a quiz with questions covering all aspects of your role – you could even have staff teams and make it a competition.
- Have an INSETT session combining giving a summary of what your role is with the opportunity for any questions.

I worked at a large school which introduced the idea of a 'RADOS' – a Rotational Assistant Director of Studies – which was an opportunity for teachers to apply for a one-year fixed managerial position before returning to the staffroom afterwards. As one teacher finished their term, another took over after a selection process. This RADOS position allowed teachers to dip their toes into management, which had the benefit of indicating to them if this was something they would like to do on a longer-term basis given the opportunity, but also to give them hands-on experience of the life of an academic manager. Of course, this is not something that most schools can offer, but even on a very small scale of teachers being involved in processes and decisions through consultation can go a long way to a greater appreciation of roles.

Something else for managers to do is to explain decisions that they make rather than just making them. Decisions taken to do with timetabling / staffing / student complaints, etc., can often be baffling to teachers, so why not say to them 'The reason I did this / had to do this was...'? It all comes down to communication and understanding. For any teacher wanting to go into management, it is important to understand as much as possible about the role and everything that it involves, and managers themselves have a responsibility to share what they do and why they do it. If they don't, then someone on the outside, such as the DELTA candidate I spoke to, is not surprisingly going to come to the conclusion that management is a 'thankless task'. It's not.

Summary

There is a lot you can be doing! We have in this book heard about many ways of developing, big ways and small ways, and in the final chapter we will discuss one of the most important in more detail – reflecting. But can you add to the list of all the ideas in this book so far? What have you done or would like to do that hasn't been mentioned? Make a list!

Whatever you do, though, don't sit still... get ahead!

SECTION 4
Global views and reflections

20

The line manager's view

I interviewed Maureen McGarvey who has worked in the ELT
field for a great many years in many different roles and has been
at International House in London since the 1970s. Her current
role includes line-managing a number of teaching and training
staff, many of whom have more than 30 years' experience. Part
of Maureen's role as a line manager is to help those she manages
develop professionally, whether they are teachers new to the
profession or those who have been working for decades.

THINKING TASK 1

Whatever your current role is in your organization, think about
the contrast between a teacher who has just completed their pre-
service training course and started their first teaching job (Teacher
A) and someone who has been in the profession for, say, 25 to
30 years (Teacher B). You may be 'A' or 'B' yourself, or a manager
(and previously a teacher) – maybe even a line manager to staff who
are themselves 'A' or 'B' or anything in between.

Make a list of possible issues each type of teacher might face, and
how such teachers could be encouraged to develop. There will, of
course, be an overlap of issues and ideas.

For example, an issue for Teacher A would be dealing with potentially
a new country and maybe a new culture as well. A development
possibility would be to observe a more experienced colleague.

Once you have done your lists, read the interview with Maureen and see which of her points are mentioned, and what additional points she raises. Depending on your own position and experience, perhaps you could take up some of her suggestions and ideas.

My experience: Maureen McGarvey

Can you summarize your career to date?

I'm a teacher and a CELTA trainer and I've been doing it for a very long time. I did my initial teacher training course with International House and then I did my diploma. I later trained to be a CELTA trainer and I also worked on the precursor of the Distance DELTA when it was still very paper-based. I had extended periods in Spain, where I was Director of Studies for teacher training, and at International House in Budapest, where I was also Director of Studies for Teacher Training, and that at the time was a completely new school. After my return to the UK I continued my career as a teacher and trainer at International House in London.

I'm also trained as an inspector for various schemes and I wrote the Diploma in Educational Management, which became a fully online program. I wrote the management module for the Aston University MSc in TESOL and I was a specialist tutor for Educational Management and a dissertation supervisor to that for a number of years. I'm also a committee member for the Leadership and Management SIG for IATEFL and the incoming co-ordinator for the scholarship working party for IATEFL, for the whole scholarship scheme.

In general terms, how important is continuous professional development in an individual staff member's career?

I think it's a blessing and a curse because there's a danger that we try to quantify it in a way that can lead to us putting a great deal of pressure on people who are already doing quite a high-pressured job in sometimes difficult circumstances. I think that most professional teachers constantly want to do better for their students, not necessarily for themselves – they want their students to do better. So, because they want their students to do better, they are reflecting and considering their own lessons. At the end of a lesson, teachers have their own mental checklist – 'That worked, that didn't work' and 'why or why not' – so I think there is a continual awareness of how we could be doing things better. How to transmute that into what would be called a CPD approach is a different set of questions and more the line manager's responsibility and the school's responsibility. The common point of view is that a teacher who is not developing is standing still and we can all say that, but there are times when the best thing to do *is* to stand still – forward motion is not always a desirable trajectory for people, I think.

For someone quite new to the profession, who almost doesn't know how to take those next steps, who may feel a bit isolated and unsure how to go forward, what do you say to those people?

When you're a new teacher, what concerns you most – and I can still remember my early teaching experience of basically being one lesson ahead of the students – is your own language awareness and technique mastery. I think one of the most effective ways for a line manager to work with those new teachers is partly through observation, which newly qualified teachers are comfortable with because it is a return to the familiarity of their pre-service training and they are often less resistant to being observed because of this. Supported lesson planning can also be a great help, through a 'buddy' system where you can work with other colleagues teaching the same level or type of class, or with a more experienced colleague who can work as a mentor.

These things can help you in the early stages but, with any CPD, for any teacher irrespective of their level, my starting point is always 'I have complete confidence in my colleagues'. If you have passed your pre-service training course, my starting point has to be 'Well, you've passed that so you must then be at that level. You're a qualified professional on a different point in your journey than I am so I have to support you, but I have to support you with confidence.'

Do you think this always happens in organizations or do some newer teachers remain feeling isolated and unsupported?

Yes, I think it's very common. I do think that many newer teachers are given their book and their level and they're left to it. Basically, it's 'No news is good news'. If you don't hear students complaining about a teacher, then that teacher can be left to work and they'll only get support if there's a problem. Of course, this isn't always viewed as support but as triage – get them into surgery and identify the problem as quickly as possible. A more considered support for those people might have prevented them from going to triage in the first place.

When you work in schools overseas, particularly, you get a batch of new teachers most years and they have different levels of experience and skills and knowledge, but they're all new to that context and there's an awful lot for them to cope with. I think it is a school's responsibility when they're inducting new teachers not only to make sure that they understand the systems and the structures of the school – because if you've been working there for five, six, seven years they are second nature to you and you can forget how confusing they can be to new teachers – but also to give support. Teaching 25 hours a week or more at different levels and possibly in different locations and to different age groups is all very bewildering when you're a new teacher. You really want to do your best but you do need support to do it.

When you're a new teacher, every day can be another mountain to climb but you learn so much and so quickly – it's like being a low-level student, where progress is identifiable. You can think 'That's the first time I've tried that' or 'I'm going to try this for the first time' – whether it's an activity or a type of class, level, age group or course book, or anything else that is new to you.

On a pre-service training course the opportunities to try out a whole range of things are often quite limited and you find yourself working in tightly defined time slots, but to have a class for, say, 90 minutes gives you much more scope to experiment. You feel a lot freer, plus it's usually your own class, whereas on a training course you would normally share the teaching of a lesson, so everything you learn and discover – your development – becomes more easily measurable.

What is your role as a line manager?

I am Programme Manager for e-learning and I line-manage a team of between seven and nine online tutors remotely, and I directly line-manage a team of six to eight teachers and teacher trainers on the school staff.

I know that some of the staff you line-manage have worked in the profession for decades rather than years, so how do you motivate them and give them ideas for their own continuing development, particularly if they feel 'stuck' or that they don't want or even need to go further? How do you inspire them?

I particularly like working with the type of teacher or trainer that you have described, precisely because of those challenges. It's also a challenge for me so, in a way, I view that part of my line management as part of my own development. My starting point for staff like that, more than anything, has to be one of mutual respect and recognition of their ability, experience and expertise because they have been in the profession for a very long time. What I want to do as a line manager is harness that before it tips into its sinister cousin of fossilization, cynicism and despair – to stop teachers and trainers from getting to the point where they're just going through the motions.

A mistake I've made before is to try and encourage staff members like that to develop by asking them to do something too big because they are very experienced. I think 'Why don't you try this?' or 'Why don't you try that?' but that can be a step too far because what you have to remember as a line manager is that very experienced staff are also apprehensive and nervous when confronted by something new.

Yes, we often talk about 'stepping out of your comfort zone' but maybe it's possible to step too far out of that comfort zone?

Yes, and for an experienced staff member (and I can't remember who said this), the more experienced you are, the more you have to lose, because you have a staffroom persona and you're perceived in a certain way by your academic management staff. If you try something and it goes disastrously wrong, your feeling is that there is going to be more egg on your face than there would be on someone recently qualified.

I think one of the things to do as a line manager is to look at development in a lot of different ways. I'm a big advocate of using the timetable developmentally and that's a bigger organizational responsibility than simply deploying staff in the manner of First World War generals in films shoving troops across a map of Europe! It's more important to look at what people have done and, more importantly, what they haven't done for a while and thinking, for example, 'Oh, it's six months since you last taught an elementary class and it would be good for you to revisit that and perhaps at the same time could you use a course book that you haven't used before and see how that goes, and while you're doing that could you perhaps look at the syllabus we have for this course and see if it is feasible because you're experienced and you can make that judgement?'

I also think that, when you've been teaching for a while, you do so many things automatically that you don't question what you're doing. I think that one of my jobs as a line manager is, through discussions with my line managees, when I find articles, or references, or blog sites, to say 'I saw this; it might be interesting.' Part of my own development is to keep abreast of what's going on and I'm quite lucky because I go to conferences and I speak at conferences so I am quite clued in in that way, but I have to bring that 'clued-in-ness' back to the people I line manage.

I know of organizations that have set up their own internal SIGs – for example on 'pronunciation in the classroom' – usually led by a senior teacher for like-minded colleagues to join. Together they share a particular interest and meet to discuss it, or to read articles about it, or even to lead an INSETT session on the topic. What do you think about that?

I think that's a great idea and it's an example of a bottom-up process. It allows teachers to explore something of particular interest to them while being supported. However, I am always slightly nervous when emphasis is placed wholly on bottom-up development initiatives. While I think that ideas that come from teachers and are driven by teachers, such as these SIGs, are 'for the people by the people', I also think that, if you are an academic manager, you have a responsibility to lead and support and manage your staff's development. You can't say 'All our development here is bottom up' because my question would be 'Don't your staff have a right to expect you to take some responsibility for the development of the staff in the school?' I think that's linked very closely to what you see in an observation and how that observation feeds into your annual in-service training.

One thing that interests me is that very often development happens almost by accident. Annual appraisals and PDIs are fine and good but much development is not planned. Too often, it seems to me, development is measured solely by whether or not you have achieved your targets, which may have been slightly artificial anyway when you are basically trying to think of something to satisfy the requirement of an appraisal record.

Well, yes, as we were saying before, development doesn't have to be a huge thing – you don't have to invent a new methodology. Development can be a very small thing. I can see the point of bringing everything together in an appraisal, in that you should know your organizational objectives and within that your departmental objectives, so that you can see how your personal objectives are aligned with those different layers – that's all well and good, the whole must be the sum of its parts – but I think if you have the view that teaching is more of an art than a science, which many people do, it's quite hard to tie these down to SMART objectives.

People always say 'achievable' for the 'A' in SMART but I prefer to say 'agreed'. If development is to happen at different times during the year, those objectives need to be consistently revisited and re-evaluated. You need to say, for example, 'OK, we're in the first quarter of the year, so by December what would you like to be doing, or have done, or be in a position to be doing?' For some people it might be, 'By then I'd like to be able to apply for a particular position' or 'I'd like to be doing something different within the school'. I'd say, 'If that's what you'd like to be doing, let's work backwards and see where we can get to' so that everything you then do throughout the year leads to that end goal, which we have now identified. When we meet again, maybe in a couple of months, we might decide that the end goal has shifted a bit so we reassess the date when it can be achieved.

Therefore, the measurability is very important. It's not just doing something but seeing its effects and its benefits.

Yes, and those effects and benefits depend on how your organization measures them. If it's in terms of increased student or client satisfaction, that's fine, but our teachers are our internal clients, so are our internal clients feeling more satisfied with what they're doing? Are they feeling more challenged? Are we helping them? As line managers, we need to be having a lot of conversations with people and the appraisal is simply a longer conversation with a lot more paperwork. We should be having a lot more 'How's it going?' conversations.

Motivation and development change during different stages of our career. When you're younger and newer, it might be 'Fling it at me, I can take whatever you throw at me', but as you get older and more established, you won't be motivated necessarily by the same things. As a line manager, you can't think, 'Oh, so and so knows a lot about X, so they can do this and it will be motivational.' The motivational bit is tagged on at the end, but will it be? Things change throughout your career, so that's why you have to keep in contact with your line managees, not only professionally but personally. Maybe it's a case of 'There's no point asking teacher X to do this for a few months, because she's in a set of difficult personal circumstances', so in that person's case, not developing for a few months is not a negative thing.

You have vast experience and have done just about everything that can be done in the profession, so how do you (a) motivate yourself and (b) continue your own development?

I'm very nosy! I find Twitter a great source of resources, with links to fantastic blogs, etc. I'm quite systematic; I look at it first thing in the morning and 'favourite' anything I think I might like to look at. In my lunch break I read the things that I 'favourited' and send anything I find particularly interesting to all teaching staff and say, 'Have you seen this blog?' or 'This might be interesting for you to read'. People might just delete it, but at least they will have an awareness of the broader world. I feel that, particularly in private ELT language schools, we can be very navel-gazing and we need to look out there and also to see what our colleagues in state schools are doing, as the majority of ELT teachers around the world are actually in state systems and not private language schools.

I'm also interested in technology – I'm self-taught in IT because I thought it was interesting. I'm interested in conferences and conference attendance and in encouraging my colleagues to speak at conferences; I think almost every colleague I have is more than capable of delivering a very good conference talk. And just reading, connecting, networking and talking to teachers keeps me very interested, particularly talking to newer, younger teachers who aren't as scared as I might be to try something. They have no awareness of the painful 'stop at the end of the drop' and when they say what they are thinking of doing I think, 'Blimey, are you really?' I think it's also because I intensely like my job and my work. Winston Churchill said, 'Find a job you like and you'll never work another day in your life', and generally, because my job is so interesting and the people I work with are interesting, and the students are endlessly fascinating, I don't get bored. I do look more to the outside world and I think this is where technology is important, to keep giving me that spark.

THINKING TASK 2

What aspects of the lists you made before reading the interview did Maureen mention and what additional ones did she include?

Below are some of the statements Maureen made. If you can, get together with a colleague or colleagues to discuss your reactions to them or, when appropriate, ask relevant colleagues what their views are.

1 'CPD can be both a blessing and a curse.'

2 'Sometimes it *is* better to stand still.'

3 'If you don't hear students complaining about a teacher, then that teacher can be left to work and they'll only get support if there's a problem. Of course, this isn't always viewed as support but as triage – get them into surgery and identify the problem as quickly as possible. A more considered support for those people might have prevented them from going to triage in the first place.'

4 'Experienced staff are also apprehensive and nervous when confronted by something new.... the more experienced you are, the more you have to lose.'

5 'While I think that ideas that come from teachers and are driven by teachers are "for the people, by the people", I also think that, if you are an academic manager, you have a responsibility to lead and support and manage your staff's development.'

6 'Motivation and development change during different stages of our career.'

7 'I'm a big advocate of using the timetable developmentally.'

8 'Winston Churchill said, "Find a job you like and you'll never work another day in your life."'

Summary

Whether you are a newish teacher or one with a few years' or several decades' experience – or whether you are in a management position or a line manager to staff – what have you taken from this interview with Maureen McGarvey and how might it influence your own development? Has it got you thinking or even inspired you in any way? Perhaps you completely disagreed with something that was said. Whatever your reaction, to have any reaction is good because it means that the interview got you thinking, and that in itself is development.

21

The school director's view

In this book so far we have focused almost entirely on the individual's CPD. Now, though, we are going to learn more about the CPD of staff other than teachers and the development of the organization itself and how individual CPD can contribute to this.

I interviewed Justin Vollmer, Director of Operations at International House in London, first about his views on the importance of individual CPD to the organization as a whole and especially that of non-teaching staff, and then about his views on how teachers and trainers can develop, and looking especially at highly experienced staff.

Before reading what Justin had to say in part 1, here's a predictive task for you.

THINKING TASK 1

Choose option A if you are a teacher with no management experience and option B if you have current or past managerial experience within ELT. Choose your task and make some notes before reading part 1 of Justin's experience that follows.

Option A

Choose a member of staff who is neither a trainer nor a teacher. This could be someone who works at the front desk or reception, a cleaner or your line manager. Find out what training or development they have had in the last year and/or what training or development they feel they need, and how such training could benefit not just them but the organization as a whole.

Option B

Think how an individual's continuous professional development can and should contribute to the development of the organization as a whole, particularly in relation to non-teaching staff, and what forms this type of development might take. Try to think of actual examples from your current organization. What training and development does your organization offer non-teaching staff, and what further training and development do you feel still needs to take place?

My experience, part 1: Justin Vollmer

Can you summarize your career to date?

At IHL I started off as a teacher, then became a trainer, then I was the ADOS, and after this I was the DOS for General English before taking on my present role a few years ago. As well as London I have worked as a teacher in Spain, and in South Africa as a trainer and as a DOS. My first job as a teacher was in Poland.

What does your role regarding training needs involve?

The role of a DOS regarding teacher development is to facilitate the teacher development (INSETT) sessions – to organize sessions and to deliver some, and to involve the staff in a coherent INSETT programme. It happens regularly here and it happened in Spain and in other places where I've worked.

In terms of identifying training needs for the organization as a whole, it's a little more complex. I do think that departments come forward and say why they need training in 'X' as things arise and we make sure that people are aware of developments and ensure that training takes place. But we also do it through looking at strategies and identifying where we think we have a shortfall or a lack of expertise in a particular area that we need to address. That can come from strategy proactively or it can come more reactively from admin staff saying 'Look, we really need more updated knowledge about "X"', or the feeling that we're not really using a system or tool effectively, such as our student database, and therefore staff need more training in that.

Training for non-teaching staff is as important as training for teachers. If admin staff need to specialize in something, then specialist training may be needed. For example, one of our admin staff is Head of Health and Safety Training and another member of staff is Head of Welfare, so there are various people with specific needs. And then there are cross-school needs, and a variety of different people in different departments need training in such things as the school's class database, so there's training across departments. Also, last year we had training in posture and ergonomics for any member of staff because a lot of people's work involves sitting at a desk for long periods and some were developing problems, so we brought in a trainer for several days and he did a number of sessions and anybody could attend. And we've also had training for general service staff – for lifting, for health and safety and for cleaners dealing with certain kinds of chemicals and where and how to store them. So there's been a whole raft of training that has benefited individuals as well as the organization as a whole.

In terms of middle managers, we've recently had project management training as we've had a number of new projects and we felt we needed to be more proactive. Management training is an example of this because in ELT, when senior teachers become an ADOS or DOS, they have a knowledge of the industry and of teaching and training, but they tend to arrive in the management position without any management background and therefore need support in all areas. This includes management of people, doing PDIs (professional development interviews, also known as 'appraisals'), and time management. So one thing we've done recently is appraisal training, which we now call PDIs to emphasize their developmental aspect, and that was in relation to a change in our system of line management and who people manage.

We've also had some reception and student-service staff observing classes and some admin staff watching what other admin staff do. The benefits of it are that there is a greater understanding across departments of what people do. You can learn a great deal from finding out what other people do and looking at their systems afresh. You can learn from the process more about how the organization works and the role of each department and the individuals within it – and we're keen to do much more of this.

For other things that need to be done, it's important in any organization to try and co-ordinate how people do things within departments, and one aspect of this is cross-departmental analysis of the processes we go through. Sometimes it is more effective to bring someone in from outside to analyse what is done and make suggestions as to how we might do things more effectively. You shouldn't do something just because it's always been done in a certain way if there's a better way of doing it. Processes can become ingrained and when you have to explain a process to someone else you can suddenly see the light and say, for example, 'Well, that stage of the process doesn't really need to be there.'

Going back to individual CPD, if there are certain teachers or other members of staff who are reluctant to attend INSETT sessions, this probably needs to be dealt with by their line manager, maybe through the PDI appraisal. Individuals need to be looking to develop themselves – it's part of the ethos, part of the job that we want teachers to be able to do this. Some teachers don't and their line manager needs to be talking to that person to energize them in a particular area or find something they're particularly interested in. A teacher who is sitting still is really going backwards. Even if is just mentoring another teacher in the staffroom or contributing to a blog site, they need to be doing something.

When we have the PDIs, there is a section on the form that is discussed that focuses on targets and the training required to meet those targets. All targets are SMART and the responsibility for the setting and achievement of those targets is with both parties, with the continuing support of the line manager. Previous training and its effects are also looked at, along with the achievement of the previous year's targets. The line manager should be asking how the person can contribute more to the organization and what training they need.

THINKING TASK 2

Do any of your findings from Task 1 match any of this director's comments, or does he make additional comments on the same topic? What would you say were the main points Justin made?

Whatever your role is now, what aspects of staff development mentioned have occurred in your organization, or which do you think your organization could benefit from? Do you think that staff are generally as aware as they need to be of how individual development needs fit into organizational needs?

CPD for senior teachers and managers

The second part of the interview focuses primarily on two areas. The first is Justin's views on how teachers and trainers with many years' experience can continue their development and maintain their motivation. The second is on how someone in a management position (and a senior management position in Justin's case) can continue their own development.

THINKING TASK 3

Choose option A if you are a very experienced teacher (with at least 15 years' service) and option B if you are in a middle or senior management role. If you do not fall into either of these categories, have a look at option A for senior teachers and try to chat to such a colleague and get their views on this subject.

Option A

1 How do you stay motivated after working in the profession for so long?

2 What kinds of CPD have you had over the last year or so?

Option B

1 In what areas have you developed professionally over the last 12 months?

2 In what areas do you still feel the need for development?

3 Do you think that identifying areas for development as a manager is easier or more difficult than for a teacher to identify her needs? Why is this?

4 What do you think is the best way to find time for your own CPD?

After thinking about this and making some notes, read the second part of the interview and see what Justin has to say about these areas.

My experience, part 2: Justin Vollmer

For teachers of between 10 and 30 years' experience, do you think there can be a problem with maintaining motivation sometimes?

Yes, it depends on the individual but there *is* a danger of this happening. Obviously, people go through troughs and peaks in their careers and maybe that feeling of comfort once you've established yourself and you know your routine and you are doing what you know you can do can quickly tail off into not developing at all – and perhaps feeling that you don't have the opportunities that you had in the past. For managers of those people, the danger is to assume that experience equals confidence or knowledge of how to further develop but with anybody, experienced or not, it is a manager's job to be providing a place to input ideas and opportunities for development and perhaps trying to stretch that person and challenge that person. That person might not want a challenge at that point and that's fine but managers should always be looking for ways in which a person can develop.

Sometimes a line manager can find it easy to see development opportunities for an inexperienced teacher but less easy with a very experienced teacher or trainer. They may not know what the opportunities are or think they shouldn't be suggesting something because the teacher is so experienced and will know for themselves already, but I think that's a mistake. As line managers we need to be there with them, suggesting things and having the 'Why not...?' conversation about various things that they could be doing, such as 'You've never done this, why not try...? OK, you don't want to do it, so what about this?' There's a danger that someone does specialize in something or becomes very good at doing something and the manager sees this and lets it continue, but this can result in a lack of opportunity for that person to do something different.

Is there a danger sometimes that you get into a comfort zone: 'This is what I do, this is what I've done, I'm good at it and I don't particularly feel the need to do anything different, so why am I being pushed into doing other things?'?

I absolutely agree that development – and this is one of the things that continuous professional development theory suggests – has to come from the person concerned rather than the line manager, so the motivation to develop has to come from them. What I do also see is that, if someone is feeling a little stagnant, they may not feel confident enough to suggest that development. It's good if someone else can say to them, 'You can do this and it would be really good for you' and can give them a bit of advice and guidance without pushing them into doing something, because that would be self-defeating. That input – for example, a suggestion to attend a conference – is a way of just giving people a little push to see whether they would like to do something but without forcing them to do it. I think that line managers may feel less able to do that when people become more experienced, and there's a danger, therefore, of more experienced teachers not getting the opportunities and advice they need.

Can you think of any specific examples of what senior teachers might do to get out of that comfort zone?

People can do a number of things, big and small: going to a conference, joining the Cambridge teachers' site, creating their own portfolio, doing a short course, teaching an IELTS class, doing a DELTA or an MA, writing an article, peer observation and having discussions with colleagues. You can also mentor a new or less experienced colleague over a period of time, using your expertise. It can be a way of reassessing your own practice by looking at someone 'further back' and thinking about how they've developed and what you can do help them develop further. By doing this you can rediscover your own enthusiasm for your profession and that can really help.

There are other possibilities that weren't around when I started out. There are many frameworks now, although I have some reservations about linear frameworks, as do a lot of people, but they offer a way of looking at your role and aspects of your role and reflecting on how you behave in those aspects of your role. So for me as a manager there is a framework for national standards of management and leadership. It describes in great detail desired behaviours in a number of different areas and what the skills are for those behaviours; and that leads to self-reflection. It's very useful to think about your job and have it described and to reflect upon it and people can do this peer to peer as well as when mentoring, whether it is teachers or managers. It can be really motivating for the person who is mentoring to take on that role.

How valuable an opportunity is a sabbatical for development?

I think, when you've been working in an institution for a long time, taking a sabbatical that includes time spent working in another institution gives you a different perspective. It shows you what works well in an institution and what doesn't work so well – it gives you that critical eye. Coming in with experience to a different organization can be really valuable.

But a sabbatical, of course, can mean many different things: it can mean writing or going into a different area altogether and that can also be strongly developmental.

Do you think it is easier or more difficult for middle managers, such as a Director of Studies, to identify their own developmental needs compared with teachers and trainers?

I think that in our industry it can be very difficult and that's where this idea of a framework of management, which I spoke about before, can give you a way of looking at your job, as can a lot of management theory. Management theory is full of ideas about how to look at your job. Recently I was reading an article about a theory that's quite well established about demands, constraints and choices for managers – demands being what you have to do, constraints being what you can't do and choices being the bit in the middle. This middle bit is where managers may make the wrong choice about what to do.

With such a huge role and set of demands, do you find it difficult to find the time to think of your own development?

Well, that's the danger for managers because if you're always 'firefighting' you can never be thinking about your own development time. Sometimes you need to allot development time away from your location and away from interruptions; it can be very useful to separate yourself completely from the daily operational side of your work. You have to find the time for self-management, and that includes managing your own development, but that's a big ask sometimes. Some people, whether managers or teachers, are very good at organizing themselves regardless of their role and experience but others aren't: they just get absorbed into things and never find the time.

Someone said to me recently that from time to time everybody needs a period of 'time off' from ongoing development and you need some time to just do what you're doing and in the way you are used to doing it, and then come back to working on your development later on. What do you think about that?

Yes, I think that's true and, especially if you've been through quite a fast period of development, to keep setting yourself new targets may not be the best thing. A target can be to consolidate what you have done recently in a particular area rather than to learn a new skill or develop a new behaviour. However, CPD cannot come from above; it can only come from the person themselves and development isn't always something you plan. Guidance and support and facilitating are the job of the line manager – not pushing people but suggesting different options that perhaps the person hasn't thought of.

How do you stay motivated?

I can see where I think I need to improve and my motivation is to do my job as best I can.

THINKING TASK 4

Consider the following statements from the whole case study interview. Either reflect on these statements yourself or, if possible, set up a discussion group with peers to discuss them and then consider the final question below in the summary.

1 'Sometimes a line manager can find it easy to see development opportunities for an inexperienced teacher but less easy with a very experienced teacher or trainer. They may not know what the opportunities are or think they shouldn't be suggesting something because the teacher is so experienced and will know for themselves already, but I think that's a mistake.'

2 'There is a danger that someone does specialize in something or becomes very good at doing something and the manager sees this and lets it continue, but this can result in a lack of opportunity for that person to do something different.'

3 '...if you're always "firefighting" you can never be thinking about your own development time. Sometimes you need to allot development time away from your location and away from interruptions; it can be very useful to separate yourself completely from the daily operational side of your work. You have to find

the time for self-management, and that includes managing your own development, but that's a big ask sometimes.'

4 'Guidance and support and facilitating are the job of the line manager – not pushing people but suggesting different options that perhaps the person hasn't thought of.'

Summary

Justin spoke primarily about how individual CPD feeds into the needs of the organization, about the development of very experienced teachers and trainers, and about the development of managers. Some of what he said might have struck a chord with you; other things he said might have been more surprising; and you may even have a different perspective about some points because of your own experience or current working context.

As a result of reading Justin's views, how might your own behaviour and/or development be influenced in any of the areas Justin talked about? It could just be a case of increased awareness of some issues, or possible actions resulting from the interview. As a manager you might have a slightly different approach to dealing with the CPD of the people you line-manage, for example. Or as a senior teacher you might be more proactive in setting yourself goals. Reflect on all this and then see how Justin's comments might themselves take you forward in some way.

22

Reflecting

In this final chapter we will look at one more aspect of development, possibly one of the most important – reflection. We will reflect on everything that has come before this moment and try to tie everything together. Before we do that, though, it is important to see ways in which reflection should always play a part in every step we take.

Why reflect?

As we have seen throughout this book, we can make progress as professionals almost without realizing it, just as learners in our classrooms sometimes feel that they have made little or no progress because they haven't really reflected on what they have done or considered ways of measuring their progress. This is why it is important to reflect – in other words, to consider and think about what we do in the classroom and why we do it, and also to evaluate what we do and be aware of what works and what doesn't, and to decide on areas that we need to develop in or experiment in – and this should be a career-long process.

Sometimes reflection might come down to emerging from a lesson and merely thinking 'That went well' or 'That didn't work as well as I had expected' or 'The students were very unresponsive' or any one of many other possible reactions. It could also involve you going through a period of feeling unmotivated, or a period in which you have done a number of things that you feel have made you a better teacher. Being aware of how you are feeling at a particular moment or how you have reacted to a particular lesson or series of lessons is, of course, valuable, but the important question is 'What should I do about those feelings and reactions?'

THINKING TASK 1

At this point it is worth asking yourself how, if at all, you reflect on your work beyond the 'That lesson went well' type. Have you done any formal student feedback, or asked a colleague to observe you, or recorded yourself, or done any action research, or anything else? If you haven't, then try designing a student questionnaire along the lines of the example below that would be suitable and appropriate in your context. Try it out and see what results you get and how you could act on them.

Keeping a journal

In Chapter 18: Get SMART, we discussed the value of having goals and clear, specific and measurable targets and of recognizing when we have achieved them. Reflecting on such achievements is part of this, but we also need to reflect on our day-to-day work as part of a continuing process. One way of doing this is to keep a journal of some kind. Any such journal might focus specifically on classroom practice and experience, or it might focus additionally on other aspects of your professional life.

On a pre-service teacher training course, candidates are normally expected to complete a reflective self-evaluation form after teaching, and that is good practice for all teachers to continue in one form or another (without literally filling out a form after every lesson you teach!). Any such journal entry could be completed once a week or month to reflect on a series of lessons, or after particular lessons. It could at various times go beyond purely you reflecting on a lesson or lessons and include such features as:

- observation feedback
- student comments
- notes on a film of your lesson
- the results of action research.

OBSERVATION FEEDBACK

Feedback from a manager's official observations will obviously suggest areas for you to work on, as well as acknowledging what you are doing well. Perhaps, though, it is peer observation feedback that you might find more useful here, given its more informal nature and the fact that as the teacher you can steer the feedback towards the area or areas about which you most want outside comments. Asking your colleague beforehand to look out for and give feedback in certain areas will be of immediate and relevant value to you. Refer back to Chapter 4 for more on this.

STUDENT COMMENTS

As teachers, how often do we ask our students to comment on our lessons, beyond the feedback given at the end of the course? There is always going to be an element of trepidation in asking a question as direct as 'What did you think of my lesson today?' so that may not be the best question to ask. To elicit feedback on your lessons generally, up to a certain point in the course, can, however, be very valuable and illuminating and help to inform your future planning. You could give out a questionnaire along the lines of the following (and this can be adapted to suit the age, level and nature of the class you are teaching):

1. Do you generally find the lessons very useful, useful or not useful? Please give reasons or examples for your answer.
2. Do you usually find the lessons very interesting, sometimes interesting or not interesting? Please give reasons or examples for your answer.
3. What do you like best about the lessons? Say why.
4. Is there anything you don't like about the lessons? Say why.
5. What could I do more, or do differently, to make the lessons more useful and/ or interesting for you?

A questionnaire such as this could be expanded or adapted in any way you want, but the general idea of getting feedback from students is illustrated in this example. What questions you ask and how you phrase them is up to you. In addition to this, or in place of it, you could also arrange for one-to-one 'tutorials' with your students. The advantage of this is that you can engage the student you are speaking to in a meaningful dialogue and explore their answers and feelings more. The disadvantage is that you might not have a written record unless you do the questionnaire as well as the discussion.

Whatever approach you adopt, having student feedback to help inform your own reflecting process can only be a good thing and, who knows, you may be surprised by what they tell you (and this could go either way!).

NOTES ON A FILM OF YOUR LESSON

If your organization has the facilities/equipment available for you to do this, and you are not camera-shy, then being able to watch a recording of a lesson you have taught can allow you in the privacy of a darkened room to watch yourself in action, and equally important, to watch your learners' responses to the lesson. This can be particularly helpful if peer observations are not really possible. Again, it helps to have a particular focus to your self-observation. If you have detected a lack of response from your students recently, perhaps sensing a lack of interest, then you could watch the recording with that as your focus and, perhaps in conjunction with student feedback, your reflection process will be that much more guided and meaningful.

THE RESULTS OF ACTION RESEARCH

In Chapter 12 we looked at action research, and this is something that you might do following a period of meaningful reflection, especially if that reflection process revealed an area that you feel you need to improve in. You can then record the results in your journal.

THINKING TASK 2

Whether you are a teacher or trainer, if you don't already keep a journal or log, try keeping one that you fill in daily, weekly or whenever you choose to. You could work with blank pages if you prefer, or you could focus your thoughts and entries with prompts.

There are two examples below. Adapt them or design your own according to your particular context and needs.

Example 1

My lessons(s) today / this week	
What went well and why:	
What didn't go so well and why not:	
What I have learned:	
What I need to do to go forward:	
My action plan:	

Example 2

- Devise a lesson around authentic materials
- Try to integrate (Maria) more so she participates and talks more
- Do more language feedback work as I don't really do enough of that
- Make sure I get all my admin done this time!
- Spend at least half an hour a day less preparing

One month later	
My thoughts on the authentic materials lesson and how it went:	
Is Maria more involved in lessons now? What else can I do?	
Am I happy I have done more language feedback? What was my students' response?	
Did I get all my admin done? If yes, what made the difference?	
Did I manage to cut my lesson preparation time without it affecting the quality of my lessons? How did I manage to do it?	

Reflection for trainers and managers

Reflection is not only for teachers, of course. If, for example, you are a teacher trainer or a manager, then you, too, should be reflecting on your practice. Let's take two examples: a DELTA trainer of a couple of years' experience, and a middle manager who line-manages a number of teachers. What kinds of reflection process could they undertake?

THE DELTA TRAINER

For such a person the process could involve reflection on the input sessions they are delivering to trainees, or on the advice and support they are offering, or on the quality and balance of feedback they are giving following teaching practice, or any combination of these areas. It could also involve reflecting on current reading and ideas or theories and how these might shape their development and overall quality of training. The trainer, like the teacher, can incorporate any or more of what we listed before in a journal: feedback from trainees, peer observation, recordings and action research.

THE LINE MANAGER

Being a reflective manager might seem less obvious than being a reflective teacher but it shouldn't. It is understandable to think why this contrast may be applied, because a teacher teaches a lesson and can reflect on how that lesson went. For a manager, though, there is no such self-contained part of the day they can reflect on and evaluate in the same way. The manager's days, weeks and months are filled with a multitude of tasks and projects that are a combination of the proactive and reactive.

To consider every area of the job at one time would be too much – there would come a point where your reflection would just lead to a headache and be counter-productive. What a manager needs to do is to isolate different aspects of the job they do regularly. Depending on the precise role of the job, these aspects may include:

- timetabling
- leading INSETT sessions

- carrying out observations
- conducting appraisals
- day-to-day support of staff
- running meetings
- prioritizing tasks and time management
- dealing with client complaints.

It is better to consider these individual aspects in turn. Let's take one example – running meetings.

Reflecting on meetings

Running a meeting involves many skills if you want those attending it to go away feeling that it was well run, productive and worthwhile. A starting point for reflection, therefore, could be asking attendees to complete a feedback form. This could include questions and answers, a multiple choice (e.g. choosing 'I agree', 'I disagree' or 'I'm not sure' in answer to a question) or a 'grading' system (e.g. '1, 2, 3, 4, 5' – going from '1', the most negative choice, to '5', the most positive). Questions could relate to the usefulness of the meeting, the organization of it, whether the agenda was helpful, if it was felt that there was sufficient opportunity for people to contribute and to ask questions, if a clear summary was given and action points and outcomes agreed.

From this feedback and your own impressions, you can reflect in an informed way on how effective and well received the meeting was and in which areas you could improve next time.

Here is a simple example of a feedback form.

Meeting feedback form	
1 = I strongly disagree 2 = I disagree 3 = I agree 4 = I strongly agree	
1. I found this meeting to be useful and relevant	1 – 2 – 3 – 4
2. The agenda clearly showed what the meeting was about.	Yes/ No
3. The meeting started and finished on time.	Yes/ No
4. Participants had the chance to contribute and ask questions.	Yes /No
5. There was a clear outcome to the meeting.	1 – 2 – 3 – 4
6. Overall, the meeting was well run.	1 – 2 – 3 – 4

7. What I liked best about the meeting was...
8. For future meetings of this type I would suggest...
9. Any other comments?

In addition, before a meeting you could set yourself targets:

1 I want to send out a clear agenda beforehand.

2 I want to start and finish the meeting on time.

3 I want to allocate rough timings to each part of the meeting to keep it on track.

4 I want to ensure that there is opportunity for everyone to ask questions and contribute ideas.

5 I want us to agree on outcomes and proposals arising from the meeting.

6 I want everyone to be clear what happens next and who will be responsible for what.

7 I want to email everyone a summary of the meeting and confirm outcomes.

You can then have your own checklist to compare with that of those who gave you feedback, thus making your reflection process more meaningful and more useful to you. Any conclusions drawn from the reflection process can then become either informal goals for yourself, or SMART targets to be reflected in your performance review during your annual appraisal.

Tip

Reflection should be far more than just a reaction to how something went or how things in general are going. It needs to be more focused and substantive, and followed by some action(s) based on your reflections, and then further reflections. Whether your reflection is guided by client feedback, observation comments, your own journal, or anything else, it needs to be based on something, and it needs to lead somewhere.

Reflecting on what we have covered

As we near the end of our professional development discussion we, too, should reflect on what we have covered in this book.

Consider the question or suggestion next to each topic that is relevant or of interest to you. The questions are simply there to encourage you to reflect a little on each area that we have looked at and to draw you towards a more global reflection on all the many avenues of development that exist and how you can go about exploiting them.

- **Being observed**

  When you are next observed, reflect on the lesson and the feedback and decide on an area to work on and improve in. What happened the last time you were observed? Think back to your last observation and how that experience helped you develop.

- **Observing others**

  Do you think doing a peer observation could be a good thing for you to do? What would you want to get out of it?

- **Day-to-day ideas and development in the staffroom**

  What was the last really useful piece of advice or discussion you had in the staffroom? What did you take from it and what did you do with it?

- **Taking part in INSETT sessions**

  Reflect on the last INSETT session you attended. What did you learn from it and how has it helped you since in your job?

- **Using online resources**

  When was the last time you found something useful online which you were able to use?

- **Teaching exam classes**

  Have you taught an exam class recently? How will the student feedback at the end inform and shape your approach the next time you teach an exam class?

- **Reading groups**

  Even if you have not participated in an actual reading group, what was the last professionally related article or book you read and what did you get out of it?

- **Attending and participating in conferences**

  Have you attended a conference in the last year, either face to face or online? What was the most worthwhile part of it, and why? Have you been able to put any of it into practice?

- **Writing**

  Maybe you haven't done any writing, but is it something you might consider or have the opportunity to do? Perhaps this could be a new direction for you to go in?

- **Action research**

  If you haven't done this before, is it something you might now consider? Is there a particular area you might like to focus on?

- **Being a student again**

  Are you thinking of taking the DELTA, of learning or brushing up on another language or of learning how to play a musical instrument, perhaps? Whatever you do would put you back in the student's chair again and, as well as learning a skill or developing your teaching qualifications, you would also remind yourself about the joys and frustrations of being a student.

- **Becoming a trainer**

  If you are already a trainer of any kind, what have you done differently recently – what have you tried out, and why? Did it work? What did you learn from the experience? Or maybe you did something that didn't work so well, or had a difficult conversation with a trainee. What did you learn from this?

- **Professional groups and journals**

  Have you read a journal recently? On reflection, what did it teach you or show you or share with you?

- **Taking a sabbatical**

  If you have been lucky enough to have one, what were the benefits of it?

- **Going into management**

  If you are in a managerial role of any kind, what have you done recently to improve an aspect of your work? What was it that made you want to do this? You could reflect now on one part of your role that you would like to do differently or better and think of what actions you could take to do this.

- **Get SMART**

  Reflect on any SMART target you have set yourself or been set. Did you achieve it, and what have been the benefits to your work?

- **Get ahead**

  In the last month, what have you done? For example, did you deliver a new type of lesson, write some materials, use a different book or have a professional conversation? In what ways have you benefited from even the smallest of events?

- **The line manager's view**

  Having read the interview in Chapter 20, what do you appreciate more about the role of a line manager?

- **The school director's view**

  Having read the interview in Chapter 21, what do you appreciate more about organizational development?

Reflecting on a year's writing and interviewing professionals who have worked all over the world, I have taken a few pointers myself from this process:

- Listening to Jan talking about his action research project on board work got me thinking about my own board work – never one of my strengths! It was reassuring to hear a very experienced teacher talking about this and it has spurred me to do some action research of my own to improve the quality of my board work. I intend to devise a SMART target and try to implement this when I next teach a class.

- Researching the chapters on professional journals and online resources led me to places I had not been to before. I have already read a number of interesting articles, which will certainly influence me in my teaching and training.
- Doing some language learning again has reminded me of some of the issues learners face, which I had almost started to take for granted, and on reflection I can focus even more on ways to help my learners cope with the demands of learning a new language.

Summary

- As professionals, we all need to continue our development to constantly improve our performance in all aspects of our work.
- We do not have to be given ideas for development all the time; to an extent we can decide ourselves what we can do – in other words, we should play an active part in goal-setting.
- Many of the ways we can develop are almost unnoticed day-to-day things that we do inside or outside our classrooms or offices – it doesn't have to be a big project every time.
- We also need to have regular SMART targets to have measurable and recordable examples of what we have done.
- We need to always reflect on what we do and how we do it, and to make those reflections more focused and with outcomes to those reflections.

I hope this book has given you some ideas, increased your motivation, expanded your awareness of the importance of both individual and organizational development, and shown you where else you can go to for professional development. If you have taken just one thing from this book that you will go forward with, then it has been worth the journey. If you have taken more than one thing, even better!

Thanks for reading, and I wish all my readers and colleagues around the world continuing professional satisfaction and development. There is always another step to take!

Glossary

Acronyms used in this book

CAE – Cambridge Advanced English, also known as Cambridge: English Advanced

CELTA – Cambridge ESOL CELTA (Certificate of Language Teaching to Adults) a pre-service course taken by more than 10,000 candidates worldwide per year

CertTESOL – the Trinity College pre-service training course

CLIL – Content and Language Integrated Learning

CP – course participant

CPD – continuous/continuing professional development

CPE – Certificate of Proficiency in English, Cambridge's most advanced language assessment qualification

DELTA – Cambridge ESOL DELTA (Diploma of English Language Teaching to Adults), a course taken by practising and experienced teachers

DOS – Director of Studies, a common title for the middle manager working in part as the school's academic manager (ADOS being the Assistant Director of Studies). Some organizations have alternative names for similar positions, and some people are 'senior teachers' with some management duties included in their job, such as line-managing other teachers.

EFL – English as a foreign language: still a commonly used term, as is ESL (English as a second language). The latter often refers to those learners who are now or intending soon to live in an English-speaking country.

IELTS – International English Language Testing System

FCE – First Certificate in English, also known as Cambridge: English First

INSETT – in-service training for teachers (INSET being more general in-service training)

IATEFL – International Association of Teachers of English as Foreign Language. Although technically an organization with thousands of teachers as well as schools worldwide belonging to it, it more typically refers to the annual five-day face-to-face and online conference that takes place around April.

IT – information technology

IWB – interactive whiteboard

MOOCs – massive open online courses

PDI – professional development interview (often called 'appraisals'), which staff usually have once a year to review performance and to set targets for the year ahead

SIG – an IATEFL special interest group. There are many such groups that, as the name suggests, focus on a particular aspect of language teaching. For example, there is a SIG for pronunciation and a SIG for young learners. Most SIGS have their own publication and talks or conferences.

TD session – teacher development session (similar to INSETT and usually internal to the place where you are working)

TEFL – teaching English as a foreign language

TOEFL – Test of English as a Foreign Language

TP – teaching practice (usually on a teacher-training course)

YLs – young learners (as opposed to adult learners)

Useful web addresses

(These web addresses were correct at the time of printing)

Chapter 6: Taking part in INSETT sessions
www.ihlondon.com/blog/posts/

Chapter 7: Using online resources
www.handoutsonline.com
www.onestopenglish.com
www.eslcafe.com
www.teachitelt.com
www.tinyteflteacher.co.uk
https://scottthornbury.wordpress.com
www.englishclub.com
www.eltjam.com
www.cambridgeenglishteacher.org
www.ihlteachers.co.uk
www.ihlondon.com/blog/posts
www.britishcouncil.org
http://eaquals.org/pages/7104

Chapter 8: Teaching exam classes
www.ihlondon.com/exam-centre/
www.ets.org/toefl

Chapter 9: Reading groups
http://eltreadinggroup.weebly.com/

Chapter 10: Attending and participating in conferences
www.iatefl.org.englishuk.com-conferences
www.ihtocmay2014.blogspot.co.uk
www.ihworld.com

Chapter 11: Writing
www.ihjournal.com

Chapter 12: Action research
www.teachingenglish.org.uk/article/action-research

Chapter 13: Being a student again
www.cambridgeenglish.org

Chapter 14: Becoming a trainer
www.cambridgeenglish.org/teaching-english/teaching-qualifications/celta/
www.trinitycollege.com/site/?id=263
www.ihlondon.com

Chapter 15: Professional groups and journals
www.iatefl.org
www.iatefl.org/special-interest-groups/sig-list
www.tesol.org
www.tesol.org/connect/interest-sections
www.tesol.org/attend-and-learn
www.linkedin.com
www.elgazette.com
www.modernenglishteacher.com
www.tttjournal.co.uk
www.etprofessional.com
www.eltj.oxfordjournals.org
iteslj.org
www.ihjournal.com
www.iatefl.org
www.tesol.org/read-and-publish/journals/tesol-quarterly

Chapter 19: Get ahead
http://eaquals.org/pages/7104
www.britishcouncil.org
www.iatefl.org